HIS OWN MAN
A Victorian 'Hidden' Muslim

The Life and Times of Robert 'Reschid' Stanley

By Christina Longden

With Brian Longden (research support)

HIS OWN MAN

First published in England by Past Truisms CIC 2019

Photographic credits: Tameside Local Studies Archives, Liverpool Record
Office (Liverpool Libraries), Abdullah Quilliam Society and British Library,
The Sphere, Brian Longden, Christina Longden, Arakan Creative Media,
Manchester Libraries, Information and Archives, © US Copyright from G.
Robinson David Urquhart; some chapters in the life of a Victorian knight-
errant of justice and liberty (Boston & New York: Houghton Mifflin Co., 1920)
Illustration credits: Tameside Local Studies Archives, Liverpool Record Office
(Liverpool Libraries), Brian Longden, Christina Longden, Abdullah Quilliam
Society.

Robert Reschid Stanley's family website and information can be found at:
www.robertreschidstanley.wordpress.com
Email: **rreschid@yahoo.com**

ISBN 978-0-9928792-4-2
Cover design: Flora Rustamova (art and layout) with calligraphy art by
Razwan Ul-Haq

*Translation from back cover: "God is the Light of the heavens and the earth. The
example of (God's) light is like a niche within which is a lamp, the lamp is within
glass, the glass as if it were a pearly [white] star."*
From the Qur'an, Chapter (24) sūrat l-nūr

CONTENTS

For Dad

'Rooted in the past, deeply personal and shaping our present, *His Own Man - A Victorian 'Hidden' Muslim* - is a necessary and timely read in the debate about identity and belonging.'
BARONESS SAYEEDA WARSI

'*His Own Man* is an essential read for anyone interested in challenging preconceived ideas of Muslim and working-class community life. Chris Longden must be congratulated for writing this highly accessible biography; one which Robert Reschid Stanley would be deeply proud of. This is a compelling socio-political portrait of one of the leading Victorian Muslims, based upon extensive archival research. This book provides a much-needed contribution towards a growing field of research on early Muslim convert communities during Victorian Britain.'
DR SHAMIM MIAH, *Senior Lecturer, University of Huddersfield.*

'History matters.
It matters because we are who we are and what we are. Not only because of our own personal history - but also because of our familial, local, regional, national and international histories.
History matters because it teaches us that life is not about 'me' and 'I'. It is about 'we' and 'us'.
History matters because it belongs to everyone and not to one person.
History matters because it brings to the fore continuity and links the past, the present and the future in a vital chain.
History matters because it brings together the local and the global and through so doing, it calls out to us of the need to understand, respect and embrace those who may appear to be different to us: for through knowing our histories we recognise the commonality of the peoples of the world.
History matters because it is not only about the past, it is about making the present and shaping the future in a more inclusive, caring and appreciative way. This book by Christina Longden matters because it embraces all those vital concepts of history. An important and pioneering work, it highlights the need not for tolerance of each other's beliefs but of acceptance: an acceptance that can only arise through the understanding of the importance of our shared histories. Herein lies the power of Christina Longden's research, writing and passion: the celebration of that which we have in common – our humanity.'
PROFESSOR CARL CHINN, *MBE, Ph.D.*

ACKNOWLEDGEMENTS

I could not have completed this book without the love and support of my husband, Ian, and my children, Ruby and Gregory. They managed to contain their collective eye-rolling during my inordinate number of 'Eureka' moments, they smiled with encouragement and they stayed away from me when, to all intents and purposes, I was acting like some sort of grumpy Victorian ghost.

I also owe more than I can say to my dad, who initially made the discovery about Robert's conversion to Islam and who had already done so much of the unbelievably hard slog, looking into Robert's life and producing his own pamphlet on his ancestor. To my mum too - who has always encouraged my love of community and of history - and who pushed for my brother and I to become 'first generation university educated'.

My brother, Steven, his wife Rozina and my nephews Eesaa and Yaaseen, have always been there, cheering both me - and this book - on. Our Auntie Gay, local historian and genealogist, has also been generous in sharing her own research into the wider history of our Stanley family - along with our Uncle David Stanley. Tameside's Local Archives department has been a tremendous source of help and resources (and never shouted at me when I forgot to return their pencils). Thanks too, to the British Muslim Heritage Centre, to the Liverpool Public Records Office and to the Manchester Libraries, Information and Archives. Stuart Vallantine deserves a special thank you for all his enthusiasm and his wisdom on anything in relation to local history, transport and faffing around with photos.

Shamim Miah, Yahya Birt and the Abdullah Quilliam Society in Liverpool provided helpful advice. Conor Ibrahim of Arakan Creative Media and director of the film 'Freesia', decided to create a short film, supported by Adnan Pervez and starring Brian Longden (available on the website).

Others have shown enormous interest in this work and deserve thanks: Afzal Khan MP, Baroness Sayeeda Warsi, Chris Gribble of the National Writers Centre, the Church of the Christian Israelites in Australia and Claude Nealy. Flora Rustamova added the icing on the cake with her talent for cover design and Razwan Ul-Haq wove his magic with the Islamic calligraphy. Finally, thanks to my wonderful editor, Graham Brown - who has the patience of a northern saint.

THIS BOOK HAS BEEN MADE POSSIBLE THANKS TO:

Muhammad Umar & Sofia Zaynab
Naila Malak
N. Latif
Ayyub Syed Qadri
Ibrahim Hussain
Maryam Hussain
Sumayyah Hussain
Mohammed Amin MBE
Rima Hadid

AUTHOR'S NOTES

Given that the audience of this book will include people who follow a religion and people who don't, and those born 'n bred in the North of England and those reading this book on the other side of the world, I have tried not to be too presumptuous. For example, I have done my best to give a brief nod to the history of the Christian church in the UK and account for the peculiarities of the North of England and Islam in Britain. I hope that the explanations are helpful, without being overly patronising to those who have come to this book with an in-depth knowledge.

I also want to acknowledge the fact that there are many people who are actively opposed to religious institutions and to any external belief systems but who are, in themselves, deeply caring people. They have helped me immensely in the development of this book. They have as much a stake in it as those who consider themselves to belong to a particular faith group. And, after all, as I state in the introduction, this is not a book about religion!

The research for this illustration of Robert's life has been carried out in the same manner that any academic publication would be. It was important to my family, however, that it should be written using a 'Plain English' approach and that its style does not exclude any readers (which, sadly, far too many academic publications seem to do). For this reason, the footnotes do not follow a formal academic layout and I have taken the liberty of not including an index. Additionally, the reader will find that my approach sometimes presumes or second-guesses elements of Robert's life. An academic book, of course, would not be permitted to do this for evidential reasons. Therefore, I have done my best to remind the reader that sometimes I am resorting to conjecture. I feel that this is my prerogative, as a relative of Robert, and I have tried to leave room for other thoughts (cynical or otherwise!) when it comes to his life, views and actions. I do ask the reader forgiveness if, at any point, I have adopted a 'rose-tinted spectacles' outlook on his character and motivations. If this seems to be evident, it will be a result of my own fascination with Robert and with good old-fashioned family loyalty as opposed to anything more sinister on my part.

Creating such a book has been a rather tricky balancing act at times, so I hope that you will forgive me for any pernickety errors which might irritate those of you who are absolute sticklers for facts. I have found it mightily irritating myself to see the (very few) mentions of Robert Stanley in other authors' books as being inaccurate. But, as with anything, we all benefit by being slow to take offence and to consider instead the bigger picture and overall intent of a published work.

The companion book to this one, *Imagining Robert - Scenes from the Life of a Hidden Victorian Muslim*, was written in parallel and uses creative fiction to bring colour to, and to dramatize, Robert's life and times. We all enjoy learning and absorbing information in different ways, so - as with the 'Plain English' approach - it was important to my family to offer a chance to learn about this incredible man in a more entertaining manner. *Imagining Robert* can be used by schools and community groups to bring his story to life in a way that a more straightforward, non-fiction history book cannot.

On Tameside
The word Tameside did not exist until 1974, when the metropolitan area of Greater Manchester was created. It consists of several towns on Manchester's south-east side of Lancashire – Ashton-under-Lyne, Denton, Droylsden, Dukinfield, Hyde, Longdendale, Mossley and Stalybridge. The notion of Tameside is still a cause for controversy amongst many who feel greater affinity to Lancashire. This too, though, is a subject for debate because the towns of Tameside fall into both Lancashire and Cheshire – with the eastern portion overlapping with West Yorkshire and the southern with Derbyshire. Stalybridge moved from Lancashire to Cheshire when the post office was moved to the other side of the River Tame. It may sound rather complicated, but the reader is warned to be careful of using this term when speaking to people from the area. Never forget that wars have been fought over this sort of thing 'up north'...

This book's research has primarily focussed on the three towns where my branch of the Stanley family spent most of their time: Dukinfield, Ashton-under-Lyne and Stalybridge. Please note also that the spelling of Stalybridge has varied throughout time.

On Roberts and Johns
Because there are a lot of Robert and John Stanleys in my family tree and who feature in this book, I have done my best to use family nicknames to distinguish them for the reader. The Robert whose life this book focusses on is always referred to as plain old 'Robert' and sometimes as 'Robert Reschid' for the parts of his life when he was a Muslim. I also refer to John Stanley, the wealthy Christian Israelite and Robert's benefactor, as 'Uncle John' in order to differentiate him from other Johns such as Robert's older brother, John, and his own son, John. The reader will note references to John 'Strongi'th'arm' Stanley – both nephew and son-in-law of Uncle John. This name causes much amusement amongst my family and it came down through the family tree thanks to Lexey Strongi'th'arm, who was Robert's grandmother and who married into the Stanleys. Often a woman's name was kept as a middle name for her children. It is nice to know that some visibility of women was allowed to remain, even if in 'name only'.

My direct line to Robert can be seen in the family tree contained in the Appendices. It comes through his own son – also a 'Robert' - whose family nickname was 'Unlucky Bob', which is how I will refer to him in this book (apparently, he was landed with this name by his relatives because both his wives died when they were relatively young. This seems a bit of an unfair burden for Bob to have had to carry around with him for the rest of his life – but then, that's families for you).

On Reschid and other non-English Spellings
I chose to use this spelling of 'Reschid' for Robert because it is the one that accompanies the photograph. At other times in *The Crescent,* and when other contemporaries have referred to Robert, it has been spelt 'Rechid' and 'Rashid'. As with many other names, the spelling is variable; often people forgot which spelling another person preferred to use and used a different form.

In terms of Islamic spellings, and where the material is quoted from its original source, the spelling contained by the author of the time is used (i.e. 'Servian' for 'Serbian'). I have tried to remain consistent throughout, but I am sure that I have not done this perfectly. I beg forgiveness from those who are experts on these matters!

Please note, too, that there are many extracts in this book which are direct transcripts from newspapers and magazines of the time, so the spelling, punctuation and grammar has been left exactly as they were written at the time.

Genealogy and Family History

I'm aware that many readers will be familiar with the terminology used during family history research – however, just as many will not. Therefore, I've tried to reduce the use of genealogy-related jargon, although the reader will see the use of the 'x2, x3' abbreviation, for example, when I refer to 'great great grandad' or 'great great great grandmother' etc. The Appendices will tell you more about researching family history.

GLOSSARY

Below are the more modern spellings and terminology used in this book. Where material is quoted from its original source, the spelling contained by the author of the time is used.

Abrahamic	Relating to the laws of the Prophet Abraham (followed by Jews, Christians and Muslims).
Anglicanism	The Church of England (or Established Church) and the Protestant church. The British monarch is the head of the Established Church, along with the Archbishop of Canterbury.
Caliph	The caliph is considered to be the leader of Muslims who follow Sunni Islam. At the time of Robert Stanley, this authority was invested in the Ottomans. The Ottoman Caliphate was abolished in 1924. Currently, Muslims are without a caliph.
Census	The census system in Britain collects data on every household, usually collecting name, age, occupation, birth.
Chartism	A movement that began in the 1820s amongst those in Britain who campaigned for various elements of democratic reform (including the enfranchisement of the working class).
Christian Israelites	A 19th century sect founded by Prophet John Wroe.
Circumcision	A medical procedure to remove a male's foreskin. Also a religious requirement practised by Jews and Muslims.
Conservatives	The Conservative Party is a centre-right party and was one of the two main British political parties of the 19th and 20th centuries. Its origin was the 'Tory' group in Parliament, which many still called themselves after the Conservatives developed as a party after 1830. The Party stood for resistance to sudden change and reform, the Establishment (Crown, aristocracy and Anglicanism) and opposition to home rule for Ireland.
Dissenter	As with Non-Conformist, a Christian who was not part of the Established Anglican Church/Church of England (i.e. Baptists, Methodists, Congregationalists, Quakers, etc).
Eid al-adha	Feast of the sacrifice. An annual festival honouring the sacrifice of Prophet Abraham (pbuh) that takes place during the Hajj.
Eid al-fitr	Feast of the breaking of the fast. An annual festival marking the end of the fasting month of Ramadan.
Established	As in the Established church; see Anglican.
Fatwa	An important legal opinion made by one qualified in Sharia Law.
Fez	Ottoman/Turkish traditional cylindrical red hat with a tassel.
Iftar	Breaking of the fast of Ramadan (each evening when the daylight has ended).

Hajj	Pilgrimage to Mecca/Makka and the 5th Pillar of Islam (obligations on all followers).
Halal	Something that is permitted for Muslims (i.e. dietary laws whereby an animal is killed with a prayer said over it and its blood is drained before consumption).
Haram	Something that is not permitted for Muslims (i.e. consumption of alcohol, immodesty of clothing and appearance, gambling).
Hijab	A headscarf. Similar to many other religions, the covering of heads in Islam is a sign of modesty.
Imam	A religious leader of a Muslim community.
Janazah	Islamic funeral prayers/service.
Jihad	The 'greater' jihad is a personal one: to overcome your inner weaknesses. The 'lesser' jihad involves armed struggle against oppressors.
Juma namz	Friday prayers.
Liberal	The Liberal Party was one of the two main British political parties of the 19th and 20th centuries. An alliance of the Whigs and the free-trade Peelites and Radicals, its members favoured social reform, free trade, personal liberty and reducing the powers of the Crown and the Church of England.
Mohammed	The last and greatest of all prophets to whom God revealed the message of Islam.
Mullah	Commonly used to describe local mosque leaders and men learned in religious knowledge in some Muslim countries.
Municipal Socialism	A movement that began in the early 1870s when public health became a priority for Britain and the new system of local government was empowered to spend local authority money in order to benefit the public. Measures included water distribution, sewers, drains, gas and baths, the demolition of slum dwellings, the erection of public libraries and the founding of parks. Not associated with the political philosophy of socialism.
Non-Conformist	See 'Dissenter'.
Orientalism	A term used to describe Western descriptions of the Eastern world, particularly in the 18th and 19th centuries. Edward Said has shown the inherent bias of Orientalists.
Orthodox	A Christian church of the Eastern Roman Empire/European tradition.
Ottoman	Of Turkey (i.e. the Ottoman Empire expanded from Turkey and beyond).
Pbuh	Peace Be Upon Him. It is tradition for all Muslims to say this phrase whenever the name of one of their prophets is mentioned.
Pillars of Islam	Five obligatory religious duties providing a framework for the life of Muslims. The Five Pillars are: Shahada (profession of faith), Salah (ritual prayer), Zakat (charity), Sawm (fasting during Ramadan) and Hajj (pilgrimage).
Poor Law	Before the welfare state was established in Britain in the early 20th century, those who fell on hard times could obtain some

	relief in the form of financial handouts or clothing etc. However, the 'New' Poor Laws of the 1840s generally involved admission to the hated workhouse system.
Prophets	Muslims follow the same prophets as Jews and Christians and much of the text in the Qur'an is identical to that of the Torah and Bible. Muslims believe that Jesus was not the physical manifestation of the son of God (or born of a virgin) but that he was the last and greatest prophet of all before Mohammed (pbuh).
Protestant	The church originally created by Henry VIII of England in order to counter the Roman Catholic church.
Qur'an	Islam's holy book, believed to contain God's exact words (Muslims believe the Bible has been muddied through translations, exclusions etc.). The Qur'an contains many of the same stories as the Old Testament and the Torah.
Ramadan	Month of fasting which Muslims must honour (unless illness or other exclusions apply).
Rechabite	One who practises temperance.
Roman Catholic	Christian who follows the church headed by the Pope.
Shahada	The 1st Pillar of Islam; a statement that must be said when someone converts to Islam: 'I declare that there is no god, but God and I declare that Mohammed is His Messenger'.
Sharia	Literally: the path to the watering hole. Often translated as Islamic law, Arabic-speaking Jews and Christians often used the word Sharia to refer to their religious laws.
Shia/Sunni	Shia Muslims believe that leadership of Muslim Ummah should be led by one who belongs to the family of Prophet Muhammad (pbuh). Sunni Muslims believe that the leader of the Ummah need not be descended from the Prophet (pbuh).
Shiloh	The Shiloh is mentioned various times throughout the Old Testament and the Torah. It usually relates to either the coming of the (new) Messiah, or to a specific locality in Israel/Palestine where the Ark of the Covenant was said to be held.
Sheikh	A religious or a tribal leader.
Southcottians	Followers of Joanna Southcott, an 18th century Christian sect that Prophet John Wroe won leadership of and developed into the Christian Israelites.
Sufi/ism	Islamic mysticism.
Sultan	Ottoman caliphs were often addressed as sultans.
Temperance	A movement promoting abstinence from alcohol. One who practised abstinence from alcohol was known as a Rechabite.
Torah	The Jewish holy book (also the Old Testament 'half' of the Christian Bible).
Ummah	Muslim community around the world.

Wahaabism	A term given to a religious movement emanating from the Arabian Peninsula in the 18th century. Wahaabism overturned Ottoman rule of the Holy Cities of Mecca/Makkah and Medina/Madinah, providing the religious identity of modern-day Saudi Arabia.
Wakes	Annual holiday enjoyed by the working class in the factory towns of northern England.

HIS OWN MAN
A Victorian 'Hidden' Muslim

The Life and Times of Robert 'Reschid' Stanley

FORWARD

This book has been written with three purposes in mind. Firstly, to bring to light for the first time the remarkable life and times of my ancestor, Robert Stanley. Secondly, to demonstrate that, through the pursuit of family history, we can bring about a greater depth of understanding of other people's choices, cultures and beliefs. Thirdly, it aims to demonstrate that some of the greatest British patriots have been ordinary men and women, people who did not have access to the internet, or to countless books or even to a formal education, but who were ferociously intelligent, who sought out justice for others overseas and were brave enough to stand up against those who embraced uncritical nationalism, or who took the attitude of 'my country, right or wrong'.

INTRODUCTION

Don't panic! This is not a book about religion. Of course, there are quite a lot of mentions of religion contained within it, but the story contained is all about one man's life and the choices that he made. Many readers picking up this book will lack knowledge of either Islam or Christianity in Britain or they may have been exposed to ignorant or prejudiced ideas of what Muslims and Christians do and don't believe or should and shouldn't believe. Hopefully, even just dipping in and out of some of the chapters might challenge the views that some readers possess in relation to people who practise a religious belief. Britain today is predominantly a very secular society and one which hardly encourages interest in spiritual matters.

But enough of the politics. This isn't a book about politics, although some readers will already be aware that my family has been – and still is – rather political, and that Robert himself was an avid follower of politics both at home and abroad. However, I do need to start the book off by quickly addressing a key issue that has led to this book being written: how British society perceives Muslims and the religion of Islam.

Today, it is nearly impossible to pick up any newspaper or to listen to any news coverage without hearing about the threat of Islamism. This book is not the place to delve into the whys and wherefores or 'what IS Islamism' or 'what constitutes Muslim extremism'; but, in order to understand the motivations behind Robert Stanley's conversion to Islam, we do need to consider the relationship that the British Government has had with Muslim communities across the globe during the last couple of centuries. This book will not provide a detailed analysis of British foreign policy set against an Islamic context, however. Instead, Robert's life and choices will be laid against the historical background and we shall see that, on the one hand, he faced a very different set of political circumstances to those of contemporary British Muslim converts but, on the other, the narrative, fear and misunderstandings will seem, to some, horribly familiar.

Many non-Muslim British citizens today may associate the word Islam with that of terrorist. Anti-Islamic sentiment has been on the rise since 9/11, largely because a warped version of the religion has received so much publicity, thereby confusing many about Islam, its history and its active practise by the vast majority. This, however, has not always been the case; Islam and its followers have not always been perceived to be a threat to Britain. The history of the Crusades, of course, provides stories of brutality – along with co-operation – on both sides and this is where we first encounter tales of British converts to Islam, although many of them were either the result of enforcement, misinterpretation or, for those living abroad, a method of gaining trading connections, wealth or power.

Once the Crusades had burned themselves out, Islam was not deemed to be a menace to Britain - and once Henry VIII had created the Church of England, for many the Ottoman Muslims came in handy holding the spread of Roman

Catholicism at bay. However, when Victoria's Empire began to expand, an increasing fascination and attraction with Orientalism began, accompanied by fear and mistrust of what the Ottoman Empire might do next. Still, for many (such as Benjamin Disraeli) the Ottomans were quite useful in keeping the Russians just that little bit further away from influencing and encroaching upon the rest of Europe.

As a result of the printed press, literate British people soon began to receive more information than ever about Islam and all-things Oriental, and the late Victorian period saw a growing number of single-minded men (mostly) becoming Muslims, with the Queen herself becoming fascinated with Islam thanks to her friendship with her Urdu teacher, Abdul Karim. Two World Wars, however, reinforced patriotism to all things Christian and Crown which meant that, for many – and probably for Robert Stanley's family – it was probably best not to dwell too much on the religion of the Musselman.

Recent years have seen an explosion of interest amongst academics researching this Victorian and post-Victorian period of conversion to Islam, with much of the excitement on the subject being spurred on by the hypocrisy of currently prevailing attitudes in Britain towards Muslims. After all, only a few decades ago the US and its Western allies were aiding and abetting Islamist militants in order to support their own struggles against the Soviets in Afghanistan. Still, whilst it is fair to say that there have always been rather inaccurate and often preposterous views on the part of the British in relation to what most Muslims do and don't believe, there has never been such negative and destructive perceptions of ordinary Muslims than exists today.

Robert Stanley, though, did not actually convert during the glory days of the Ottoman Empire, when relations with Britain were better and when Ottoman Islam was seen by many as esoteric and admirable. In fact, by the time that Robert met Abdullah Quilliam, Britain's most famous Victorian convert, the tide was turning against the 'friendly Muslim neighbour' outlook. The conversions of both Quilliam and Robert took place at a time when turning to Islam and rejecting Christianity, as a British-born individual, would not have been seen as a peaceful, private belief. Instead, those who converted in the last quarter of the 19th century would probably be viewed in a similar light to many who have chosen to convert in today's post-9/11 environment: people who have taken an oppositional stance to Western society and who might well become the 'traitors of tomorrow'.

It is unusual to hear of anyone converting to another religion just a few months shy of their 70th birthday. We tend to identify religious conversion with youth, with those who are impressionable and who lack life experience and perspective. No matter how patronising this attitude might be, the statistics do bear it out. How much more remarkable, then, for someone born of the working class, with no formal education to speak of and living in a notoriously conservative, patriotic and provincial Victorian town, to drop a lifetime of religious conviction and nail his colours to the mast of those who were increasingly being seen as 'the enemy'?

The question of 'why' Robert converted is always first on the lips of anyone who hears his story, whether they are Muslim, belong to another faith or have no belief system at all. This book marks the first attempt to guess (and we can only guess) at why Robert changed his faith so late on in life. It is nigh on impossible to reduce the reasons why someone changes their religion (or joins one) to a few bullet points or soundbites, although scholars have researched the various psychological elements that cause individuals to decide that they have converted. And of course, the level of conviction, practise and 'true' conversion will vary from individual to individual.

I hope that this book will successfully examine the many and varied strands that pulled Robert towards his own conversion (without discounting, of course, what some would see as an overriding spiritual force), but I deliberately shy away from providing the reader with definitive answers as to 'why'. Whether Robert converted for experimental, intellectual, fraternal, political or mystical reasons – or a combination of all of these - I don't know. I don't suppose that he did, either. But the fact remains that he only became a Muslim after living 'a very British life' for nearly 70 years and therefore the bulk of this book focuses on this portion of his life. I hope that the research demonstrates that Robert's conversion never seemed to change his love for his land and for his family: if anything, it was simply a natural progression for him.

Re-discovering Robert
In 1999, my family made an astonishing discovery. Our ancestor, Robert Stanley, had converted to Islam in 1898.[1] My brother, Steven, and I had always known that Robert had been mayor of Stalybridge during 1874-76, but no surviving member of our family knew anything of any involvement with Islam. It seemed to us, therefore, that his family had either tried to forget this part of Robert's life, or had deliberately worked to conceal it.

That a working-class-born man, a well-known member of the Conservative Party, residing in an overwhelmingly white, Christian, Victorian and extremely traditional Northern mill town, chose to change his religion is remarkable. But what makes our family story even more astounding is the fact that Robert's own great x 3 grandson - my older brother, Steven – converted to Islam in 1990, knowing nothing of the religious convictions of his ancestor.

The revelation about Robert occurred shortly after my father, Brian Longden, was made redundant from his job as a lorry mechanic in Stalybridge. Dad had always intended to delve into his family history and used his new waking hours to visit Tameside's Local Studies and Archives Centre (see Appendix 4). He also got in touch with other relatives who had begun to unravel the various branches of our family tree.[2] Family history is a very common pursuit for many from our hometowns; the Workers' Education Association courses on genealogy in the

---

[1] Muslims believe that the natural state of all human beings is to be at one with Allah (God), that all are born Muslim but that, through sin or mistaken beliefs, people turn away from Allah. Many Muslims, therefore, refer to 'reversion' to Islam rather than to 'conversion'. Because a large proportion of this book's audience will not be familiar with Islam, the word 'convert/conversion' is used.

[2] Our auntie, Gay Oliver, married Mike Oliver, Brian's cousin and great x 2 grandson of Robert Stanley. Gay is a family historian in Tameside and her research has been of huge importance. Our uncle, David Stanley (great grandson of Robert), has also been incredibly supportive with sharing family history.

north west are enormously popular. Soon, word got out that Brian was seeking to find out more about the maternal side of his family – the Stanleys. One of his relatives, Noel Stanley, got in touch to say that he had something that may be of interest to Brian.[3]

This 'something' turned out to have been a possession of our ancestor, Robert Stanley, who was born in 1828 and who we knew had been one of Stalybridge's first mayors. At that point we had only one photograph of Robert: his mayoral portrait showing a slightly balding man, looking distinguished and composed, complete with a big beard and his mayoral chain. The new item that came to light was a papery-thin and frayed magazine dated 3rd April 1907. This turned out to be an edition of Britain's first Islamic publication – *The Crescent*. It contained a photograph of Robert wearing a fez and the caption underneath the photo describing 'Bro. Robert Reschid Stanley'.

The magazine featured Robert and described him as a 'Most Distinguished British Musselman'. My father, Brian, had not heard of the term 'Musselman' before, but from the content of the article it was clear that it meant 'Muslim' and that his ancestor had, indeed, become a Muslim. Brian asked his mother, my grandmother Edith Longden (née Stanley), about it and she was just as surprised. She had never been led to believe that Robert's life had followed anything other than a straightforwardly conservative and Christian path.

Brian then contacted his son, telling Steven, "You'd best sit down, I've got some strange news for you." My brother's reaction was one of absolute amazement. When he had first converted to Islam it had, in some respects, felt like quite a lonely action for him to take. In the 1990s, white working-

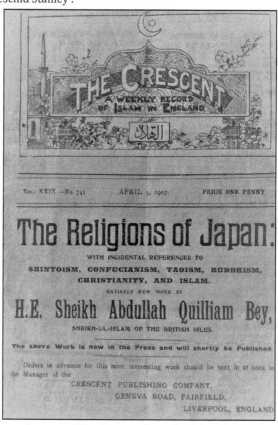

Our copy of The Crescent, featuring Robert in 1907

---

[3] Noel is David Stanley's brother; both were grandsons of 'Unlucky Bob' Stanley – i.e. great grandsons of Robert Stanley.

class lads in Manchester, who had received no exposure to interfaith practices or different religious backgrounds, just didn't do that sort of thing. So, for Steven to find out that his ancestor had made precisely the same change in his own life, and in a time where it would have been such an unusual thing to have done, was astounding; using my brother's own words, "It really knocked me for six."

Steven's own conversion occurred at a much younger age than his ancestor's (Robert was 69, Steven was 21) and by the time that the new revelation about his ancestor had been made Steven had been a Muslim for over eight years. He had studied Islam, made great friends amongst the Islamic community and was married to a Muslim woman, Rozina, of Pakistani heritage but who had been born and bred in the same town as us. But he had never dreamed that anyone in his own family would have had a connection to Islam.

After we were both born, our parents had taken the decision not to have us christened within the Anglican church. They felt that this would have been hypocritical. Our mother, Yvonne, had been raised in the Methodist tradition but had not gone to church for some time. When she was 40, however, she started attending Dukinfield Baptist Church and regained an interest in the faith that she was born into. Our dad holds little regard for religion and describes himself as an atheist. Despite (or perhaps because of) the lack of church attendance on behalf of

Robert Stanley's fez

our parents, our Auntie Enid took it upon herself to influence her teenaged niece and nephew to attend church. Together, we went to a C of E church in Stalybridge, New St George's, which followed the Anglo-Catholic tradition of worship.[4] As a teenager, I went to an evangelical Christian school in Stalybridge and then, as an adult, I joined the Quakers. So, for both my brother and I, it is fair to say that there was absolutely no childhood interest in, or exposure to, Islam; we were either exposed to Christianity or immersed in secular life.

Steven and Rozina's first child was born just a few months after our discovery about Robert's life. They named him Eesaa Robert Rasheed.[5] But the story of Robert Stanley did not stop with Eesaa's birth. Over the next few years, Brian made it his mission to find out as much as he could in relation to the facts of Robert's life, along with Auntie Gay and Uncle David. As a newcomer to the discipline of family history, I have to say that their collective efforts have been nothing short of outstanding. Without their help I could not have

[4] The Anglo-Catholic tradition of the Church of England is very similar to a Roman Catholic style of service, but it remains strictly Church of England/Anglican – i.e. no connection with the Pope, less veneration of Mary, less focus on transubstantiation (the belief that the wine and bread become the physical blood and body of Jesus). New St George's of Stalybridge was famously engaged in a battle with Old St George's of Cocker Hill, attended by Robert Stanley and the following generations. See Chapter 3.
[5] Steven and Rozina opted for the phonetic version of the name; i.e. 'Rasheed'.

written this book. Between them, they have barely left a stone unturned when it comes to finding out about the basic facts of Robert's life, and as word got out amongst the Muslim community in the north west we also saw an increasing number of approaches from academics and journalists who were eager to hear our family's story; in particular, the synchronicity of Robert's conversion with that of his great x 3 grandson.

In 2008, our grandmother Edith sadly passed away and in her jewellery box, we found a tie pin, bearing a star and crescent emblem. Brian knew that it had belonged to his great great grandfather and we began to wonder if it had been a gift bestowed upon Robert by the Muslim community of Liverpool. Then, in 2009, Ronnie Stanley, Brian's elderly great uncle, got in touch. Ronnie had heard about Brian's search for information on Robert and invited Dad to visit him. Brian and Steven drove to his home in Macclesfield and were stunned to be presented with a fez, the very item which Robert had worn in the Liverpool mosque as he prayed alongside Sheikh Abdullah Quilliam. Ronnie had no idea of the significance of this find; an astonishing item which had been kept in the family for 'no apparent reason'.

Writing About Robert

By 2011, Brian had compiled two pamphlets containing his research into the Stanley family history; one focussing on his own life and childhood, and the other outlining the facts of Robert Stanley's life. Reading both was quite an emotional experience for my brother and I. Dad had left school at 15 and always claimed to be uneducated and not confident in his writing or public speaking. But for the first time, Dad's booklets allowed us to see that this was not so. His writing was excellent and, also for the first time, Robert's life had been revealed to the world after being hidden for so long.

Brian's pamphlet proved to be in great demand amongst local history enthusiasts in the Tameside area and amongst our Muslim friends, and the number of nudges and not-so-subtle suggestions that it was 'time you wrote a full book on Robert' increased in intensity.

At this point, I should be honest and state that I never wanted to write this book about Robert. I had always felt that this was a story belonging more to my brother – and that if anyone would work closely with my dad on furthering the story, it would be him. However, during the time that Brian was beginning his research on the life of Robert, I had started to write books myself. In the end, I began to see their point, particularly when I witnessed the enthusiasm reflected in other peoples' eyes when I told them the story of Robert. People from many different walks of life had questions for us about the impact of Robert's conversion on his family, why his faith was shrouded in secrecy for so long and – of course - the million dollar question that nearly every woman asks: "What on earth must his wife have thought?"

I was aware that there was plenty of room in academic circles for further work on the life of Robert and I have been met with much enthusiasm should our family want to take our work in this direction. In my research to produce this book, I have certainly found a wealth of new material on Robert, unearthing details that provide us with a journey from Cardiff to Stalybridge, Chartist murders, the Seven Virgins scandal of the Christian Israelites and onto the Pankhursts' corner of

Manchester. We take in Quilliam's first mosque in Liverpool, Parliament's debate over enfranchisement, Robert's stance over Bulgaria, Urquhart's dabbling with the Ottoman Caliphate and Robert's stint at owning a pub. Not to mention all the minor local events which might sound petty: the stolen mackerel, the gruesome corpses at the train station, the streetlamps, the giddiness in the council chambers, the seven-year-old boys sent down for prison with hard labour and the girls who didn't need to go to school. And last, but by no means least, the ever-present drunken women of Stalybridge; all of which add colour and character to this life story.

In coming to write *His Own Man*, my family were agreed on one thing: it should be *an accessible read for all* and not present itself as an academic book. So, although the research contained within it has been conducted in an academic manner, and I have done my best to add accurate notes and annotations, it does not set out to try and impress upon the reader anything other than it being a thorough, non-fiction investigation into the life and times of Robert Stanley.

Beyond Non-Fiction

The companion book to this one is called *Imagining Robert – Scenes from the Life of a Hidden Victorian Muslim*. It uses creative fiction alongside the factual, utilising scripts and monologues to tell another side of the story. Robert was born into the working class and, although he had strong views on the different segments within the working class, like practically all lower-class people during the Victorian period, the recording of information, thoughts and views was not something that he did (or if he did, nothing was kept!). This has made our research much more difficult than, for example, if Robert had been middle class. It made perfect sense, therefore, to try and fill the gaps of his life, the parts that we can only imagine, using creative fiction. This approach allowed me to bring the lives of 'Robert's women' into the story. Women, of course, always linger in the shadows of history and none more so than working-class women (see appendices).

Hoping for Change

My personal aim in writing 'His Own Man' is to encourage others to investigate their own family history and to seek out the ordinary-yet-wonderful inspirations amongst our ancestors (see Appendix 4.) But, as a family, we also have deep concerns over the rise of the far right and anti-Muslim attitudes in the UK. So, it would be good to hear that this book has perhaps demonstrated that we cannot learn about the practise of Islam solely from the newspapers, from the internet or from the TV. The only way that we can learn how a faith is really practised is to examine the lives of others and to get to know, personally, the people who have chosen to follow that particular religious path.

Although it focuses on someone born in 1828, I hope that *His Own Man* perhaps challenges readers' views about what being a Muslim means in British society today. Writing it has certainly made me think about the fact that history is in grave danger of repeating itself if we can't learn – as Robert did – to take the responsibility to educate ourselves and to get to know people who may have different beliefs to our own.

CHAPTER 1

The Tale of William and Ann
1788 - 1838

Leech's Mills, Stalybridge - built 1806

A Cotton Context

By the end of the 18th century, south-east Lancashire's woollen industry was no longer the dominant industry; it had been usurped by cotton. Consequently, during the 19th century, the north of England experienced rapid expansion, both in terms of its economy and the size of its population. Villages such as Stalybridge and Dukinfield had grown to become towns, and most of their industry and trade was based on cotton. The towns of Ashton, Stalybridge, Dukinfield and Hyde – the hometowns of our Stanley family branch – were the earliest towns in northern England to experience the profound social, political and economic effects of the Industrial Revolution.[6]

The first cotton mill in south-east Lancashire was built in Stalybridge in 1776. Stalybridge was also the first town in England to use steam to power its factories, marking it as the cradle of the industrial revolution. Ashton and Hyde soon followed the example of their neighbour and, by 1835, these three towns collectively produced almost the largest quantity of steam output in the whole of Lancashire. All were located close to the banks of the River Tame. Hyde and one-third of Stalybridge were situated on the Cheshire side of the river whilst Ashton remained in Lancashire. Coal was present at Ashton, Dukinfield and Stalybridge and a network of canals, along with the turnpike roads to Huddersfield and Manchester, meant that the area had many of the conditions necessary for growth of the cotton industry and its factory system.

---

[6] Dukinfield was originally an outgrowth of Stalybridge. It is now a town in its own right but during Robert's time it did not have borough status and part of Stalybridge was known as 'Dukinfield ward' – this was Robert's first constituency.

'King Cotton' became the nickname for Manchester, which had become the industrial centre of the world during the early years of Robert Stanley's life, lying six miles to the west of Stalybridge, Ashton and Dukinfield. Whilst the economic boom that accompanied textile production lined the pockets of the wealthy, it also increased the gap between rich and poor. Elaborate new mansions and exquisite town houses belonging to the newly-monied sprang up along the main roads in south-east Lancashire towns and along the main routes towards Manchester, but conditions were horrendous for many people. Low wages, fluctuating unemployment and the threat of the workhouse provoked discontent amongst the factory workers, who were already resentful at being hemmed into dangerous, horrible workplaces and forced away from their families and from traditional home-based piecework. Children as young as ten were expected to work over ten hours a day and, as the power loom quickly pushed the much smaller production output of the handloom to one side, Luddism and violent antipathy towards the nouveau-riche factory owners flourished.

In south-east Lancashire, the great majority of the population was working class, as observed by Friedrich Engels when he visited the towns, and was engaged in the cotton industry, mainly in mule-spinning and power-loom weaving. However, because of the ease with which the new skill of power-loom weaving could be acquired, and due to the ready availability of work in these towns, the redundant handloom weavers were often absorbed more easily than in some other areas. This did not mean, though, that the workers of these towns settled peaceably into the new regimes or prospered accordingly.

From 1825 to 1850, these three towns saw not only a rise in the numbers employed in the cotton industry, but also in the number of combined firms employing large workforces. Ashton proved to have exceptionally 'giant' firms, with 29 employing over 100 people – a larger percentage than that of Manchester and considerably greater than Oldham. These larger firms also prevailed in Stalybridge and Hyde where, due to their considerable power, the cotton masters were able to enforce the truck system upon their employees.[7] Prior to this period, a protectionist economy had been the status quo for Britain. The 1815 Corn Laws were keeping food prices artificially high, which depressed domestic manufacturing markets and led to higher unemployment. The working class suffered as a result of indirect taxation and income tax was abolished in 1816.

After the prosecutions (and executions) of Luddites, who had taken it upon themselves to destroy hated factory machinery, many of the working class turned to trade unions, but the early attempts in the north of England failed as unions were outlawed. However, in 1824 and 1825 parliamentary legislation legalised unions again, but they were weak, and employers easily defeated strikes, countering them with 'lock-outs'. The economy was in constant fluctuation, as the real value of wages decreased, and a series of harvests failed. So, the strike weapon was simply not viable for most factory workers, and unions had insufficient funds to support those who were sacked by the cotton masters.

---

[7] The truck system was a method used by mill owners to ensure that as much money as possible was returned to them i.e. a portion of a worker's wages would be paid in coupons for food etc. which could only be redeemed at the mill shop.

The 1830s were witness to a series of fiscal crises – the Whigs (Liberals) were in power from 1830-41, but their economic strategy was weak. They left a £7,000,000 deficit on departing from office and made no attempt to perform much-needed reform of the banking sector or of British currency. Subsequently, between 1836-38 over 60 banks crashed in England, resulting in even higher levels of unemployment and food prices. The gap between rich and poor was ever-increasing, an ongoing feature for commentary and not just by pro-revolutionaries, such as the French rebels and Marx and Engels, but by figures of the British Establishment, such as Charles Dickens (a Liberal) and Prime Minister Benjamin Disraeli (a Conservative) in his own novel about the time, *Sybil Or The Two Nations*.[8]

By the early 1830s, the condition of the nation had become a deep concern for those who felt a moral outrage on behalf of the poor. The Ten Hours Movement found massive support amongst the working class and the more paternalistic elements of the middle and upper classes, but the 1833 Factory Act proved to be a bitter disappointment: regulating child labour but not the hours that adults spent confined in those places. They also only applied to textile factories.

The threat of sacking and of transportation overseas was a very real deterrent to any working-class person who wanted to become more closely involved with the unions; the names of the Tolpuddle Martyrs became forever etched in the minds of any family who dared to become too engaged in trade unionist activism during this period. The residents of both Stalybridge and Ashton – the towns where Robert spent half of his childhood - preferred union action whenever they experienced particularly harsh economic circumstances or were being treated more cruelly than usual. They were not by nature, however, given towards revolutionary politics; rather, conservatism prevailed for most of the time, although in times of distress the areas displayed a strong proclivity towards flashes of violence. By the time that Robert Stanley had become mayor in 1874, the Home Office had marked them out as towns which were somewhat 'notorious'. This mode of behaviour might be seen as a sign of the truly oppressed: a passive-aggressive people fearful of longer-lasting upheaval and change.

Nowt to be Ashamed of?
What was Robert Stanley's immediate family background? Prior to the revelation of his conversion to Islam, several of our Stanley relatives had been working on their own family history trees. Collectively, we could trace quite a large amount of information going back at least nine generations and to Robert's own great-grandfather, another Robert Stanley, who had a farm in Dukinfield. The Stanley farm was next door to Plantation Farm, which was owned by a Mary and Robert Moffatt, who spent much of their time as missionaries in South Africa. Their eldest daughter married the famous Dr Livingstone in 1845, when Robert was 17 years old. Perhaps these neighbours - their experiences and talk of foreign travel, of

---

[8] Disraeli's most telling quote in 'Sybil' could apply to 21st century Britain, *"Two nations; between whom there is no intercourse and no sympathy ... who are formed by a different breeding, are fed by a different food, are ordered by different manners, and are not governed by the same laws: the rich and the poor."* Disraeli, *Sybil, or The Two Nations*, 1845.

other cultures and religions - piqued the interest of the young Robert after he had returned to live in the area?

When looking at the information available on Robert Stanley's parents, William and Ann, it becomes clear that something is amiss. We know that William Stanley was born in 1788 in Dukinfield and that his firstborn - and Robert's eldest sibling, William junior - was born in 1808. This means that William would have fathered the child at the age of 20. Ann, William junior's mother, was listed as being aged 44 in the 1831 census, with every following census affirming this age each decade. Therefore, she must have been born in 1796 or thereabouts. No record of her birth can be found, however, although each census gives her place of birth as being in Hereford. The birth of William junior in 1808 meant that Ann would have been either 12 or 13. We can only assume that the couple met in Dukinfield but, because their residence there pre-dates any census data collection, it is impossible to know why young Ann – born in Hereford – was living close to William in Dukinfield, where William junior was christened.

To the modern eye this situation appears to be quite shocking, although there were incidences of marriages occurring in some parts of the country of those aged 14 or 15. However, it was illegal to get married below the age of 21 unless a parent had given specific consent. And whilst women got married at a much younger age than at present, a girl of 12 or 13 becoming pregnant would not have been tolerated by a conservative community if the pregnancy had taken place outside of marriage.

By the time that Ann's next child was born she was living with William (although we have never been able to find proof that they married) and the family were based in Cardiff. Why Cardiff? Had William been pressured to move to Wales, with Ann following him later? Or had the couple met there originally, with Ann moving to Dukinfield by the time that this (potentially) illegitimate first child was born? More intrigue arises around Robert's birth family when we notice that there was an eight-year gap between the birth of William junior and their second child in 1817- John, who is set to feature much more in this story. Following John, Ann had given birth to another eight children by 1836.

Why was there such a gap between their first and second child and then so many in relatively quick succession? As with many aspects of Robert's background, we can only guess. Perhaps William was sent away until Ann came of an age where their union was deemed to be respectable, or perhaps Ann had other children that did not survive infanthood and it simply took that long for them to have another child that survived. However, thanks to the census, we can be certain that Robert was the seventh surviving child of ten and that all other siblings after the eldest were born in Cardiff.

A Cardiff Life – but Links to 'Home'

We know that William was a hatter, one of the most respectable and flourishing trades in the north of England, and that his firstborn, William junior, worked alongside him for at least some time until he moved to Manchester, where he became a miner.[9] Given William's profession, it seems strange that he relocated to Cardiff, as it was Stockport – which shared its boundaries with Dukinfield – which was the centre of the British hatting industry. But perhaps this points again to a 'need to leave' theory. It could have been that William wanted to prove himself as a sole trader in a different region; perhaps Ann's family were in Cardiff and he thought that the Welsh capital would be as good a place as any to demonstrate his ability to create a viable hatting business. Certainly, by the time that Ann fell pregnant, William's older brother, John, was already on the road to becoming one of the most successful and wealthy businessmen in Ashton, and his achievements were even more impressive given that he did not come from a rich family or was born of the landed gentry.

There is no proof that Ann and William ever married, although thanks to the census data we know they lived together as man and wife in Cardiff, where they both died in old age. After his wife, it seems likely that William's older brother, John, would have been the most significant adult in his life, for several reasons. We know that John Stanley was a member of the Southcottians at the time when William and Ann set up home in Cardiff (see Chapter 2) but, because there are no written records produced by either John or William in relation to their lives, it is difficult to decipher the brothers' personalities. From what we can deduce about John Stanley, he was stable, focussed, had an excellent talent for enterprise and business, was comfortable mixing with wealthy industrialists in the Manchester area and was deeply religious. In some respects, it seems that the two brothers could not have been more different, as William's life was perhaps less conservative; even as an elderly man he comes across as sounding like quite a character and somewhat a charmer (see Chapter 7). Later, we shall see that John Stanley came to be the key parental figure in Robert's life, which might cause us to wonder whether Robert's character was formulated with no thanks to his father's influence – or, perhaps, even despite him? It could have been that Robert preferred to mirror the more respectable and civically-inclined characteristics and examples of his Uncle John.

We can learn a little bit more about Robert's father's character from two incidents that took place in Cardiff. In 1818, records show that William Stanley owed a debt 'to our sovereign Lord the King in the sum of Twenty pounds'. Then, in 1825, the following was contained in the Cardiff Town Clerk's Memoranda:

William Stanley has carried on business in the Borough of Cardiff as a Hatter, for these last nine years, and has during that period sold goods in the public Market. He himself, as well as all others, erecting every market day, their own standing in the street. About a year and a half ago ("Christmas 1823") a person calling himself Collector of the Corporation Tolls, for the first time demanded 4d. for Corporation dues. Stanley having never paid this before or ever heard of it, refused. He refused also on the following days, on which the same was demanded. And on each of such successive dates the Collector and

---

[9] William Stanley junior was a miner at Newton Heath colliery, Manchester, in the 1850s according to the 1851 census. He would have been in his 40s at this time. It is likely that he was one of the four brothers who came back up north to be helped by Uncle John Stanley, who by this point had become owner of Standard Pit in Moston, Manchester.

Constables seized one of his hats.

A toll of 1d. is admitted having been paid from time immemorial to the Serjeant at Mace, and no other, and the oldest persons in the Town who have stood the Market between 30- and 40-years last past, never paid any other toll but 1d., nor was any other demanded of them.

From the information that William presented, it seems that a rival market house had been set up and that its owner charged tolls. This led to a collector being introduced to do the same on William's pitch. William quoted a King's Charter that stated that those who were burgess of the area should be free of additional tolls on top of the usual taxes and, although he did not have the burgess status, as an inhabitant, he argued that he fell under the Charter's ruling. The judge agreed with him, and he won his case.

William Stanley must have come away from this experience feeling more than a little vindicated. He was not a wealthy man; he was engaged in a struggling industry at a time of economic downturn and high unemployment in the region, but he had stood up to the Establishment for the rights of the street market trader and had won. In doing so, he would have caused others to think more carefully about the fairness of taxation and the boundaries of identity, citizenship and even nationality. This incident took place three years before Robert was born and, no doubt as a small child, he would have been regaled with the tale of how his father placed his trust in the judicial system, argued his case and had been victorious. So, even if life as a son of William Stanley in Cardiff did not provide the sorts of economic or educational advantages that being the nephew of John Stanley in Ashton did, he probably learned some valuable lessons from his family of origin in relation to justice and equity, perhaps spurring him on to become a magistrate in the late 1860s. This case bears all the hallmarks of the beliefs that were required to create Robert's political conservatism: an interfering state should not persecute the small but hard-working businessperson.

By 1836, when Robert had reached the age of eight, life seemed to have become more difficult for the Stanleys. According to the 1851 census, William Stanley was no longer employed as a hatter and yet he still had a large brood of children to feed. Perhaps his attempt to build a long-standing hatting trade in Cardiff had failed; maybe the problem was that his skills centred on the art of making beaver-skin hats (top hats made of felted beaver fur) and by the early to mid-19th century men preferred to wear hats made of silk. It seems likely that William and Ann would have sent the inevitable 'need a bit of assistance again' letter to William's now extremely wealthy older brother, John. The 1851 census tells us that William had now become a proprietor of houses and that his family was living on David Street in the heart of St Mary's district - Cardiff's bustling market area. Other than receiving help from John Stanley there are no other obvious answers as to where the money needed to purchase houses to rent out could have come from.

Going Back to His Roots
The rest of William Stanley's family had remained in the Dukinfield and Ashton areas. When his own father, John, died just a year before Robert was born, William had been a clear favourite in the will, indicating that he had kept a strong and

regular connection with his parents and siblings up north. Robert would probably have been familiar with the hometowns of the Stanleys and with his Stanley grandparents. Thanks to the census, we know that at least three of William and Ann's sons moved up north for employment reasons; it seems likely that all three were taken under the wing of their Uncle John.[10] When he came to live in Ashton, Robert moved in with his older brother (another John) which we know because in 1841 a 13-year-old Robert is listed as living with newlyweds John Stanley, aged 21, and his new wife, Betty (nee Miller) of the same age, on Oldham Road in Ashton.

Children under the age of ten were not legally obliged to attend school until 1870, but the 1841 census tells us that Robert's older brother, John, had clearly done well enough for himself to become a bookkeeper – no mean feat if he had not received an education himself when he was in Cardiff. In all likelihood John Stanley insisted on providing his nephews with both jobs and elements of an education. Perhaps with this in mind, the young Robert was also dispatched to the area to reap the benefits from their benefactor. In Britain today the average ten-year-old is not even allowed to walk to school on their own; independence and moving away from parents is practically unheard of, so it is hard to imagine what was going through the mind of this young lad when he journeyed north in order to live away from his mother and father. Still, if Robert had been around today to ask about this monumental change in his life, he might well have said to others about this period in his life that, "It was the making of me."

---

[10] Robert's younger brother, James, moved to Stalybridge from Cardiff when Robert first set up his grocer's business. He is listed in the 1851 census as being ten years old and employed as a grocer's assistant to Robert. Robert clearly wanted to do for his younger brother what his Uncle John had done for him. James moved back to Cardiff when he was a young man, and in the 1861 census was listed as an Outdoor Officer of Customs.

CHAPTER 2

The Christian Israelites Connection
1821 – 1838

Which Church?

Readers not from the Tameside area may be unfamiliar with the sect known as the Christian Israelites and with their founder, Prophet John Wroe. However, after carrying out more research into their beliefs and the historical context, it seems to me that their values and the persecution that they faced were crucial in shaping Robert Stanley's view of the world: that they played an important role in setting him on his long path towards Islam.

Robert Stanley's involvement with the Christian Israelites was only discovered when my father, Brian Longden, retrieved the wedding certificate of Robert's marriage to Emma Meredith. It transpired that the couple had been married in the Sanctuary of the Christian Israelites. For these reasons, this chapter focusses exclusively on the Christian context of the area and in detail on the Christian Israelites, the person of Uncle John Stanley and the now rather infamous debacle surrounding John Wroe in Ashton-under-Lyne.

Brian Longden himself never had much interest in religion or in religious history. Not a believer, he would be the first to say that he placed little value on church life other than its architectural and community contributions. Brian was born into the Anglican church but stopped attending as a teenager. His father's side of the family (the Longdens) possessed no particular religious beliefs or loyalties and, according to Brian, his dad's only interest in the church was The Church Inn in Stalybridge! Brian and his brother, Ted, however, had attended Old St George's in Stalybridge whilst children. Usually accompanied by their grandfather, Dean Stanley (Robert's grandson and also a mayor of Stalybridge), they both became members of the church choir and then the Boys' Brigade. The tradition of attending Old St George's was something that Dean had inherited from his own father, 'Unlucky Bob', so when Brian decided to find out more about Robert Stanley, he supposed that Unlucky Bob's father – Robert - would have had a similar life-long involvement with Old St George's before he became a Muslim. This turned out to be only part of the truth.

Old St. George's Church, at Cocker Hill in Stalybridge, was a flourishing Anglican chapel by the time that an excited – and perhaps nervous – ten-year-old Robert arrived in the area in 1838 from Cardiff. As he moved in with his older brother and new sister-in-law, Robert would no doubt have been aware of the type of work that lay ahead of him, and of the personality of his new benefactor – the highly respected, religious and rather curious figure of Uncle John Stanley.

John Stanley was a resident of Ashton-under-Lyne, and his name is mentioned in many of the town's history books. He was one of the area's leading industrialists but, until Brian was presented with the 1908 copy of *The Crescent*, there was no information about the nature of any relationship between Robert and

Uncle John. However, in the interview with Robert that Quilliam printed, Robert mentioned that he had been sent to the area to become an apprentice for his Uncle John, though he made no mention of the Christian Israelites. When Brian decided to locate Robert's grave (see Chapter 11) he found that he had been buried in St Paul's Parish Church graveyard - the second parish church of Stalybridge after Old St George's, consecrated in 1839. This led him to wonder whether Robert and his family had been lifelong members of St Paul's Church rather than Old St George's, as Robert's son and later descendants were.

After having found two of the three most important documents in relation to Robert - his birth certificate for Cardiff and his death certificate and burial in Stalybridge - Brian was astonished to discover that Robert and Emma Meredith's wedding certificate showed their marriage took place at Ashton's Christian Israelite Sanctuary in 1847. Thanks to the debacle surrounding Wroe and the Christian Israelites, Brian – like many Tameside residents – was already familiar with the name of this unusual sect. But his own family being involved with this group came as something of a surprise. It seems that Robert and Emma's marriage in the Sanctuary could only have meant one of three things: firstly, that Robert had been a member of the Christian Israelites; secondly, that Emma Meredith had been a member; and thirdly, that neither of them were members, but perhaps attended there sometimes and simply chose to get married in the Sanctuary in order to please Uncle John. Emma had moved to Ashton, and the 1841 census tells us she was living with the Knott family as their live-in domestic servant at the age of 16. This family's home was close to the area where many of the Christian Israelites lived, only yards away from the Sanctuary. So, the family that she lived with and worked for may well have been Christian Israelite members themselves.

In terms of the latter theory, there is enough evidence to show that Uncle John Stanley demonstrated very generous sharing of his good fortune with others, and not just in terms of his family. He invited and hosted his nephews from Cardiff to come and live in the area and helped them find work. We also know that Robert's parents, William and Ann, had become property owners and landlords in Cardiff by 1851. It was highly unlikely that they had come into large amounts of money themselves through William's hatting business, which probably failed because beaver fur-trimmed hats were no longer in vogue. It seems plausible, therefore, that Uncle John continuously helped his younger brother and family out on a financial basis.

Uncle John's sons from both of his marriages turned out to be extremely wealthy and successful: the benefits of having an industrious and generous father. In many ways, it seems that John Stanley treated his nephew, Robert, as another son. We also know that Robert owned property and did not simply rent the shop premises that he lived and worked in after his marriage to Emma, as he was listed on the electoral register (being a property owner was a prerequisite at this time for being able to vote in elections and was the reason why most working class men were, in effect, still disenfranchised). It looks very much like Uncle John bought the property for Robert – who could not have afforded such an extravagant outlay at the age of 20 and on a grocer's assistant's wages. Robert, however, was not provided for in Uncle John's will in 1855, perhaps because John had already furnished him with a shop and a trade during the course of his life.

Given that John had been so generous towards his nephew, getting married in the Sanctuary may well have been both the polite and the political thing to do for the young couple, particularly if Uncle John had offered to pay for the wedding in such a sumptuous setting. By the time of Robert and Emma's marriage in 1847, the history of the Christian Israelites in England had suffered all manner of slanders and persecutions. Even before the allegations made against Wroe, the group was seen as an unusual, rather eccentric and inward-looking sect, although their kindness and generosity had been noted by outsiders, such as the secularist and free-thinker Richard Carlile. Their views were perceived by mainstream Christians to be controversial, if not downright heretical. It would have been highly unlikely, therefore, for a couple who had no connection to the Christian Israelites to get married within this church.

And yet, this church had always attracted wealthy and highly respectable residents. Robert's mentor, employer and father-figure, Uncle John, was one of the Number Four – the four men who governed the church - and Jonathan Andrew, one of the town's Poor Law guardians, was the presiding priest for their marriage. The rest of this chapter will examine the religious history of the area but will mostly concentrate on the 'Wroe years' of the Christian Israelites so that we can consider the influence that this fascinating congregation would have had on the young Robert.

Radical, Conservative ... and Dissenting

National historians who have studied the towns of Stalybridge, Ashton and Dukinfield during the late 18th and 19th centuries have always viewed the locals as either radicals or conformists. Those who follow a leftist tradition have pointed to the people's involvement in Peterloo, the length and strength of the 1830-31 strike and the Plug Riots (General Strike) of 1842. Even the murder of Thomas Ashton, a rich mill owner in 1830, and the killing of an Ashton police constable in 1848, have been tied to popular radicalist groups such as the Chartists. The imprisonment of firebrand Methodist preacher, Joseph Rayner Stephens (see Chapter 3), Lancashire's Cotton Famine, the Bread Riots of 1863 (which began in Stalybridge and spread to Ashton and Dukinfield) have all also been claimed as popular radicalist victories. Those historians who prefer to dwell on working class conservatism, however, highlight the fact that the striking workers ultimately failed and note that many mill owners were paternalists and very popular amongst local workers. They point to the fact that the poor were not united; for example, the bitter divisions between working class Protestants and Irish Catholics that exploded into Stalybridge's Murphy Riots in 1869. And there is no denying that even the most violently anti-Poor Law campaigner, Joseph Rayner Stephens, ended up becoming a Poor Law guardian himself and stood as a Conservative parliamentary candidate.

But the fact of the matter is that the people of these – our - towns are not easily explained away in terms of Leftist and Rightist political sentiments. There may not have been much formal education during Robert's life in these towns but there was a strong tradition of informal education, discussion and debate.

The sentiments of the people could never be assured in these areas and, even today, these places still demonstrate a huge independence of thought. Non-conformism and the determination to dissent were – and still are – the order of the day. Robert is perhaps one of the finest that the area has ever had, in terms of a man who thought for himself and who always refused to be boxed into any sort of political or religious corner.

The towns of Dukinfield, Ashton and Stalybridge have always been some of the strongest dissenting areas in Britain, dating back to the English Civil War when Colonel Robert Duckenfield proved himself to be one of the North's leading Roundheads. A much-admired member of Cromwell's New Model Army, Duckenfield set up the first dissenting church in the area – his own domestic place of worship, named Dukinfield Old Hall Chapel. This church changed hands over the years between various dissenting groups, such as the Unitarians and the Congregationalists, but it was also the only place of worship in the area for a long time, and our original branch of the Dukinfield Stanleys lived less than a mile away from it.[11] The next church to be built in the area was known as Old Chapel. It was equally close to the Stanley family farm and proved to be another strong non-conformist church that switched hands between various non-conformists.[12] Another group of famous dissenters, the Quakers, also had some following in the area, with their founder, George Fox, said to have preached his first sermon at Colonel Duckenfield's Old Hall Chapel as far back as 1647.

In addition to the presence of protestant Anglicans, Roman Catholics and Dissenters, many new and unusual sects were gaining hold in the region from 1700-1850. The Moravians, who created their own communities and settlements in Dukinfield and Fairfield, and the Mormons (Church of the Latter-Day Saints), had a considerable following around the central Manchester area, with thousands embracing the faith and choosing to leave England for a new life in Utah. The Christadelphian church was also growing at this time.

Those who have found their way to this book because they are already interested in British Victorian and early 20th century Islamic converts may be aware that the more well-known recorded converts had previously been members of various mainstream British churches. Many of them were non-conformists who were dissatisfied with the Established church. The growth of early Islam in the north of England under the direction of Sheikh Abdullah Quilliam developed greatly as a result of the weaknesses of the Anglican church, and the Muslim faith benefitted

---

[11] The Church of England - also known as 'Anglicans', the 'Established' church or the 'Protestant' church - was set up by King Henry VIII in order to create a new state-governed Christian church and to break away from Papal influence. Dissenters, also known as non-conformists, were the other branch of Protestants that predominated in England, but they were not associated with Parliament or royalty. Mainstream examples include the Methodists, Baptists, Congregationalists, Quakers and Unitarians to name but a few, although there were, of course, many smaller sects and groups.
[12] Many Muslims feel a natural affinity with Unitarianism due to the focus on the oneness of God/Allah as opposed to the Trinity-centric attentions of Protestants and Catholics. Many Muslims also feel close to the Quakers, who have no excluding creeds. The Stanley family's dissenting roots may have caused Robert to feel more predisposed towards Islam. Some of the wealthiest families in Stalybridge (the Bayleys, Leeches and Harrisons) were Unitarians and peers of Robert: fellow politicians, philanthropists and mayors.

considerably from the strength of the temperance movement.[13] Very little has been written, however, about the role that the more fringe elements of Christian sects have played amongst those who abandoned Christianity in order to follow Islam.

The Christian Israelites were one of the smaller millennialist groups who had grown out of the Southcottian church and had formed part of the dissenting movement; their story is intriguing - and not just because Robert and Uncle John were involved with them. After spending much time researching this period of the Christian Israelites and their influence on Robert's life, it seems to me that their treatment at the hands of the press and by local people very much shaped Robert's local and national views on justice and fairness towards those who possessed a different set of religious beliefs.

The Southcottians

One aspect that the Christian Israelites had in common with other non-conformists was that they believed the Established church of England had become corrupt and misled. More than this, they felt that mainstream Christianity's teachings had moved too far away from the original intentions of God and from the Abrahamic laws handed down by Moses to the Jews. Their millennialist approach centred on a literal belief of the New Testament: that Christ would physically return to earth before the dawn of the next millennium.

The Christian Israelites were drawn from the Southcottians, an 18th century sect named after Joanna Southcott, who was born in 1750 at Ottery St. Mary, Devon. She had been raised in the Church of England but in later life claimed to have been chosen by God to receive divine revelations. Unlike 19th century sects, which were primarily instigated and led by men, the 17th and 18th centuries bred some highly charismatic female religious leaders: fervent about their faith and who took bold steps to share it with others. Perhaps once the capitalist system set about defining much stronger gender roles in the 19th century, women were permitted less freedom to think about religious interpretations.

Joanna, known as Mother Southcott to her followers, shared prophecies and attracted several thousand to her fold. She was an unmarried, older woman who travelled the country, providing revelations - even writing some of them down and sealing them in a box so that they might be opened by future generations. One of her most startling prophecies was that, after reaching the age of sixty, she would give birth to the Messiah – or the Shiloh.[14] On 14th October 1814, the prophecy appeared to be coming true when she began to display all the signs of a heavy pregnancy. Preparations were made to welcome the child (including a special cradle being carved for it), but on 29th October, with no sign of a baby, Joanna died. A doctor confirmed that there had been no pregnancy and that she had died from

---

[13] Temperance was a movement of people who were opposed to any consumption of alcohol and who were said to have taken the pledge in order never to touch alcohol. Most were non-conformists but there were also Anglican groups. See Chapter 8 for more on 'the booze question'.

[14] The Shiloh is mentioned various times throughout the Old Testament and the Torah. It usually relates to either the coming of the Messiah or to a specific locality in Israel/Palestine where the Ark of the Covenant was said to be held. Shiloh also means 'bringing peace' or a 'sanctuary' in a place of desolation. Perhaps this is why the Christian Israelites chose this name for a church in Ashton!

a fast-growing tumour which certainly would have made it look as though she was pregnant.

After this, the Southcottians entered a long period where the group was divided over who was worthy enough to be the overall leader: prophecy and visions were the order of the day. In Ashton, the Southcottians continued to meet in the Charlestown area, in a building belonging to John Stanley – part of his iron and brass works.[15] John Stanley never claimed to be a prophet or visionary, but from early on he was a leading governor of the Southcottians and then the Christian Israelites. At the time of Joanna's death, he, along with his wife Sarah, believed that the successor to Southcott should be George Turner – an Ashton man himself, who was said to have the gift of prophecy. By now, there were several contenders for leadership: Samuel Walker, Thomas Stone, Robert Harling, William Shaw, George Turner and two men with the names of Towrt and Twigg. Later, another famous rival for the prophetic leadership emerged – John 'Zion' Ward - but it was John Wroe who managed to fight his way forward as the strongest candidate for leadership in 1821.

Wroe: Bradford Lad - Christian Israelite Founder

At a Southcottian meeting held in Bradford, Turner announced another expected birth date for the Shiloh; this time the Messiah would arrive on the 14th October 1820. John Wroe attended the meeting, although he was not a Southcottian. He publicly disagreed with Turner over the proclaimed date for the Shiloh's arrival. This fascination with the millennium and the coming of a new, holy child did not die a death with Mother Joanna, and for the rest of his years in England, differing interpretations on how and when the Messiah would appear, and fissures over who was fittest to be leader, would chequer the life and work of John Wroe and of the history of the Christian Israelites in England.

Very few people outside of the Ashton, Bradford and Wakefield regions may have heard of Prophet John Wroe. Those of a certain age, however, may recall the BBC TV series starring Jonathan Price, Kathy Burke and a very young (and pre-Hollywood) Minnie Driver. The TV drama was based on a book by the author Jane Rogers, who was herself a local resident. Rogers produced a dramatic and provoking work of literary fiction, offering a creative interpretation of the scandalous case surrounding Wroe and the allegations of mistreatment of seven virgins. The Christian Israelite church today, however, feels that much that has been written in recent years about Wroe is the product of biased and clumsy historical research which has not adequately challenged the media reports and other prejudices of the time.

John Wroe was a Bradford boy, born in the West Bowling district of West Yorkshire. When he was in his mid-thirties, he claimed to have received divine revelations from God and during the years 1820-22 began gaining his own followers. The West Yorkshire folk were the first to pledge their allegiance to him, with 50 Southcottians from Almondbury in Huddersfield declaring that he was their leader. This was followed by larger numbers in Sheffield and in Stockport.

---

[15] This building is where Ashton swimming baths is now located; the venue, too, where circumcisions of male Christian Israelites were performed by John Stanley and Henry Lees.

The Southcottians in the London area, however, were rather more reluctant to throw their lot in with him. Soon, though, the Southcottians of Ashton decided to interview Wroe as a prospective candidate for leadership and, in 1822, the most prominent members of the group – presumably including John Stanley - visited Wroe in Bradford.[16] Afterwards, Robert Blackwell of the Ashton group wrote to Wroe to declare that there was, *"no doubt of thy visitation from God."*[17] By 14th December 1822, Wroe was in a strong enough position to be able to formally break the sect away from Joanna's cult of personality, renaming the group the Christian Israelites.

On Christmas Day in 1822, Wroe arrived in Ashton, having travelled over 40 miles over the Pennines to speak to the Southcottian congregation. By this point in time, it seems that he had temporarily fought off the other contenders to become Joanna's successor. John Stanley had changed his allegiance from Turner to Wroe and was appointed as one of Wroe's Number Four, the four men who upheld the beliefs, practices and finances of the congregation.

Illustration of Prophet John Wroe, 1831

Ashton-under-Lyne proved to be fertile ground for the Southcottians and the Christian Israelites for several reasons. At the time of Wroe's arrival, the town's original parish church was St Michael's - the only Anglican church in the borough - and it had fostered a disastrous reputation amongst the community. Its parish boundaries simply could not deal with the enormous growth that Ashton's population had experienced as a result of the industrial revolution. The church had also gained a reputation for a lack of empathy with the poor, and its clergy hailed solely from the very privileged classes. From 1816-70, its priest was the Reverend George Chetwode, son of the Earl of Stamford. The Reverend Chetwode made a tidy profit from his stipend at St Michael's, which included a parsonage and monies made from the sale of coal reserves beneath the church's glebe land. He spent hardly any time in the North,

---

[16] One of them, Samuel Walker, was sceptical about Wroe; Wroe predicted a trial and death awaiting Walker. On his return to Ashton, this married man found that his affair with a much younger woman had been discovered. He subsequently fell from a position of prominence within the church and became a travelling fortune teller.

[17] John Wroe, *Divine Communications*, v 1, 22 Nov 1822.

preferring his home and tiny parish in Chilton, Buckinghamshire (with just 315 residents, in comparison to Ashton parish's 33,500). In 1869 it was reported that he hadn't been to Ashton in ten years, nor presided over a service in 30 years.[18]

Although non-conformist churches existed in Ashton, these had fast become the home of the newly prosperous mill owners (most of whom were Liberal voters) and many working people were not comfortable with worshipping alongside those that they were increasingly perceiving to be their oppressors. For those who felt threatened, concerned and confused, millennialist religion provided a much-needed source of comfort. Individual glory could be gained alongside justice for the new and greedy oppressors which the Established church – controlled by the dominant aristocratic classes - simply could not offer. Groups such as the Southcottians and Christian Israelites also offered a sprinkling of excitement and hope with their prophecies and mystical elements.

Along with Uncle John Stanley's family, many other rich and respected members of the town chose Wroe as their leader. But why? By all accounts he was poorly dressed, eccentric in habits and was more than a little outspoken in his condemnation of those with whom he disagreed. However, it is all too easy – especially after the sexual allegations – to portray Wroe as some sort of Rasputinesque figure whose apparent hypnotic eyes entranced people. The truth of the matter has more to do with the neglect by the Anglican church and because the Church of England, at this time, was impossible for newly wealthy men to break into; Anglicanism had always been the natural home of the landed gentry. Men of new wealth such as John Stanley (a factory, shop and coal mine owner), Samuel Swire (a coal mine owner) and the Lees family (cotton mill owners), might have been able to possess a good deal of Ashton's revenue, but, in terms of traditional forms of power, many remained voiceless. Furthermore, if they had Tory tendencies, they often would not have felt particularly welcome at the other pro-Liberal dissenting churches. Until the Reform Act 1832, it is important to note that even those who had created great wealth thanks to industrialisation still had no vote and no say in the running of the country.

John and William Stanley's Dukinfield family of origin had mostly had their children baptised at the non-conformist Old Chapel, so Uncle John would have felt no great affiliation with Ashton's Anglicans. He married his wife, Sarah, at Stockport parish church and it may even have been Sarah who had been involved with the Southcottians, given that this town was a stronghold for Mother Joanna.[19] It seems that he became involved with the Southcottians at the beginning of his early business successes and, given his status, he would have found it easy to exert power and influence within this comparatively small religious organisation. He would have found it difficult to wield the same level of influence if he had decided to change his worship preferences once Joanna had died (a more cynical perspective on John's involvement with the Christian Israelites, but one that nevertheless should be considered).

---

[18] E. Green, *Prophet John Wroe: Virgins, Scandals and Visions*, 2005, p.74.
[19] Whether a follower of Southcott or not, at the time of John and Sarah Stanley's marriage in 1845, the law only allowed weddings to take place in Church of England establishments.

Building a New Jerusalem

By 1823, the vast majority of Southcottians in the North had been won over by John Wroe, although he faced constant battles for control of the congregations. During the 1820s, it was estimated that the number of Christian Israelites in Ashton was at least 500.[20] Wroe's interpretation of Christianity based itself on a return to Abrahamic origins, with a strong connection to Judaism, and the church's rules included dietary, behavioural and dress codes, many of which would be familiar to most Jews and Muslims today.[21] Throughout the Manchester area, Christian Israelite males were often referred to as 'the Beardies' because they were not permitted to cut their hair (and subsequently were rather unpopular with the local barbers).[22] The Prophet organised his church by dividing the congregation in Ashton into 12 'tribes', representing the 12 tribes of Israel, each being led by 12 men and 12 women.

Wroe wanted to create a physical manifestation of this return to Abrahamic roots and he ordered that Mosaic Law should be followed from 1824 to 1864. After this, he predicted a period of 40 years where Gospel observance should be followed. To mirror the real Jerusalem, he decreed that the group should build actual gatehouses at four strategic points on the roads into Ashton. One was later named Taunton Lodge in the Waterloo area, and another was on Mossley Road (later becoming a public house –The Odd Whim - rather cheekily named after Wroe and his followers). The third came to be known as Moss Lodge on Manchester Road and the fourth was built in the Shepley area, close to Dukinfield Hall. Although the grand gatehouses were built, the mammoth enclosing walls of

---

[20] Green, p.7.

[21] Wroe's aim was to serve the 'scattered children of Israel' in addition to Gentiles. He created several tests; some with clear Abrahamic origins, others less so. Followers were to adhere to Mosaic Law; not consume animals that chewed the cud and fish (i.e. to eat kosher food only); take no tobacco, snuff or spirits; not cut or shave hair (for men) and to grow beards (as in Numbers 6:5); not wear red or black and to primarily wear yellows and blues (for women) and only wear clothes with side seams; possess no portraits or images of a living creature; observe the Sabbath on both Friday and Sunday; circumcise all males. At the time, the group was also accused of a strange practice of punishment whereby women were to beat male sinners, although this has always been denied by the church. Samuel Swire, one of Ashton's leading coal owners, was Mayor of the Manor in 1841 and a Christian Israelite. Along with John Stanley, he was one of the Number Four under Wroe. On 10 November 1827, *The Manchester Guardian* describes the church members at the funeral of Swire's daughter, saying that the men; *"appeared in blue coats, drab trousers, and brown hats, their usual costume. The ladies were dressed in white, with Leghorn bonnets trimmed with large white satin roses ... The ladies had on blue shoes and white silk shawls; the coaches were not covered, but green and yellow painted."* The men wore collarless coats with vests buttoned high up the throat over a linen shirt and ruffle, along with broad-brimmed beaver hats or brown felt hats, sometimes trimmed with green. The women wore bonnets, often with veils that had Hebraic characters embroidered over the portion below the eyes, and on religious feast days church members wore white linen vestments.

[22] Prophet Wroe made an exception for the wealthiest 'Beardie' followers; those (perhaps John Stanley) who were required to move in commercial circles and who traded on the floor of the Old Corn Exchange in Manchester were permitted to shave, as otherwise their businesses would have suffered. These non-Beardie Beardies were, however, made to pay a tax to the church for the fact that they shaved.

the gatehouses were never started, because the debacle involving Wroe put the project off somewhat (although even if Tameside Council and its ever-vigilant planning department had existed at this point in time, it is likely that the people of Ashton would have objected to having their land enclosed in such a way. A few gatehouses? Fair enough. But not a ruddy great wall).

But why did Wroe choose Ashton for his New Jerusalem? Why did he zone in on this medium-sized town, east of the increasingly sprawling Manchester metropolis? Why not Manchester itself? Or Bradford? The cynic might say that Wroe needed a substantially populated place where social and economic conditions were ripe for his prophecies to fall onto fertile ground. The early 1820s were cruel years for the ordinary working people of Bradford, and none more so than the wool combers, yet Wroe chose not to dwell in this place, perhaps because he was already too much of a familiar figure with the West Yorkshire folk. He would also, no doubt, have been aware of the words of Jesus Christ himself, *"Truly I tell you … no prophet is accepted in his hometown".*[23] It seems that Ashton possessed the needed spiritual vacuum required to develop a new and unusual church, thanks to the neglect of the established church within that town.

Ashton was also a well-renowned centre for radical political agitation during the 19th century and a hotbed of trade union activity and activism (see Chapter 3). But for those who were tired of politics and of the mainstream churches, the coming of Christ offered a captivating promise during harsh economic times. Following the end of the Napoleonic Wars, British trade plummeted and the appalling harvests of 1816-19 drove down wages, with a subsequent rise in unemployment. The Southcottian church had already shown that it could flourish in places where there had been a rapid change from home-based industry to factory production.

Many in Ashton would have been drawn to the new group by the charisma and predictions of John Wroe himself. In April 1823, he travelled on a self-directed mission to Gibraltar, France and northern Italy where he experienced divine communication which, he said, had led him towards the Lees family – one of the richest families in the Tameside area. His prophecy was for the wealthy widow, Hannah Lees, that her youngest son,

Is to become a Methodist preacher in Gibraltar, and I will order the Methodist preacher to send him unto thee … for I will deliver him from the paw of the lion and out of the mouth of the bear … I tell thee, if his mother refuses to deliver him up unto me, the Lord, I will return evil unto her as I had thought to return good. [24]

Mrs Lees consequently permitted her youngest son, William, to accompany Wroe on his next trip overseas. Wroe then became very close to the Lees family, as he soon did with other wealthy non-conformist families such as the Swires and the Stanleys, both of whom had already been associated with the Southcottians. Whilst on this voyage with William Lees, Wroe predicted that the young man

---

[23] *The Bible*, NIV, Luke 4, 24.
[24] Wroe, *DC* v 1, 21 May 1823.

would meet his future wife, which he subsequently did when they attended Southcottian meetings in Chatham and Gravesend, Kent. William Lees's bride returned to Ashton with him, and both became stalwarts of the Christian Israelite church there. John Stanley's second wife, Mary Deane, who was some 28 years younger than him, also came from this Gravesend group.

The prophecies of Wroe came thick and fast and ranged from the every-day humdrum to the wildly dramatic. Some were in relation to the socio-economic issues of the day, such as predicting Luddite activity, which Wroe recorded on 5th January 1826. He had left the Park Bridge area of Ashton in order to wander in the wilderness for 14 days, and stated in his Divine Communications that local people who had refused to offer him bread when he was hungry would be forced to,

> ... break one another's machinery til they had to beg their bread ... this was fulfilled: witness John Stanley, of Ashton-under-Lyne, he being chosen a valuer of the machinery that was destroyed in various parts of Lancashire, within a year or soon after. And the public are witnesses to the weavers being out of employ, and taking bands of music, and going about the streets, playing, singing, and begging, in various parts of England.

Beyond the religious, Wroe also had strong opinions on the personal and the political – whether it be on the enfranchisement of the working man, trade unions or in relation to the encroachment of Russia. When Wroe first came to Ashton he had predicted further wealth for John Stanley, and many of the prophecies were recorded and signed by John Stanley himself.[25] However, he was certainly no po-faced old prophet, as some newspaper reports of the time seemed to indicate. He allowed marching bands and picnics, encouraged women to be adorned in beautiful and unusual dresses, staged grand events and had extravagant and elegant buildings erected for use by the Christian Israelites.

The Two Johns: Prophet and Loyal Follower (With Big Wallet)
John Stanley's business empire in Ashton was primarily as an iron and brass founder, producing machines that supplied parts to the cotton industry. He entered business with one of the other richest families of the borough, becoming a partner with Henry Lees, the eldest son of the Lees family. Together they owned a property on Oldham Road, and the meeting rooms of the Christian Israelites were kept above these premises.

Wroe was not averse to attracting publicity during his early years as leader and he arranged a public baptism for himself in the River Aire of West Yorkshire in April 1824, but then decided to have another – this time in Ashton in the River

---

[25] Wroe's predictions included the personal (greater wealth for John Stanley), the political (the passing of the Reform Bill 1832, that Lord Morpeth would win the parliamentary seat etc.); local business (the location of the future Ashton Gas Company); and even disease (plague – one of the New Jerusalem gate houses was converted into a cholera hospital). Wroe had also talked of his wife's jealousy and said that their unborn child would die as a result of her rebellious nature - which it subsequently did. He predicted the downfall of Samuel Walker. And the two publishers of *The Voice of The People* came to a sorry end; one dropped down dead not so soon after their explicit reports on the Seven Virgins and the other hanged himself.

Medlock, with hundreds of onlookers. He decided to be publicly circumcised at John Stanley's and Henry Lees's premises on Oldham Road. This ceremony was preceded by a parade of the newly assembled Christian Israelite musicians and Wroe preached a sermon (which presumably took place prior to the circumcision rather than afterwards, as he might have been rather uncomfortable...) where he stated that, *"a light shall break forth out of this place where I stand, which shall enlighten the whole town; with a light also to enlighten the Gentiles."*

Afterwards, these words were interpreted by many as yet another prophecy which came true, because the site of Stanley's buildings and the Christian Israelite meeting rooms became the Ashton Gas Company – undoubtedly responsible for lighting up the whole town.

In addition to being one of the Number Four, it seems that Uncle John was very much 'hands-on' – quite literally – as he was responsible for performing the circumcisions on male Christian Israelites. Together with fellow rich industrialist Henry Lees, the two men carried out this 'holy surgery'. It might sound strange to the modern ear that a non-medically qualified person should carry out such a personal operation but even today the rite of male circumcision in many communities is entrusted to people who are respected and trusted but who hold no medical qualifications. Following Wroe's public circumcision, it seems that the practise became an important one for all males who belonged to the church. In September 1824, however, an eight-day-old child died after having been circumcised by Henry Lees. Lees was subsequently charged with manslaughter at the Lancaster Assizes in March 1825 but was acquitted.[26]

In 1825, John Stanley paid for the construction of a magnificent sanctuary in Church Street at the west end of Ashton's most fashionable area and the main shopping route of Stamford Street. The walls were thick and contained no windows, the light being provided by two glass domes in the roof. The Judaic symbol of the Christian Israelites - the Star of Judah - was carved over the separate entrance doors for the men and women. The floors were of polished oak, the seats and galleries were made of Santo Domingo mahogany and all fittings were cast from silver or bronze. Two imposing pulpits, one on each side, reached up to the level of the gallery. Music for services was provided by a group of 30 people, singing or playing wind instruments.

The Sanctuary was officially opened by Wroe on Christmas Day, 1825, and a polygonal organ was later installed, its 12 sides representing the 12 tribes of Israel. The cost of John Stanley's bill was £9,500; compare this with the cost of construction of Ashton Town Hall some 15 years later, which was £4,000. In today's prices, building the Sanctuary for John Stanley would have meant taking three-quarters of a million pounds from his bank balance.[27] During that same year,

---

[26] He was acquitted as a result of a disagreement between the doctors called as expert witnesses, the argument being that the baby had already been sickly. Lees continued to carry out circumcisions for many years, presumably alongside John Stanley.

[27] The Sanctuary was built in a prominent position on Church Street, on the main route towards Manchester. For a short time after Wroe's departure from Ashton, the Sanctuary was occupied by the United Methodists. It became The Star Theatre and then The Star Cinema, taking the name from the Judaic Star of David carved above the door. Brian Longden spent many a happy hour there, watching Charlie Chaplin, Laurel and Hardy and John Wayne.

an Ashton residence for Wroe was built, a Doric pillar-fronted mansion close to the Sanctuary and to John Stanley's own very fine home on Park Parade.

Virgin Obsessions?

The virtue of the state of virginity (only amongst women, of course) has always been a source of importance for many religious groups, and in March 1831 British newspapers were gleefully condemning Wroe and the Christian Israelites for possessing a fanatical and deviant obsession with the subject. *The Voice of the People* railed against the group the most, reporting that in 1830 Wroe had told his congregation that the Lord had instructed him to take seven virgins to, *"wait upon, nourish and comfort him and be as wives unto him, except that he should not carnally know them,"* and that the young women were appointed by a Christian Israelite committee after a sermon by Wroe on the coming of the Shiloh.[28]

Whilst we do not know the names and identities of all the women who were said to be involved in the so-called Seven Virgins sexual scandal, the names of three who made allegations against him were made public. To this day, the Christian Israelite church in Australia feel that this tale of Wroe and his seven virgins is fictitious and unfair.[29] If we try and understand their perspective, we might even compare it to what is referred to today as fake news as part of a media frenzy and a vendetta against Wroe and his leadership. Today's Christian Israelite church believes that the alleged sexual scandal began as the result of bitterness on the part of one of the women, who was a servant to Wroe and who was not some sort of concubine at all. She was said to have been accused of stealing and was subsequently threatened with

The Sanctuary, Ashton under Lyne

demotion. Some of the details reported by the press – and refuted by the Christian Israelites as being untruthful have been included in this book in Appendix 2.

Wroe was called to a church hearing on 24th October 1831, in order to answer to the allegations against him. The hearing was comprised of 12 influential men, including John Stanley, and 12 married women and it was held at the Mossley Road

---

[28] *Voice of The People*, 5 March 1831, page 22. Green has pointed out that this virgin-companion phenomenon was not a new preoccupation for Wroe and that, in Bradford, Wroe was said to have paraded from his farmhouse with 12 virgins dressed in white, with long veils.

[29] The Christian Israelite Church established by Wroe still exists in Victoria, New South Wales and Queensland.

Gatehouse (later The Odd Whim pub). Almost immediately, arguing began amongst pro- and anti-Wroe factions and several were dismissed, one of them being William Masterman, for displaying extreme bias against Wroe. The hearing then sat more peaceably for another six days. Many of the allegations related to conduct at Wroe's Bradford home, with newspapers present at the meeting reporting that one of the women - whose literacy had led her to become a scribe for the illiterate Wroe – had experienced clandestine moments with Wroe, "satisfying his lustful inclinations" and that on one occasion they were caught in the act by a furious Mrs Wroe. Indeed, for its time, the reporting of details by *The Voice of The People* is nothing short of astonishing for its raciness (see Appendix 2).

So, what really did happen between Wroe and these women? None of the other alleged seven virgins came forward with testimony against him. Was this situation a matter of false accusations and a vendetta directed against a very famous man? Or was Wroe the charlatan and deviant that many believed him to be?

Whatever the truth, the fact of the matter is that there was never a legal case brought against Wroe. The Church carried out a lengthy and very public investigation into the allegations and at the end of the week stated that they had found that he had merely "shown laxity of right principles". These related to more peripheral wrong doings than sexual abuse (such as the consumption of alcohol and various Christian Israelite shopkeepers stating that Wroe had not paid his bills). But there was no guilt declared and no dismissal from the church for Wroe. As far as most Christian Israelites were concerned, the case was over.

After the hearing, Wroe embarked upon a prolonged trip to Huddersfield and then to Wakefield, but he returned within four months in order to preach at the Sanctuary. However, when Masterman and Walker – who had previously been two of Wroe's Number Four along with John Stanley - heard that he was going to make a post-sermon public address to the Ashton townsfolk about the allegations, they decided to make plans. They printed and distributed hand bills declaring the date and the time of Wroe's speech and stated that if Wroe went ahead with it he, *"would be charged there and then with lying, perjury and even worse."*

Wroe ignored the threats. But thanks to the publicity meted out by the men, on the date of his sermon the Sanctuary was filled with non-Christian Israelites, excited to see what might transpire. As Wroe descended the steps of the pulpit to read out his statement, Masterman began to shout out charges against him. A full-scale riot ensued. Almost every fixture and fitting of the Sanctuary was torn up and used as either weapons or instruments of vandalism against the Christian Israelites; pews and doors were ripped out and windows were smashed. The rioting spilled out onto the streets of Ashton, with the homes of Christian Israelites being vandalised as people searched for the preacher, who seemed to have vanished into thin air amidst the chaos.

It turned out that John Stanley had perhaps had some prophetic talents of his own. His house was located on Park Parade – where many of Ashton's notables chose to reside – and in recent years he had had two secret tunnels built leading from his home to the Sanctuary.[30] According to the Christian Israelites, he led Wroe and other members of the congregation through the tunnels to safety, just a few hundred yards away. The tunnel escapes were mentioned by newspapers at the time. As soon as the town grew quiet, Wroe fled across the moors and to the comparative safety of West Yorkshire.

Although Wroe had more or less been acquitted of wrongdoing by the Christian Israelites, and even though English legal forces had felt there was no case that needed to be brought against him, the townsfolk of Ashton remained unimpressed. By Easter Sunday of 1831, the Christian Israelites in Ashton were divided in relation to their leader. The press reported that many had left the group, with *The Manchester Guardian* joking that the barber shops in Ashton were raking in a fortune as men jettisoned their beards. But Wroe once more planned to preach at the Sanctuary and, once again, the people of Ashton heard about it. Rioting commenced both outside and inside the Sanctuary and this time Wroe was severely beaten. Yet again, Uncle John came to the rescue, leading church members and a bleeding and limping Wroe through the tunnels to the liberation of Stanley's home.

By now, some members of the congregation had clearly had enough of life in Ashton. A group of them headed out from Ashton, accompanied by the Christian Israelite printing press, which was carried by a cart pulled by four of John Stanley's finest black horses. However, the group was determined not to be cowed by the townsfolk. As they travelled, they played their instruments and upon arriving at the Mossley Road Gatehouse, where the church trial had been held, they were singing Hebrew hymns. Wroe met them at the building; he had been keeping a low profile at John Stanley's house until five in the morning so that he could slip away with a minimum amount of attention. But like a bad pantomime villain, Masterman decided to make a final show of it, arriving with a few other anti-Wroe-ites and seized the prophet by the collar. Wroe and the others managed to escape but, shortly after this, Mrs Wroe's gatehouse home at Shepley in Dukinfield was ransacked by Walker and others. In Wroe's Divine Communications, he noted that John Stanley retrieved a silver plate owned by the family from the ransackers and urged Mrs Wroe to take it back (she had at first refused it, due to Christian Israelite strictures on receiving stolen goods).

The next day, the traditional Black Knight pageant in Ashton-under-Lyne took place - a festival involving an effigy being paraded on horseback throughout the streets. This time, however, the event took on a rather more contemporary twist when the stuffed figure on the horse was not the Black Knight but was dressed as Prophet Wroe instead. When Wroe arrived at his Bradford home, news of what had occurred in Ashton had travelled ahead of him and he was subsequently attacked and trampled underfoot. He left Bradford and headed for Wakefield, where he railed against the people of Ashton, declaring that, *"and for Ashton, I will show it its nakedness; and those that have risen up against my word there – where they have tried to slay my messenger, may be a place for their dead*

---

[30] Tunnels in this area were discovered in the 1970s when workmen were building the extension of the Parade, which is now a main dual carriageway from Ashton towards Manchester.

bodies to lay in." [31] His anger at the people of Ashton did not, however, prevent him from being close to death after a furious Wakefield mob seized him, demanding to know the truth about the seven virgins, and they very nearly drowned him in a local beck.

Picking Up the Pieces: Meeting Robert?

Was Wroe a prophet or a charlatan? Wrongly accused or justly vilified? Perhaps, over the years, too many historians have let the motives and the scandalmongering of the press go unchallenged. In many respects, it seems

Mossley Rd 'Gatehouse', became the 'Stamford Arms', then 'The Odd Whim'

regretful that the Christian Israelites, who had been peaceable citizens and had contributed a great deal to the local economy through their businesses and who had demonstrated great kindnesses to the poor, were collectively tarnished by these events.

Whatever the truth behind the allegations surrounding Prophet Wroe, Uncle John seems to have been his most loyal supporter in Ashton. He remained involved with the church when many of the original members faded away and, like the other Christian Israelite businesses in the area, his Israelites' shop (known as Th'owd Joanna's shop) was remembered with great affection by local people. Even into the next century, memories remained of the kosher food which was sold there and of the fact that it was run on an extremely fair co-operative system, long before the Rochdale Pioneers came along; a business model that benefitted not just John Stanley, but local people too.[32]

Some accounts state that Wroe was advised by Ashton church members to stay away from the town for a long period until the dust had sufficiently settled. Whether he did or not is uncertain, although Wroe's diaries note that by 1839 the attitude towards him was much less hostile and that if he had shown his face in

---

[31] John Wroe, *Revelations on the Scriptures*, 1849, p.62.
[32] Letters to local newspapers reflecting on shops of the past mention John Stanley's and other Christian Israelite businesses with much affection in 1942, Evans, p.153.

Ashton rather more publicly before this date, *"he would have been almost murdered and ill-treated … he was now allowed to do so peaceably and although well-known to some of those who saw him, yet he was not treated with a disrespectful word."* [33]

On the night before Wroe journeyed to Ashton to make a very public appearance to preach a sermon – Sunday 6th January 1839 - the town had been shaken by an unusually violent hurricane, which Wroe said that he had predicted. By this time, a ten-year-old Robert was living in the area on Oldham Road, just a couple of minutes' walk away from the Sanctuary. He would have been working with, and spending a great deal of time alongside, his Uncle John and he would have been aware of this controversial prophet who was still famed throughout the region. Perhaps Robert's young imagination was captivated by the fact that even the forces of nature heralded the presence of John Wroe?

Wroe the Matchmaker

Unfortunately, there are no written records available from Uncle John Stanley himself and the only mention of John by Robert Stanley does not refer to Wroe. But it is likely that both Johns would have been key influences in Robert's life, until his uncle's death in 1855. Wroe may even have played a part in influencing the match of Robert and Emma, as he seemed to take a great deal of interest in other peoples' marriages and was clearly very close to Uncle John.

John Stanley and his first wife, Sarah Greenwood, had been married in 1806 at Stockport's parish church. They were both followers of Southcott, then George Turner and, lastly, Wroe. The couple had three children and 38 years of married life together. Sarah died in early 1845 and on 29th April, only weeks later, John remarried at the age of 59. Perhaps even stranger than this fast remarriage is the fact that he married Mary Deane on the 29th April – the anniversary of his first marriage! And if this doesn't sound unusual enough, his first-born child with Mary was subsequently named Sarah. This might have startled the people of Ashton, but perhaps the couple would have claimed to have named the baby after Mary's own mother, Sarah. Mary Deane herself was from an important Christian Israelite family, part of the Gravesend, Kent, faction. She was 28 years younger than Uncle John and soon bore him four children.[34] All in all, there was a gap of 42 years between John's eldest child from his first marriage, and his youngest from the second.

Why did John remarry so quickly? At first, I presumed that this could have been because the Christian Israelites – as many groups who closely follow Abrahamic teachings do – believed that a man has earthly needs that are best fulfilled by the sanctity of holy matrimony (a sentiment borne out by the apostle Paul in the New Testament)[35]. It seemed probable that such beliefs might take precedence over the usual 19th century mourning period and not be too much of a cause for comment. However, there is some information that can inform us about John's first marriage with Sarah Stanley, as Sarah herself was explicitly mentioned

---

[33] Wroe, *DC*, v2, pp 5-6.

[34] Their first child was named Sarah. Was this after John's first wife? Or after Mary Deane's mother, Sarah Deane? An interesting question!

[35] *"To the unmarried and the widows, I say: It is good for them to stay unmarried, as I do. But if they cannot control themselves, they should marry, for it is better to marry than to burn with passion,"* St Paul the apostle's letter to the Corinthians, *The Bible*, NIV, Corinthians 7, 1-9.

by Wroe in his records. For the entries in his Private Volumes on 26th/27th September 1821, Wroe wrote,

> *How often has the Lord ordered John Stanley to cease wrestling with his wife; let him give her up, for she is not for the kingdom on earth, for she adulterates the Lord's word, for she is a wolf among the Lord's sheep; and when one of the Lord's children comes unto her, she says, I have just been told such a thing by one of our friends, and she gets the very thing out of that person, which she said another had told her: let the committee warn the people to guard against her.*

What had Sarah done for her to have had Wroe declare against her in such a way? The style of the writing seems to indicate that he was reprimanding her for gossiping or manipulative behaviour. Given the timing when it occurred, it may have been to do with the fact that Uncle John had decided to follow Wroe, which would involve him donating a vast amount of money to Wroe's new church. If Wroe had not been a particular favourite of Sarah's – if she had still preferred George Turner – she might well have been concerned about the fact that she and her family were very soon going to lose close to a million pounds in today's prices to the construction of the extremely opulent Sanctuary.

Wroe's advice to John Stanley, that he should give her up because she is not for the kingdom on earth, is particularly interesting. 'Not for the kingdom on earth' implies either that Wroe felt she was not one of the chosen few selected by the Shiloh on his return to earth (i.e. doomed to hell) or that she did not believe in the same strain of millennialism that Wroe dispelled. Wroe advising John to 'give her up' is also a rather strange thing to say, given that Christian Israelites could not divorce. The couple were still living together at Park Parade in the 1851 census, but this does not necessarily mean that they were happy together. Perhaps, as many have done before them, they had begun to live separate lives. This would also explain why John was quite keen to marry again only a matter of weeks after Sarah's death. And it might also provide an answer as to why their son – John junior – was left only £100 following the death of his father in 1855. John junior had gone on to become a successful businessman in his own right and his father, therefore, may have felt that he did not need the money, but John junior had also previously been a leading member of the Christian Israelites and lived at one of the New Jerusalem's four gatehouses (Taunton Lodge in Waterloo, Ashton). However, in 1845 - the same year that his mother died, and his father quickly remarried Mary Deane - he left the church and relocated to Wales, where he set up his own iron and coal works.

Marriage was incredibly important to the early Christian Israelite church, both physically and symbolically.[36] As with many minority religious groups, a

---

[36] George Turner, for example, visited various branches of the Southcottians across the country to perform spiritual marriages between himself and female church members. It was said that Turner walked more than 2,500 miles across the country and was married 1,556 times to the same number of women in order to symbolise the privilege of being married to the Lord. After the wedding was performed, he apparently would kiss the woman/women in front of the congregation and then be permitted to place a hand upon their knee: imagery that she should bow to the Lord's commands.

great deal of intermarriage occurred between the early Christian Israelite families. In the Ashton area at this time, we can see that the Stanley, Corry, Farrand, Gill, Wood and Wroe families all intermarried. Wroe himself seemed to have had strong opinions in relation to the partnerships that combined to form his congregation and the wider Christian Israelite family. For example, he felt that his son and successor, Benjamin Wroe, should marry Mary-Anne Deane from the Gravesend area and that his other son, Joseph, should marry Mary Deane, her cousin. However, Joseph did not want to marry Mary; he had his own choice of bride in mind and ignored his father's wishes. Wroe's own records show that he had ordered these two little girls – Mary Deane being only seven years old at the time - to be brought before him so that he could betroth them to his sons. This sounds rather disturbing to the modern, Western mindset, but we should also consider that the marriages did not go ahead until both Miss Deanes were fully grown adult women. In the end, because Joseph Wroe rejected Mary Deane, she ended up becoming John Stanley's much younger second wife after the death of Sarah.

I have often wondered how Robert's new Aunt Mary had felt about being a cast-off of Wroe's son! It is all too easy to feel, however, that the women involved in this church must have been mere pawns in the religious patriarchy: being treated as property or chattel, being recruited as servants, having no priestly or leadership role within the church and having Wroe rail against them if they perhaps dared to upset him. As with all the situations regarding the women in Robert Stanley's life, we are left only with the ability to contemplate what their existence and situations must have been like. It is certainly difficult not to think of them as victims at times – but would the Christian Israelite women have been treated any worse than any woman was within Victorian society? Probably not. In fact, it could be argued that women born into these congregations had a greater sense of security and belonging than those who were not.

My auntie, Gay Oliver, has a letter written by Sophie, daughter of Uncle John Stanley and his second wife, Mary Deane, who was writing to her new daughter-in-law. In it, she states how happy her own parents' marriage had been. Of course, this could well be a result of the nostalgic view that many of us have in relation to our parents' marriage, but it does seem that Mary Deane – chosen as a small girl for a future husband – was certainly capable of making her own decisions, because less than two years after Uncle John had passed away, she took her children to the parish church of St Peter's in Ashton in order to have them baptised. All three children were still small, and this seems a curious decision to have made for someone who had been born into and brought up within the Southcottians and Christian Israelites. Perhaps she wanted to end her connections with the church now that John had passed away, or maybe she was hedging her bets. Robert Stanley was her contemporary in age and her nephew by marriage and he would also have moved away from the church – physically, if not spiritually – by this time, because he and Emma were living in Stalybridge. So, it seems likely that with John's death, any direct Christian Israelite influence in the Stanley family's life would have come to an end.

Echoing Influences

The figure of Wroe must have seemed quite a formidable one to the young Robert Stanley. His Uncle John and Prophet Wroe would have remained close until John's death in 1855. Wroe felt a strong regard for the wealthy industrialist who had saved his life on no less than two occasions and who had funded the Ashton church. Unfortunately, there are no letters from Wroe to Uncle John in existence, but throughout the rest of Wroe's life in England, when he is giving sermons in Ashton, John Stanley is directly addressed by Wroe in the transcripts and answers his scriptural and spiritual questions. Uncle John also signed and dated a great deal of Wroe's visions and prophecies during this time, as did Mary Deane. It seems plausible that the two men continued to correspond with each other even when Wroe moved to Australia to lead the new church there, although at the current time there is no evidence for this.

In the next chapter we will consider Robert's education a little more, but we can feel certain that he had a sound knowledge of the Bible and – thanks to the Christian Israelites - probably also of Hebrew. He would have been knowledgeable about the rudiments of biblical theology and may have developed an interest in Semitic language, history and religion from this portion of his childhood.

But what would Robert's views have been on Wroe? Many who encountered him described him as having an exceptionally strong, charismatic and magnetic personality. However, it is all too easy to take the newspaper accounts and the words written by his detractors at face value. As someone who has known about Wroe – a curious and colourful local character – since my teenage years, the Rasputinesque caricature is exactly the sort of picture that I had of him in my head. However, researching the life of Robert Stanley has caused me to view Wroe and the Christian Israelites in a rather different light. It has certainly led me to consider that history may have done them a disservice and to ponder what Robert's views would have been in relation to the outcry surrounding Prophet Wroe.

In later life, when Robert Stanley chose to criticise the British Government's actions overseas, he, unlike Quilliam, never explicitly attacked the actions of Christians or of the church itself. It is likely that some of Robert's own views on mainstream Christianity could have come from Wroe and that his fascination with all-things Abrahamic can be attributed to him, causing Robert to instantly feel comfortable with Islam when he first began to meet Muslims. Robert's deep suspicion of Russia and his perceptions of Muscovite spies and influencers may also have originated from Wroe, a man who also held grave reservations about the influence of Moscow.[37] Having grown up around a good-hearted community of devout people, who deliberately chose different rules of worship and living to mainstream practises, and who were all too often persecuted because of it, Robert could well have felt a strong affiliation for those who were marginalised and misunderstood. Whether he took the experience and learning that he gained from knowing the Christian Israelites and moulded his own life path from it consciously or subconsciously, we can only guess.

---

[37] Wroe often made references to Russian interference in his writings and sermons.

CHAPTER 3

Disturbed Towns, Exciting Youth
1838 – 1847

The Great Leveller

Robert had arrived in Ashton at the age of ten and would have worked a long day in his uncle's shop. By the time that he was 46, he had become a grocer, tea trader, magistrate, councillor and then mayor. How did he manage to achieve all of this, coming from a large working-class family that had struggled economically with no privileges available to them? Due to the lack of Robert's own words in relation to his life, we can only draw some broad conclusions but from the sources that we do have access to it seems clear that his key to advancement was education: the great leveller. However, Robert's education lacked the sort of formal schooling which the middle and upper classes would have received during the 1830s and 40s. Rather, his education was more about self-learning; absorbing reading material such as newspapers and books, Robert was also exposed to, and involved with, some of the most explosive events of the 19th century. He would have taken his lessons from carefully watching the behaviour of the people around him in Ashton and Stalybridge, both rich and poor alike.

Educating Oneself

Robert was born some 42 years before the Elementary Education Act 1870, which introduced formal schooling at elementary education level, and which made attendance compulsory for children aged 5 to 13 years old. For Robert and Emma's own children, too, there would have been no legal obligation for most of them to attend classes, given that only the very youngest of the ten was born within the requirements of the Act.

Prior to 1870, wealthy families accessed personal tutoring or could pay for their children to be sent away to boarding schools. But unless a working-class child was born into a family determined to provide them with an education, the child was more likely than not to be completely illiterate. Where poorer families desired literacy, schools were run in the homes of local people in return for payment. Often, these home schools in the north of England were no more than glorified child-minding services, whilst the parents grafted for long days in the mills. Education in these homes was usually rather unimpressive due to the quality of learning that the teacher had accessed themselves, but also because of the large numbers of children - of varying ages - present in one room. Some churches provided schools for children, but again, this depended on the parent wanting to send a child to school and whether they were happy for a child to be taught within a denomination that they may not belong to - denomination and education was an extremely contentious issue during this period (see Chapter 5). There were fees, too, to attend such schools and often even a few pennies a week was impossible for many people to find.

Robert may have been more fortunate than many, though, because the towns of south-east Lancashire during this time had quite a good reputation in relation to the provision of part-time schools and associated learning opportunities.[38] Prior to the 1870 Act, Stalybridge, for example, had an excellent track record on stimulating working-class interest in science and the arts. But despite this, the fact of the matter was that Robert received no formal or regularised education. Still, by the time that he was first elected to Stalybridge Council in 1863, and certainly by the time he gave evidence to Parliament in 1869, his words and his contributions to civic life were outstanding in terms of clarity, quality, depth of knowledge and intellectual reasoning. In his personal recollections dictated to Quilliam in 1908, Robert made it clear that he was an avid letter-writer. Indeed, his eloquence when faced with the MPs and aristocrats of Parliament in 1869 was nothing short of impressive.

On moving up from Cardiff to Ashton at the age of ten, Robert lived with his older brother, John, and John's new wife, Betty, on Oldham Road, in a house that was probably owned by his Uncle John and was part of the Stanley ironworks complex. In the 1841 census, his brother John was working as a bookkeeper whilst living there. It is likely that he came to Stalybridge before his little brother, Robert, in order to gain employment under his Uncle John Stanley. As a bookkeeper, Robert's older brother would have needed to have sound literacy and numeracy skills. No doubt he would also have encouraged young Robert to follow his example. Uncle John – a man of great standing and prestige within the town – would probably have expected both his young nephews to gain the basics of education in order to support the family business further and to make a success of the opportunities that he was offering them.

There were several after work classes near Uncle John's Th'owd Joanna's shop where Robert worked and others, too, in the vicinity of the Oldham Road. There were Christian Israelite Hebrew schools in Mottram (Stalybridge area) and in Ashton, and it is possible that Robert attended one of these at the expectation of his Uncle John in addition to going to after-work classes dedicated to the 'Three Rs'. Robert himself grew up to be a man who was not averse to children having a day-job; on 20th February 1875, whilst a magistrate, he told the mother of a seven-year-old boy who had been hauled into the Petty Sessions for stealing oranges that he, *"had better work as a half-timer than get into mischief."* Robert's perspective on education and on work ethics is also evident in the way that he responded to the famous Stalybridge 'Educate A Girl' case in 1872 (Chapter Five.) Although some may feel that his attitude was archaic and chauvinistic, we might also take the view that he was simply applying what had worked for him – an honest day's work and grab whatever self-learning opportunities come a person's way.[39]

The level of knowledge and understanding behind Robert's words, in council minutes, parliamentary records, newspapers and in Quilliam's publications, go far beyond the rudimentary education received by a little boy who managed to snatch a few hours' learning a week thanks to part-time schooling after work. But neither would he have been able to rely on public libraries; they did not become a feature

---

[38] A Lock (ed), *Looking Back at Stalybridge*, see Harrop's 'Why was Stalybridge First?' TMBC, 1989.
[39] *Stalybridge Reporter*, 20 February 1874.

of British civic society in Ashton and Stalybridge until the late 19th century. However, private subscription libraries were available that could be accessed by anyone who valued the chance to read books and magazines and who was willing and able to pay a few pennies for the opportunity. Uncle John Stanley would certainly have had religious books in his household, but even religious fame and notoriety such as the kind possessed by Prophet Wroe did not necessarily mean that a person was literate. Wroe himself regretted not having a good level of literacy and mentioned this in the hearing before the Christian Israelites in 1831 (his practice of eventide dictation to one of the women involved in the seven virgins scandal was a cause for comment at the time). For a working-class boy to become literate during this era, therefore, took some real effort. By the time that Robert had arrived in Ashton, the Working Men's Mechanics' Institute (WMMI) movement was growing, attracting the working class into their buildings with reading opportunities, seminars, lectures, courses and debates, all of which were designed to improve the character and the life chances of the working class. Although we have no information that Robert was actively involved with the WMMI in Stalybridge, in later life he was asked to chair debates there and probably thought of the institution as an essential component to a town that encouraged people to better themselves.

It must have been something of a shock for such a young boy to have to move so far away from his parents, becoming separated from a large and noisy family and moving into the home of his older brother and new bride. It seems reasonable to imagine a little boy dealing with this upheaval by filling his time with books and with self-taught learning. His long journey towards Islam and his lifelong interest in the regions and races of the peoples associated with it also indicate that he had a solid knowledge of biblical studies. The one book that most working-class people had available to them during the 19th century was the King James Bible, not only a source of spiritual comfort and wisdom, but for many the only method of learning the English language. Perhaps the Bible's tales, complemented by newspapers with plentiful information on foreign affairs and exotic distant lands, led Robert to a lifelong interest in Semitic religions.[40] Ultimately, though, we can only guess at how Robert became literate and well-educated, but perhaps - as his own great x3 grandson found in 1990 – childhood exposure to biblical text and church-going, along with meeting intelligent people who offered a different take on international politics and justice, eventually led to a rather different faith path than that of the average Victorian Briton.

Political and Civic Life

When Robert was 21 years old, John Strongi'th'arm Stanley – Robert's cousin, who had caused a family scandal by eloping with his other cousin, Uncle John's daughter, Hannah - became one of Ashton's first town councillors and Poor Law guardians. Strongi'th'arm was accepted back into the family by Uncle John, and he turned out to be a good businessman. He was entrusted with running parts of his uncle's/father-in-law's family business. Strongi'th'arm's political party of choice was the Conservatives (Tories) whereas most other men who had new wealth

---

[40] Note that the definition of Semite is not just in relation to the Jewish faith; there are various groups that speak Semitic languages, including Jews and Arabs.

tended towards the Liberals (Whigs). He had chosen a party that was more affiliated with the landed gentry and less willing to embrace progressive social reforms. Robert Stanley also chose to follow the Conservative Party, becoming a councillor and then a Tory mayor of Stalybridge. This family tradition of voting Tory probably preceded both Strongi'th'arm's and Robert's political careers; William and John's father had originally owned farmland in Dukinfield and William himself was a hatter by trade. His sympathies would probably have been with the upper working class, the small artisan strata who were more likely to be in favour of free trade and low taxation (as evidenced by his clash with the law over unfair taxation in Cardiff in 1827). Today, there is a temptation to presume that people from the working class - or upper working class – should be more left-leaning in their political outlook, but time and time again the people of these south-east Lancashire towns have shown that working-class conservative attitudes prevail.

There is perhaps no better example of this than that of one of the most famous northern champions of the poor, a Wesleyan Methodist minister and local firebrand from Dukinfield, Joseph Rayner Stephens. Although a non-conformist, Stephens was a Tory, although his words initially come across as more Marxist-derived than Conservative affiliated. Stephens was famous across the land for his passionate speeches attacking the Poor Law and the cruelty of many factory owners, plus his campaigning for political reform alongside the Chartists. He was subsequently imprisoned for his incendiary rhetoric against the Establishment. Growing up in the area, I was familiar with the life and words of Stephens and had noted the similarity of his views with those expressed by Robert Stanley. However, it was only

Rev. Joseph Rayner Stephens

through carrying out the research for this book that I finally unearthed evidence that the two men knew, and had great regard for, each other, frequently appearing as speakers at civic and social events together. Interestingly, before Rayner Stephens got to know Robert Stanley, he had famously clashed with Robert's older cousin, Poor Law guardian Strongi'th'arm, when he intervened on behalf of a poor widow who Strongi'th'arm had refused to assist with burial costs. Perhaps Stephens felt that Robert was something of an improvement on his cousin!

Both Joseph Rayner Stephens and Robert Stanley felt the need to stand up as moral guardians for the poor. Whenever the disenfranchised and marginalised were being oppressed by the callous rich or by an overbearing state, these two men could be found at the front of campaigning or advocacy. Neither of them were socialists or nailed their colours to the trade union masts, though, and in many ways, they were classic working-class Tory representatives of the 21st century, with a focus on hard work and enterprise and a sense of patriotic religious duty. But they also had a desire to prevent too much social reform too soon. Robert was suspicious of easy talk of redistribution of wealth and of promises that he felt could not be carried out without being ultimately detrimental to the masses. Why did he take this approach and not break away from it and towards the growing new trend towards socialism? The unusual political and economic context of these towns during the 1830s to 1860s best explains what drove his sentiments and probably led to his sometimes-deferential beliefs being passed down through the generations.

Class Conflict: Charter, Factories, Strikes and the Poor Law
Stalybridge, Ashton and Dukinfield are not particularly well-known British towns today, but during Robert's lifetime they were very famous, if not notorious, both as the birthplace of King Cotton and the industrial revolution and as towns that courted working-class radicalism and unrest.

These towns frequently came under the spotlight from national government and the media. By the time that Robert came to live in Ashton, the area had already experienced considerable disquiet. In 1819, the Peterloo Massacre took place in Manchester, which involved thousands of people from Ashton and Stalybridge who had walked to the city centre in good spirits and in good faith. They had been accompanied by the Stalybridge Old Band, who were chosen to play to the 80,000-strong crowd that had gathered from across the other Manchester towns. The mass meeting called for parliamentary reform and an end to the Corn Laws that were affecting the working class dreadfully, but it ended up with at least 18 people being killed and between 400-700 injured when the Yeomanry Cavalry charged the crowd. The anniversary of Peterloo was a sacred event in these towns for many decades afterwards and bitterness towards those in authority lingered, a sentiment that Robert would have seen reflected in the faces and in the words of those amongst whom he lived.

Robert seemed to have arrived in Ashton as a result of William and Ann Stanley feeling the pinch in Cardiff. By 1837, the economic situation was dire, as trade took a downturn alongside an economic depression that lasted until 1839. Robert's parents would have seized any opportunity to have one less mouth to feed and to obtain some much-needed experience in life and work for their son. Robert would have earned a small wage in his Uncle John's shop, and this would have made an important contribution to the household coffers back in Cardiff.

In addition to the aftermath of Peterloo, just 19 years before, Robert's arrival in Ashton in 1837 came only a few years after huge disorder in the district. Most national historians only associate Stalybridge and Ashton with the famous General Strike of 1842 (also known as the Plug Riots because the strikers smashed the plugs from factory boilers in order to stop the machinery) but the strike that took place here in 1830-31 has received little attention and yet was far more ferocious and protracted.

The three towns of Ashton, Stalybridge and Hyde were known as the most radicalised – and potentially the most violent – across the Manchester area by the time that Robert moved to Ashton. Throughout the economic downturns of 1828-31, 1837-39 and then 1841-42, the spectre of revolution had haunted the upper class, but the responses of the factory owners always veered towards crush, rather than conciliate. The wealthy men of Hyde were perhaps the most notorious; in 1829, they forced their mill workers to contribute to a fund that would pay for any legal costs should they, the factory owners, be prosecuted for flouting new legislation that reduced the number of hours in the working day. Shortly after this, the operatives were required to sign a document agreeing that they would not join a trade union. In outrage at this, the working people of Hyde met on 3rd April 1829, at the Norfolk Arms, where a horrific disaster occurred; as hundreds of people crowded into the upper storey of the pub, the floor collapsed, killing 29 men, women and children, and injuring 200.[41] Not long afterwards, the power-loom weavers of all three towns went on strike in response to a reduction in wages, with the action lasting from December to February, during a bitterly cold winter. In 1831, one of the Hyde factory masters, Mr Thomas Ashton, was murdered by workers – with unfounded allegations of union involvement in the crime.

To date, historians who have focused on the attack on John Wroe and the Christian Israelite Sanctuary seem to have overlooked that it took place in the same year that this all-out strike occurred. Passions were running high in the area; people were feeling desperate and powerless. Like many religious groups before them, and many after, Wroe and the Christian Israelites would have been an easy target for misdirected rage. Not helped, perhaps, by the views of John Wroe himself, who was critical of trade unions and of the actions taken over in Bradford by the wool combers, although he sympathised with the terrible distress caused to the workers when the strikes occurred.

By the time that a very young Robert arrived in Ashton in 1837, the working class was more politicised than ever. In 1832, the government had passed the Reform Act, extending the vote to certain areas of the country but only to people who met a property qualification. This legislation was a huge disappointment to the working class, who primarily lived in rented houses and therefore were still disenfranchised. The town of Ashton was awarded a member of Parliament for the first time as a result of the Act, however, and even though the working people had no say in who represented them, there was eager interest in which person would be put forward for election and which party they belonged to. A man like Uncle John Stanley would have been greatly interested in the new system and how the concerns of his class would be reflected at Westminster, an interest that may have been passed on to his new, young protégé who had already been exposed to the

---

[41] This incident became known as 'May's Downfall' (Mr May being the landlord of The Norfolk Arms.) Sadly, hardly anyone in the area now remembers this incident, even though there is a blue plaque at the site of the disaster. It seems that, once again, these small but once mighty towns have lost out in the remembrance stakes in comparison to Manchester and to Peterloo.

politics of injustice, thanks to William Stanley's railing against the authorities in Cardiff.

In parallel to the growing interest and hopes for political change came the drive for factory reform. For some time, progressives had been attempting to protect children from excessive working hours and appalling conditions. The Ten-Hour Act movement for factory reform found its saviour in Reverend Joseph Rayner Stephens, who quickly achieved national notoriety. Although many of the religious leaders of the area were becoming involved in social, economic and political reform, Stephens stood head and shoulders above the rest in terms of his outspokenness and the loyalty that he commanded from amongst the working class. He worked tirelessly for factory reform and, by the time that Robert began work in his uncle's shop, Stephens was famed throughout the land for his inflammatory words and no-compromise attitude on behalf of the working class.

Stephens was also one of the most outspoken critics of the hated Poor Law Amendment Act 1834. This legislation was created by the Whigs (Liberals) in response to increasing numbers of people who needed relief from poverty, but it was perceived to be a method of cutting the cost of the poor rates in a brutal way. Its solution was to turn away from providing financial hand outs and instead to provide more workhouses. This measure invariably treated poverty as a sort of sin or crime, ushering those who were already suffering into despicable conditions and tearing them from their families and homes. Even before the Act was implemented in 1836, its opponents were horrified, and the Anti Poor Law Movement gained much support. The new Act also centralised the distribution of Poor Law relief, alienating many of the middle and upper classes who were concerned about the loss of autonomy in the Stalybridge and Ashton areas and who were resentful that they would be subjected to decisions made by central Manchester.

Even before Robert moved to his new home, he would have been very familiar with the name of Joseph Rayner Stephens and given his own father's inclination of championing the underdog it is likely that he admired the preacher for his quest for justice. Such veneration of Stephens, however, may not have been encouraged by other members of his family - his older cousin, John Strongi'th'arm, for example, was one of the original Poor Law guardians appointed for the Ashton area prior to the new workhouse measures being enforced. Strongi'th'arm, too, gained a somewhat callous reputation in relation to his actions with Poor Law implementation. This would have been an interesting puzzle for the young boy to contemplate; was his older cousin some sort of villain, as many visitors to the shop may have felt? Or was Stephens a misguided man of the cloth?

Long-standing involvement in trade unionist activity, however, was deemed to be too risky for the average factory worker in the area during this time. There was perhaps a safer outlet for unhappiness at the current state of affairs in the country, though; that of pursuing the Charter.[42]

The Chartist movement had gained massive support in the north of England by the time Robert took up his new job in Th'Owd Joanna's shop on Stamford

---

[42] The six demands of the Charter were: universal manhood suffrage, equal electoral districts, vote by ballot, annually-elected Parliaments, payment of members of Parliament and abolition of property qualifications for membership.

Street. Regular meetings and activities calling for the People's Charter were taking place just yards from his home on Oldham Road. The Charter was extremely popular across Ashton, with 14,200 people signing it before its submission to the 1842 Parliament. However, even though the general desire of the working class was for peaceful political reform, the campaigning in south-east Lancashire towns was often infused with violence. At the time, central government perceived no differences between any of these campaigns; as far as they were concerned, violence and agitation were a matter of law and order and were to be dealt with harshly. As a child and as a youth, Robert would have witnessed the mushrooming interest in the Charter. He would have seen first-hand the demonstrations and drilling that many of the Chartists were involved in throughout Stalybridge and Ashton each evening. Their actions of preparing themselves for aggression – arming themselves with pikes and other rather terrifying homemade weapons – proved to be a cause for great concern to the Home Office, which was in frequent contact with authorities in the area. After all, revolution was looming on the continent now and the working class was seen as having been bitten by the bug. Despite the fears of the authorities, however, it is amusing to note from the local newspapers of the time that the Chartists themselves were none-too-happy about the behaviour of some of the teenage boys involved in their movement. The older Chartists often grumbled that the youths were too intent on practising with their pikes and play-acting as soldiers than honing their skills of discourse in relation to the quest for political reform. Perhaps Robert Stanley would have agreed with these older men, believing that his peers would be far better served by finding themselves a job or a more intellectually rewarding pastime.

In 1839, Joseph Rayner Stephens was arrested for sedition at a Chartist meeting. Peter Murray M'Douall, a Scottish surgeon who had built a medical practice in Ashton and who had an interest in the effects of factory work on health, became the natural successor to Stephens during his incarceration.[43] Here was another militant firebrand figure that Robert would have been more than familiar with at a very young age. Then, in 1842, the General Strike – or Plug Riots – occurred, as newly-formed trade unions attempted to forge solidarity and to force the hand of the masters by rolling strikes throughout the country. The cry across much of Lancashire, Yorkshire, Derbyshire and Cheshire was for 'a fair day's wage for a fair day's work' and soon the issue of the Charter became inextricably linked with the General Strike, when the National Charter Association voted to back it. Full scale riots took place at nearby Oldham, Blackburn, Stockport and in Ashton itself.

---

[43] After Stephens's prison sentence was served, he was bound over to stay away from such activities. He rejected Chartism, turning back to the call for factory reform and creating his own newspaper - complete with a children's section on factory reform and the Poor Law - which a young Robert Stanley would probably have read. He eventually became a Poor Law guardian himself when he began to feel that his influence on the plight of the poor might be more powerful than engaging in political activism. Perhaps similar to Robert's life, his life contained a curious mix of conservatism and a drive for equality; for example, he was described by *The Stalybridge Reporter* as a political puzzle when he declared that he was in favour of Irish home rule.

1848: Revolutionary Rumblings

The 1842 strike achieved little. Support for Chartism trailed off for a while, but widespread discontent remained. Even two days before Robert got married on 20th October 1847, *The Manchester Guardian* reported that there was a severe cotton depression and that in Stalybridge five mills were not working, with 2000 cotton operatives unemployed and that, *"Much excitement appears to be created in the minds of the public generally. Many of the shopkeepers are feeling much alarmed as a result."* This was the context surrounding the wedding of Robert and Emma – who themselves were embarking upon becoming the very same shopkeepers mentioned by *The Manchester Guardian*. And in the same edition of the newspaper, the editorial noted an "agitation" at the Stalybridge Town Council, a debate over whether Stalybridge should have its own MP, *"On the first resolution being put, in favour of the town being represented, strange to say, it was negative"*.

Just at the point when Robert and Emma were settling down, the rest of the world seemed to be waking up. The People's Spring of 1848 saw widespread and violent upheavals across Europe, spurred on by a popular press and by the publication of Karl Marx's *Manifesto of the Communist Party*. A heady concoction of liberal reform blended with radical politics culminated in the overthrow of old governments and the deaths of thousands of working-class insurrectionists. Widespread crop failures across Europe during 1846, along with the Irish potato famine, convinced many of the working class that existing governments and the absolutism of all-too-many monarchies had to change – and fast.

The revolutions that caught fire across the continent in 1848 were incoherent and ill-organised. Their ingredients included a mix of new political thinking: concepts such as nationalism, socialism, popular liberalism and democracy came together to be used by both the middle class and the working class as they sought to overthrow the old orders. In February, the French revolted against the aristocracy and a republic was founded, whilst many of the Italian and German states began to form unified nations where liberal constitutions were granted.

Whilst there is no information whatsoever on Robert and Emma's life together from the 1840s into the early 1860s, it is likely that this period – with its backdrop of revolution – would have been crucial in formulating Robert's own political views. British undergraduates studying modern history are often tasked with at least one essay where they are required to explain why Britain did not experience revolution during the 19th and 20th centuries. But it is all too easy to point to the very logical economic, social and political reasons why the country clung so steadfastly to conservatism so much more than its continental counterparts did, because these ruminations are, of course, coloured with the benefit of hindsight. Perspectives in 1848 would have been very different; British citizens could only look to what was sweeping across Europe and wonder if this new phenomenon of insurrection was infectious. Whilst many historians prefer to focus on the violent actions occurring outside of Britain at this time, those living in Ashton and Stalybridge would have had more cause than most to fear that revolution was imminent within the British Isles. Certainly, Robert Stanley – a man whose family of origin was conservative in thought and in party-political affiliation – would have been gravely concerned that open revolt might be on his own doorstep. And out to deprive him of his newly created profits, to boot!

Following hot on the heels of The People's Spring in Europe came an event of incredible importance to the working class in Ashton and Stalybridge: Parliament had rejected the third petition for a Charter in April 1848. As a result of this, the national organisation of the Chartist campaign collapsed. The rejection was met with fury in Ashton, and in May, the town's chief constable informed the Home Secretary that 300 to 400 men in the town had formed a Chartist National Guard. By July, these men were meeting regularly at the Charlestown Meeting Room, just yards away from where the Christian Israelites had met. Like Rayner Stephens before him, M'Douall had been arrested for sedition and his trial that summer was so strongly supported in the area that even Ashton Council's Town Hall Committee allowed his followers to use their hall to raise funds for his trial.

Whilst the disintegration of the national Chartist leadership continued, the rank and file in the North were looking to national action, when 'all of England would rise' in support of the Charter and in solidarity with the plight of the working man. As in 1842, the August of 1848 saw plans to 'draw plugs' and to generate a national strike across the land, and once more hundreds of working men in Ashton and Stalybridge were out and about on the streets, practising military manoeuvres and drilling with their pikes and homemade weapons. Tragedy struck Ashton, however, on the evening of 14th August, when Police Constable Bright – a popular man with the Chartists by all accounts, it seems – was shot, just yards from John and Betty's home amidst the marching and the gathering of the Chartists along the Oldham Road. Robert would have been 20 years old at the time and he and his new bride had probably just moved to Stalybridge, although they may still have been living with John and Betty. Perhaps they watched from the windows of the house and saw the events unfold. Robert himself may even have been on the streets, witnessing the violence first-hand.

Compared to many, Robert had been one of the more fortunate members of the working class. Although sent away at the age of ten, he had enjoyed the stability of living with his older brother, the guardianship of a rich uncle and the security of belonging to the closely-bound fellowship of the Christian Israelite church. During his childhood years he might have felt it an exciting time to be British – with a new, young Queen on the throne as Britain rode the crest of her Empire's waves. And, on the very streets of Ashton where he walked every day, there was an ever-present threat of demonstrations, anger, violence, strikes and a growing threat of revolution on the horizon. The young Robert must have felt that there was never a dull moment in the town. However, once he had become a man, a husband, soon to be a father and the owner of a new fledgling business, any thrills accompanying such social unrest would probably have died away. Thanks to the status and the presence of a wealthy uncle in his life – a man who had demonstrated that it was possible to rise from poverty, to become rich and to generously share it with others – Robert's political conservatism could well have kicked-in during the year of the 1848 revolutions. This period might have shaped a character that – perhaps ironically in retrospect – looked to British traditions and values as a mighty bulwark against revolutionary tendencies or anything outside of the norm.

Early Married Life

We should be like man and wife, whatever the husband says the wife says the same, and being but one fire it does not burn long, unless it be fed - but two fires will destroy: but when one holds their peace the fire burns but very little; when the cries are heard the neighbours come and interfere by feeding the fire. (Post-marriage sermon by John Wroe at Ashton Sanctuary, just one month before Robert and Emma Stanley's wedding there on 17th October 1847.)[44]

Like Robert, Emma Meredith came from a poor background. She was born in Tewkesbury to Margaret and Thomas Meredith, a bricklayer. Although today's Church of the Christian Israelites in Australia has no Emma or Robert on their records as being official members, it seems extremely likely that Robert was an attender - perhaps with his uncle. He could have met Emma there, who may have attended of her own volition or with her employing family. Robert's marriage to Emma Meredith took place the day after she turned 22 years old. He was two years younger, just 20 himself. It is likely that the marriage itself would have been heavily influenced by Robert's relationship with Uncle John Stanley and with John's second wife, Mary Deane. The couple chose to get married only 18 months after Mary Deane and John had done the same. Mary was some 33 years younger than Uncle John and, although born into a Christian Israelite community, she had more in common with Robert and Emma in terms of age.[45]

Wroe was still a frequent visitor to the Sanctuary and transcripts of his sermons were signed and dated by those that he trusted the most. These transcripts show that Wroe often directly asked spiritual questions of John Stanley during his preaching and that Mary Deane – now Stanley – was more of a favourite with Wroe than Sarah Stanley had been, as she was also permitted to sign and date the words of the prophet. Wroe continued to preside over the Sanctuary until a few years later when he moved to Australia permanently and, although he did not conduct their wedding, Robert would have been very familiar with Wroe's preaching style and with his personality. Uncle John was described on their marriage certificate as a gentleman and Mary Deane would have come to live a rather different life to that of Emma Meredith, who had married Robert – who was declared on their wedding certificate as a grocer and newly established in his own shop.[46]

When Emma married Robert on 17th October 1847, she was still working as a servant, but now for a family in Hyde. Her marriage to Robert would have liberated her from one form of servitude but, unlike Mary Deane, Emma's life would have consisted of back-to-back hard work as she supported her husband in their new

---

[44] John Wroe, *DC,* v 3, 1847 p.90.

[45] Such an age gap was cause for less comment in genteel Victorian society and certainly would not have had a whiff of scandal within the Christian Israelite community, where there were many Biblical precedents for a man having a much younger wife (or wives).

[46] Robert chose the same description of grocer in 1869 when he appeared before Parliament – although by then he could have decided to have claimed councillor or magistrate; evidence, perhaps, of genuine humility or of not being too obsessed with titles and occupations.

family business. It seems that they were able to set up their grocer's business more or less straight away, as the 1851 census shows us that they were running their shop in Stalybridge just three years later. Stalybridge had been visited by Karl Marx's closest comrade, Friedrich Engels, when he lived in Salford and was undertaking research for *The Condition of the English Working Classes.* Comparing Dukinfield, Ashton and Stalybridge with Manchester, he wrote, *"the working class, if possible, forms a larger part of the population ... they are inhabited only by working men and tradesmen, while Manchester has a very considerable commercial population, especially of commission and 'respectable' retail dealers."* There was clearly a stark economic divide between the city and its outlying towns; in Manchester, wages remained constant between 1836 and 1841, but in Dukinfield they had been reduced by 30%.[47] Engels decided to use Stalybridge as an example of the worst kind of conditions amongst mill towns in south-east Lancashire, writing that it had, *"multitudes of courts, back lanes, and remote nooks arise out of [the] confused way of building ... Add to this the shocking filth, and the repulsive effect of Stalybridge, in spite of its pretty surroundings, may be readily imagined."* [48]

Rather rude, perhaps, coming from a well-heeled middle-class revolutionary who probably enjoyed a bit of voyeuristic slumming, but for Emma, Stalybridge offered something far more than filthy back streets and repulsive nooks; it provided her with the chance of social mobility. No longer a domestic servant, she would have enjoyed the fact that her new married life allowed her to be her own boss. The physical distance from the Christian Israelite Sanctuary, although only a couple of miles, might have caused the couple to drift away from any regular involvement with the church, which was now declining steadily in numbers. The new Mr and Mrs Robert Stanley may also have felt that it would be best not to be so close to Uncle John and to his family anymore. It seems that Mary Deane's marriage to Uncle John had caused some ructions within the family - as Uncle John's eldest son (another John) from his marriage to Sarah left for Wales during the same year that his mother died, and his father had very quickly remarried. Records show that this son had also been a leader of the Christian Israelites alongside Uncle John, but that another disaffected member of the Church had persuaded the son to leave during this time. It is likely, too, that Uncle John felt that it would not have been wise to fund his nephew's own grocer's shop and locate it directly in competition to his own in Ashton.

The move to Stalybridge made good business sense. The growing population of Stalybridge was demanding new outlets for the necessities which Robert's grocery business would offer. Thanks to the brand-new railway station which connected Liverpool with Leeds and Manchester with London, moving to a new town and setting up their new enterprise must have marked a thrilling time for the couple, despite the poverty that Engels had encountered there.

A Not-So Christian Example: The Battle of St George(s)
Robert and Emma's arrival in their new hometown came at a time when Stalybridge had, yet again, become rather infamous. This time, however, the popular radicals could not be blamed; rather, the fault lay at the feet of the

---

[47] Dennis, *English Industrial Cities of the 19th Century*, CUP, 1988, p.20.
[48] Engels, *Condition of the English Working Classes*, 2007, p.73.

churchmen. By 1840 – and for reasons too ecclesiastical and lengthy to explain here - the town had two Anglican St George's churches. They were only a few hundred yards from one another and immediately competed for congregational loyalty and pew rents. One was the original parish church, known as Cocker Hill Chapel or now Old St George's, and had been consecrated in 1776. The other was referred to as New St George's and was consecrated in 1840.

The trouble began in May 1847, when Reverend France, the vicar of the 'new' church – and who had previously been incumbent of the old church - decided that he wanted to return to preside over the 'old'. The locals had proven to be far more loyal to the original chapel and consequently Reverend France was sorely lacking in pew rental income. Inevitably, the wardens took sides and the situation soon broke down, to the degree that when France tried to gain access to the old church, he was locked out. This led to a repeat performance: locks and doors being smashed by France's wardens, replaced by the old chapel's members and the church soon becoming an exciting side-show for the people of Stalybridge. Between 2-3,000 folk were turning up daily to the church and trampling in and out of the graveyard, accompanied by barking dogs, drunkenness, smoking, cursing and general hilarity. Everyone seemed to want to see Reverend France receive a good collaring at the hands of the Cocker Hill Chapel loyalists. The law enforcers became alarmed and soon France required a police escort during his daily parades to gain access to the chapel. Eventually, local magistrates Harrison, Cheetham and Platt (soon to become familiar with a young Robert Stanley) summoned the warring factions to court.

The Petty Sessions from this case make for extraordinarily lengthy reading, but at times they are enlivened by comments such as those made by one man who referred to a warden as, *"a ******* little monkey and said he would kick his ****."* [49] But in terms of the reputation of the town, Stalybridge's civic leaders were not impressed – particularly when several MPs in Parliament commented on the disgraceful behaviour by these northern churchmen.[50] Similar scenes continued for nearly four years, although the chapel remained officially closed, and this colourful situation would have marked Robert and Emma's arrival to Stalybridge, just a few hundred yards from their new home.

At some point after the reopening of Old St George's chapel, and when the scandalous scenes had subsided, Robert decided to worship at Old St George's. Perhaps he made his decision when the new vicar announced that the previous wardens had been fiddling the pew rents. Apparently, they had been keeping them artificially low so that the rich-but-cheap men of the town had been packing the church out at the expense of the poor, who were struggling to be able to access a pew. The cost of the pew rents was raised to a normal level and, according to the vicar, 'real gentlemen' were able to preside once more. Given the more dissenting tradition of the Stanley family, it might seem strange that Robert wanted to join the Established church, but examples such as this may have warmed his heart towards joining the church. Old St George's, too, was of a low Anglican tradition, which would have felt more familiar to Robert than the Anglo-Catholic New St

---

[49] Denby, P, *Two Into One Will Go – A History of the Parish of St George, Stalybridge,* Trinity Press, 1990. p. 49.
[50] Denby, p. 49.

George's. The Cocker Hill Chapel was also the place to be for a man who wanted to become more involved in civic society, as we shall see later.

It is hard not to wonder what Robert might have thought of some of the strange debacles and incidents associated with the Christian churches he had known when he looked back at his life and finally decided to become a Muslim.

Tea and Bread (Riots)

Fifteen years passed following their move to Stalybridge before we know anything more about the life of Robert and Emma. Important international events affecting the British Empire at this time included the Crimean War of 1853-56 and the Indian Mutiny of 1857, both of which would have been central in shaping Robert's early views on the way Britain was responding to some of its global positioning. It is likely that the horrors of the Crimean War coloured Robert's growing mistrust of the Russian Empire, which might well already have been filled with doubt thanks to the views of men such as John Wroe. Robert would have known young men from the local area who were killed in Crimea and he would have read reports from the conflict. It was around this time, too, when Robert told Quilliam that he had first encountered David Urquhart, whose words on Britain's errant foreign policy and mistreatment of the Turks were beginning to receive more attention in the press (see Chapter 8).

On the home front, Uncle John Stanley remained a faithful member of the Christian Israelites until his death in 1855. His second wife, Mary Deane, however, took the unusual decision to have her children re-baptised into the Anglican church immediately afterwards. She and the remaining family continued to live in the area, though, with their son, Deane Stanley, becoming a particularly successful businessman thanks to his Ashton-based Turkish towel company. No doubt in later life, Robert's younger cousin, Deane, would also have regaled him with interesting tales of life in Turkey and the economic and political situation there.

By 1863, Robert and Emma were running their grocer's shop on Princess Street (later Melbourne Street - the main shopping area of Stalybridge), but he had also developed a specialism in the tea trade and seemed to have gone into partnership with a man by the name of Robert Miller.[51] Robert Stanley had registered his tea business at one of the world's foremost centres of commerce: the awesome building of Manchester's Old Corn Exchange - a hotbed of economic activity and news from around the world. This would have made good business sense, having a base in Manchester to work from as he collected, sampled, traded and brought teas over to Stalybridge.

Although we have no evidence that Robert ever travelled overseas, his involvement with the tea trade would have exposed him to people of a far different type than the usual Stalybridge customer who frequented his grocer's shop. After stepping off the train from Stalybridge at Manchester's Victoria Station (which was directly adjacent to the Old Corn Exchange), Robert would have found himself surrounded by not only some of the wealthiest traders in the country – dealing in

---

[51] In the 22nd October 1874 edition of the *Liverpool Mercury*, in the same sentence 'Robert Stanley and Robert Miller, tea dealers' were described as having their business dissolved. Given the context (the other businesses mentioned were partnerships), this does point to the two men working together. It is likely that Robert Stanley decided to change the nature of his tea business if he felt that he had a strong chance of becoming mayor.

butter, sugar, cloth and other commodities – but also traders from many countries across the globe. The chances of him meeting and getting to know Muslims in Stalybridge itself would have been very slim indeed, so we can assume that Robert began to find out more about Islam within, or close to, the building of the Old Corn Exchange. These would have been men who made a profession out of travelling, selling and networking; many of them were foreigners who came to Britain to sell their wares and to establish a regular customer base at the British end of an international supply chain. For a man who was an avid reader of newspapers and periodicals, such people would have provided a different perspective on international situations, conflicts and on British foreign policy (see Chapter 8).

Following the trend of the previous two decades, life for the Stanleys in Stalybridge would have involved a more mundane day-to-day existence and then, suddenly, more radical extremist shake-ups. In 1862, a brickmakers' strike took place in the town and the strikers adopted the habit of using the cover of darkness to visit the brickyards of those who were not members of the union (otherwise known as 'scabs' to the strikers). There they damaged newly-made bricks and attacked any lingering master brickmakers; even the horses suffered injuries. Yet again, here was an example of bitter feelings on the part of the strikers. Often, the masters themselves did not even feature in social unrest in these towns – there could be enough division and animosity at times between the workers themselves, not to mention anger directed towards the newer figures of authority: the police. Indeed, two of Stalybridge's police officers were shot at early one morning whilst trying to stop a brickyard from being attacked, with one of the officers being killed.

The same year saw an even greater and more protracted series of civil disturbances amongst Stalybridge's working people; this time, however, the cry was not for improved wages and conditions, but to aid the suffering of the poor. The cry was simply for bread.

In 1862, King Cotton's economy was facing crisis as a direct result of the American Civil War, which had begun in 1861. President Lincoln had declared a blockade on cotton being shipped to the UK from the Confederacy (the south of the USA), in the hope of economically sapping the rival army's strength. The effect of this, however, proved to be terrible for the poorest workers in England and, as the supply of cotton from the USA dried up, slowly but surely the Lancashire mills began to close their doors to workers. Most of the working class in Lancashire was outspoken in condemning a cotton industry that was built on the backs of African slaves - even though the boycott was effectively starving them. In recognition of this, Lincoln took the unprecedented step of addressing a collective letter to them, which was read out in Manchester, and which sympathised with their plight, thanking them for their support in the fight against slavery. The burden of relief fell to the Poor Law guardians throughout 1861-62 and by January 1863 no fewer than 460,000 people across the country were dependent on such handouts.

The towns which suffered the most during the Lancashire Cotton Famine were Ashton, Dukinfield and Stalybridge, where thousands were laid off. By the winter of 1862-63 there were 7,000 unemployed operatives in Stalybridge; only five of the town's 39 factories and 24 machine shops could employ people full-time. There were 750 empty houses in the town and the population became severely depleted as over 1,000 skilled people left in what came to be known as

The Panic.[52] One answer to prevent further contraction of the industry was to replace American exports with Indian cotton – a far inferior crop and more difficult to weave – but this was deemed to be better than nothing and so, by the second winter, the situation seemed to be contained. In October 1862, a meeting was held in Stalybridge Town Hall which passed a resolution blaming the Confederacy and their actions in the Civil War for the cotton famine. Joseph Rayner Stephens, who had been keeping a low profile after his prison sentence, was horrified by the impact of the Cotton Famine and was soon making frequent appearances in public. At one meeting in Stalybridge Town Hall, he gave a three-hour speech where he emphasised the nobility of the working class, telling the people that the American Civil War was not to blame for the crisis; rather, it was the result of overproduction and the greed of the cotton masters.

But things were set to get worse again. On the Prince of Wales's wedding day on 10th March 1863, an act of solidarity towards the hungry poor of Lancashire was shown - with some 10,000 loaves made from American flour being shipped across to Manchester. As the crowd gathered to collect the food, a feeling of resentment grew as it seemed that there was, *"something derogatory in being drawn after these bread-laden waggons, like donkeys after a bunch of carrots ... a row ensued. Loaves were thrown about, were trodden upon ... and the meeting [was] broken up."[53]* Letters to both local and national press made it evident that the Poor Law guardians – noted as parsimonious hypocrites – were increasingly being made the target of anger and resentment. *The Bee Hive*, a moderate trade union publication, commented in December 1862 on the attitude of Poor Law guardians towards the recipients, who were, *"treated as if they were standing in the dock of a criminal court, or rather worse; not only are they presumed prima facie to be rogues and imposters, but they are addressed in the coarsest and most insulting language..."* [54]

The Bee Hive protested by urging a resolution which was passed at a public meeting in Stalybridge in relation to the guardians and which was then sent to the Home Secretary, explaining that, *"language of a harsh, brutal and disgusting kind is habitually used, not merely by the agents of the [Poor Law] committee but by some of the gentlemen who composed it; and not merely to men but to their wives and daughters."* [55]

The huge numbers of unemployed in Stalybridge were already required by the Poor Law to attend emergency schools when, in March 1863, seven miles away in Manchester, the executive committee of the Poor Law declared a new directive for this town. They ordered that the 17,000 men and boys in the schools should have their relief cut from 3s 4d to 2s 5d in anticipation that the economic distress of the cotton industry might continue for some time. To add insult to injury, most of the remaining amount was now to be offered in vouchers, to be exchanged in local shops for food items.

Clothes handed out via Poor Law relief also had to be marked out – or branded - so that the wearer was identified as wearing a donated item. The

---

[52] Hill, *Bygone Stalybridge*, Rigg, 1987, p.88.
[53] Longmate, *The Hungry Mills*, Maurice T Smith, 1978. p. 190.
[54] Longmate, p.190.
[55] Longmate, p. 191.

outrage at this was taken up by non-conformist ministers, with one of them waving a pair of ragged trousers from the pulpit, scorning the branding system. On 19th March 1863, those in receipt of relief held a meeting and decided to refuse both the reduction and the ticket system - and then the rioting began. The newspapers and the ensuing government investigation stated that most of the protestors were men and women - described as boys and girls - in their teens and twenties, many of them were Irish immigrants and as such deemed to be 'nowt but trouble.'

Bread Riots in Stalybridge - The building on the left being looted (with sign 'Canton Tea Warehouse') was Robert's first shop on Princess/Melbourne St

The first act of civil disobedience involved breaking the windows of a cab which was transporting two members of the Stalybridge Relief Committee. The mob then moved onto the main streets of Staybridge, smashing windows, vandalising the police station and targeting certain individuals unpopular with the working class. The first to receive such attention was Mr Bates (who was later a mayor in the town). His mill was surrounded by the crowd, with every window being smashed. This led to the first charge by the police constabulary. The crowd retaliated with a shower of bricks and stones and moved onto Bates's private residence at Cocker Hill, which received the same treatment. Mr Ashton, another member of the committee, had his shop looted, with the stocks of tea, coffee, sugar and spices being carried off. Dyson's Eating House was similarly attacked and then the people broke into the Poor Law Relief Stores themselves – seizing clothing and throwing items out of the windows to those waiting below whilst attempting to set fire to the place. By now, a local magistrate was in attendance, along with troops on horseback (hussars) from Manchester, who galloped into the streets and protected the magistrate as he read the Riot Act out to the town.

The next day, the magistrates of Stalybridge charged 29 of the 80 prisoners who had been rounded up, but events were not over yet. Twenty-four hours later, the disturbances began again. Whilst several crowds began to roam the streets of Stalybridge, the mayor announced that he would try and get them food tickets, but cries for 'money and bread' began and the rioters began to target even more shops, beginning with Mr Ridgway's who, in response to having his shutters forced, began to throw out his loaves and cheeses to the people below. Another 20 shops followed suit – amongst them Robert's, which was only several doors down from the Poor Relief Stores. One of the more amusing stories told at the time by a journalist involved a young man in the crowd who seemed to be rather disgruntled with the jar of mustard that had been tossed out the window towards him. Swearing, he dashed it to the floor declaring that he wished, *"He'd ha' summat different to that."*[56] By the evening, the police, foot soldiers, and hussars had once more managed to gain control of the town.[57] Many of the perpetrators, however, made their way to Ashton and commenced with attacking shops in the same manner – leading to the Riot Act being read in Henry Square. Dukinfield also received a throng of looters and was met with the Riot Act. Hyde, too, was targeted, with prisoners being carted off from all three other towns to the Chester Assizes for trial. Back in Stalybridge, the following day experienced similar disturbances and the disorder was now giving way to a different sort of thirst: demands for beer and a scramble to 'sup', with pubs and beer shops being besieged.

Robert, Emma and their young family would have witnessed the riots first-hand, as their shop was at the centre of the uprising on Princess Street and located between the shops mentioned by the press and the government inquiry. Indeed, one of the illustrations produced for the national press clearly shows the row of shops where Robert's business and home were located. The picture shows a scene of chaos with soldiers lashing out at the mob with swords, and clothing and food raining down from the windows onto the crowd. Indeed, the first shop on the left being attacked by the crowd is the very one that Robert and his family had, until recently, been living in (they had moved from No. 27 Princess Street down to No. 5 next to the River Tame). And one of the very rare anecdotes that we have of Robert's life - from his own family – mentions this event. David Stanley (my great uncle) told me:

> Well, your dad's grandad, Dean Stanley, told us that when he were growing up, his grandad - 'Unlucky Bob' as he were known – used to tell him the tale of the Cotton Riots in Stalybridge. He said that the shops were under attack from some of the people and that so to stop them smashing up the place like they were all the others – his dad [Robert] decided to throw all the food and that out from the top windows – to keep the people at bay.

This tale certainly chimes with the written records of the time, highlighting the desperation and danger in the air.

---

[56] Longmate, p.195.
[57] The cutlasses used by the hussars can still be seen on display at Stalybridge Civic Hall (the Victoria Market Hall).

It must have been a terrifying experience for the Stanley family to witness the looters below – especially as some of the crowd had been attempting to set fire to adjacent buildings. No wonder that Robert and Emma decided to fling their stock out of the windows! At the time of the picture illustrating the riots, the family would have been living above one of the shops further down the row, on the left (overlooking the bridge on Melbourne Street.) It is interesting, however, that Robert is not named as one of the many business owners who were unpopular in the town and deliberately targeted. Perhaps Robert – similar in attitude, politics, and outlook to Joseph Rayner Stephens - was a man with a good reputation already amongst the townspeople. Not long after the riots, the people of Stalybridge received a special visit from Mr and Mrs Gladstone, who were invited as guests of fellow wealthy Liberal, and soon-to-be sparring partner of Robert Stanley, Robert Platt. According to *Bygone Stalybridge*, Mrs Gladstone went to some of the sewing-classes, *"and expressed surprise and delight at the excellent needlework and knitting done by the scholars. Mr Gladstone went through some of the schools where the male operatives were being taught."*

However, it seems that for these unemployed scholars, the novelty was wearing off, *"knowing that the connection between the work done and the relief-wages to be procured was ... a make-believe."*[58]

The evidence that Robert provided to the Parliamentary Reform Committee in 1869 does seem to indicate that he had gained a reputation for championing the underdog. These experiences of being besieged and intimidated, though, did not seem to lead to an embittered attitude on his part towards the mill workers and the unemployed. In fact, the opposite seems to be true and his words in 1869 to the committee display a noble regard for those who had fallen on hard times (although it has to be said that, in his pre-Muslim years, he typically separated the 'respectable' working class who did their best to educate themselves from those poor who were deemed to be feckless or undesirable).

The American Question

By 1863, Robert had experienced many social and political disturbances on the streets where he lived. In November that year he was elected as a town councillor for Stalybridge and it is difficult not to conclude that this was a culmination of all these disturbances: he wanted to influence changes in society. Soon after this, he was appointed as a new magistrate for the town, most likely because of his level-headed attitude during the Bread Riots and because of his interest in judicial matters.

Even before he became a councillor or a magistrate, Robert was highly regarded in Stalybridge – and not just because he ran a reputable grocer's shop and offered the townspeople tasty tea blends. In June 1863, the *Ashton Chronicle* and the *Stalybridge and Dukinfield Chronicle* reported that Robert Stanley had been asked to chair a debate on the American Civil War. An interesting choice of a chair, as foreign affairs are, perhaps, not the sort of hobby that the average small shopkeeper in Britain today would be interested in. However, the economies of Lancashire's mill towns were completely reliant on foreign events and the

---

[58] Hill, p.97.

progress of the American Civil War had a crucial bearing on the wellbeing of the poor.

Although the people of Stalybridge had shown solidarity for the emancipation of African slaves, support for the Unionists versus the Confederates was never a given. In November 1861, Britain suddenly moved the closest to war with the USA than it had ever done since the American Revolution itself. The Trent Affair involved two Confederate diplomatic envoys, James Mason and John Slidell, being captured by the Federal army whilst they were travelling over to Britain aboard the Trent, a British mail steamer. The British had not taken sides in America's civil war and the government was outraged when word of the interception reached London. Britain demanded an apology and release of the prisoners and began mobilising its army. It sent 11,000 troops to Canada and commenced with plans to attack an American fleet that was blockading the South. Faced with British fury, Lincoln backed down and had the prisoners released. This – and the Bread Riots - provided the context for the debate in Stalybridge in which

Robert's descendants outside his first shop, looted in the Bread Riots. His second shop was further down the row and was also attacked.

Robert was asked to chair. It was reported on 23rd June 1863 by the *Ashton Chronicle* and by the *Stalybridge and Dukinfield Chronicle*:

> *On Tuesday evening last, the Rev. E A Verity, rector of Habergham Eaves, delivered a lecture in the large room of the Town Hall, Stalybridge, the subject being "The American war: its crimes and curses". The chair was occupied by Mr Robert Stanley, who after a few appropriate remarks, introduce the Rev.*

An eager crowd of 500 people assembled at a meeting chaired by a humble grocer whose shop had nearly been vandalised and torched just a few months previously, thanks to the Cotton Famine: evidence that Robert was not the only person in the town fascinated by international politics. But in addition to his experiences during the Bread Riots, it is also likely that Robert was asked to chair the meeting as a direct result of his involvement in David Urquhart's Foreign Affairs Committee, an aspect of his life which is explored more in Chapter 8.

The people of these mill towns were acutely aware that foreign affairs had a massive impact on people's livelihoods; ironically, interest in the outside, international world was perhaps even more pronounced than it is today, at a period in history when we have more information than ever at our fingertips.

CHAPTER 4

Town Hall, Parliament and ... More Riots
1848 – 1869

Councillor Beginnings

The first document that our family ever saw in relation to Robert's civic achievements was an article on Robert's life written by Abdullah Quilliam in the April 1907 copy of *The Crescent*, in which Quilliam directly reproduced an extract from *The Stalybridge Municipal Yearbook* of 1907 (see Appendix 1). We are not sure exactly why Robert was featured in the *Yearbook* in 1907, but it could be that he was soon to turn 80 years old and was, by then, the longest surviving mayor of Stalybridge. The *Yearbook* includes the photograph of Robert in his mayoral robe and chains but there is no mention that Robert changed his faith to that of Islam; unsurprising, really, given that becoming a Muslim for even the most famous figures of the Establishment (such as Lord Headley and Lord Stanley) was not something that people wanted to shout about at this point in British history.

However, the fact that the *Yearbook* chose to celebrate Robert's life does indicate that his conversion had not caused enormous waves amongst those who held the reigns of civic power within the town in 1907. If he had been deemed to be a traitor, or a person of ill repute, the Yearbook would simply have overlooked him. This further suggests that it was his family who decided not to speak of his conversion and, instead, to simply remember him as 'the mayor'. But it is thanks to both articles that we have been able to engage in further research about Robert's life in addition to his years as a Muslim.

The arrival of the railways connecting Ashton and Stalybridge to Stockport, Manchester, and Liverpool in October 1846, and then Stalybridge across the Pennines to Huddersfield in 1847, underscored the importance of the area as the beating heart of the North of England. The second half of the 19th century saw dramatic changes to the political landscape of Britain as population levels, class consciousness and demands for reform expanded. Robert probably spent this first full decade of his adult life building up his grocery business and raising a young family, as there are no records of his involvement in civic life before 1863, when he was first elected as a councillor for Stalybridge Town Council. During this period, he would have spent a good deal of time observing the events unfolding around him as Stalybridge moved towards borough status.

The years from 1848 to 1861 were dominated by two major foreign policy issues: the horrors of the Crimean War from 1853-56 and the Indian Mutiny (or Sepoy Rebellion) in 1857. On the home front, the news did not fare much better: in July 1857, 40 men and boys were killed in an explosion at Heys Colliery, which was located on the edge of Stalybridge. The New Inn, which Robert later became landlord of, was the nearest public house to the disaster and the subsequent inquest was held there.

But international battles and local tragedies aside, democracy began to creep slowly forward. Of the three towns that the Stanley branch of my family were involved with, Ashton was the largest. It received its own parliamentary borough and then a charter of incorporation in 1847, thanks to the Great Reform Act 1832. Dukinfield town - originally an outgrowth of Stalybridge – continued to be a civil parish until much later, in 1894, when it finally received its own charter. Stalybridge was granted its charter in 1857, with the document declaring that the town council should consist of a mayor (the first elected mayor was William Bayley), six aldermen, 18 councillors and should be divided into three wards: Lancashire, Staley and Dukinfield wards. At the time of Stalybridge's first elections for the council, Robert was 28 years old and the contesting parties in the town were known as the 'whites' and the 'yellows'. However, it was not until after the Second Reform Act 1867 that Stalybridge received its own MP, Conservative James Sidebottom in 1868.

Motivations of an Interloper
Local political representatives at this point in history were a very different breed to those of today. At the beginnings of the country's early local government system, the governing men were all drawn from the historically wealthy and landed families. The aristocracy were generally represented by the Conservatives, and the Whigs (who later became the Liberals) mainly consisted of those who had acquired their riches through industrialisation. Both groups possessed a sense of entitlement in relation to governing local affairs, with true universal suffrage rarely being met with serious consideration by either local or parliamentary-level politicians. These men - for they were all men, of course - were unpaid for the duties that they carried out on behalf of the town.

According to *The Stalybridge Reporter*, Robert seems to have been the first ever 'non-wealthy' mayor elected in Stalybridge – if not the entire country - and this makes his decision to stand for council even more interesting; was he motivated by the chance to rise above his working-class origins and to wield power within the town or was he more influenced by the thought of exercising fairness, leadership and innovation in local affairs? We have no way of knowing the true answer to this, but his responses to the parliamentary committee on voting reform in 1869 hint at his reasons: he tells the MPs and Lords that he felt that the calibre of local councillors was sorely lacking and that they did not possess the skills and experience that he felt an MP should have. In October 1874, Stalybridge Borough's Finance Committee reported, just before Robert's election as mayor, that more knowledgeable and qualified councillors were desperately needed; that, although there were plenty of men fulfilling these criteria in the town, none were willing to put themselves forward because they did not have the *"political fire"* required. Robert obviously felt that he was up to the job, however, and was probably acting on a sense of personal civic responsibility when he put himself forward as a candidate in 1863.

His eleven years of service were then rewarded with the post of mayor and this action succeeded in paving the way for a new batch of councillors – snobbishly lamented by *The Stalybridge Reporter* as being too young, too thin and from the more 'common trades', such as grocer.

The same old family names appear in the records of Stalybridge municipal life for the first few decades of the borough: the Cheethams, Bayleys, Lees, Leeches, Storrs, Platts and the Harrisons, to name but a few. All were extremely wealthy mill owners, employing hundreds of people and living in the town's finest mansions, but it would be wrong to suggest that the business of this new local government was not taken extremely seriously by them. Each councillor and alderman was required to declare their financial standing, their ability to vote and the property qualification required in order to enable them to stand for council. Any other declarations of interest which might affect their work within the council were also recorded.

Given that these family names appear again and again in the workings of civic, judicial, economic, and social transactions of Stalybridge life - and that all were rich families with a long connection to the borough - it is quite remarkable that Robert Stanley was not only taken seriously by fellow councillors but was quickly adopted into the fold of political life, soon rising to become their mayor. Thanks to the reporting by local newspapers, it is clear to see that Robert Stanley's achievements within the council chambers were quickly noted by others and, although he was never directly critical of those who had achieved the position of councillor due to connections rather than their own merits, the records and minutes of these meetings show that he quietly went about displaying quite formidable skills and knowledge, often highlighting the flaws and weaknesses amongst other, less rational, men without needing to point it out explicitly in exact words.

Although Robert held steadfast to conservative beliefs throughout his life, he

Robert's second shop, shown today on Melbourne St, Stalybridge

was in every sense an interloper when he was first elected to Stalybridge Town Council, and not just because he had been born in Cardiff and attended the

Christian Israelite church when growing up. His domestic circumstances would also have been a world away from most of his fellow councillors. From the 1861 census, we know that he was living above his shop with a family of eight children (aged one to twelve years old) and in 1871 - only a few years before he was elected mayor - there were still nine in the household (aged two to twenty years old). Unlike most of the other great men of the town, he had been forced to start work at the age of ten, with no access to private tuition, boarding school or university. His daily work would have been filled with moans and groans about the cost of food prices along with the day-to-day gossip about other shopkeepers or petty crime in the town. For a man of great intelligence and understanding, perhaps he had had his fill of this sort of tittle-tattle after more than a decade and wanted to influence the workings of his hometown.

As we saw in Chapter 3, the Bread Riots of 1863 were probably the final nudge that pushed Robert towards fulfilling this role, and to be so readily accepted by a group of wealthy old families would doubtless have been flattering for him. Robert, though, must have had high levels of confidence in his own abilities by the time that he was in his early 30s, perhaps in part thanks to the convictions of his own father (a poor man but full of the fight for justice) and, later, a result of his Uncle John's influence. Although not wealthy himself, as he grew older he would have been aware that he had the backing of his uncle, and the inevitable self-assurance that comes with money and status may have rubbed off on him. His interest in foreign affairs and his exposure to David Urquhart, as well as the experiences of rubbing shoulders with wealthy businessmen on the floor of the Manchester Old Corn Exchange, would have given him confidence alongside the middle and upper classes. My only family recollections of his personality come from his great-grandson, David Stanley, and emphasise firmness, *"I were told he were strict. As a child, you didn't mess about with him. But then, they were all a bit strict in them days, weren't they?"* His work, words and actions within the borough demonstrate a person who had an extremely kind and fair aspect to his character, perhaps elements that the Stalybridge Town Council felt needed to be kept close to home and fully utilised after the Bread Riots in order to prevent any such occurrences happening again.

After his election for the Dukinfield ward in 1863, Robert became a member of several council committees and, alongside his day job juggling grocer with tea-trader, his work as a magistrate and as an official (later chairperson) of the Stalybridge Parliamentary Reform Association (otherwise known as the Conservative Association) would have kept him extremely busy. Those who were enfranchised kept re-electing him, so he was clearly deemed to be trustworthy and level-headed. This is also borne out by the local press; where most Conservative councillors over the years received a good deal of criticism from the Liberal newspaper owners, very little negative commentary was ever levelled against Robert. Although a Tory, at times it was obviously difficult for the press to place Robert on the political spectrum, given his capacity for independence of thought, logic and the desire not to be swayed by bun fights. This seemed to render him an extremely popular local politician.

Robert's family would probably have been proud of his election as a councillor. The women in his life might well have found this new elevated status to be of great interest and enormous use. Certainly, the level of work involved with the many committee meetings, the court hearings and the other events requiring attendance would have taken their toll on Robert's presence within the home, but the advantages of his work and status would probably have outweighed the disadvantages for Emma.

Committee Life

In addition to the town council-scheduled meetings, most municipal authorities in Victorian England delegated certain functions to various sub-committees. This tradition still occurs for all local authorities in the UK (although it is now more of a necessity than a tradition, due to the enormous scale of their operations). These sub-committees usually sat prior to the monthly town council meeting, reporting back to the full meeting a few days later. Councillors were delegated to these committees according to their seniority in council, their experience, their interest and, often, they had no choice in the matter (as with Stalybridge's Finance Committee, where volunteers were regularly hard to come by). Robert's appointments to the various sub-committees varied slightly over the 33 years that he served as a councillor and alderman, but they generally included involvement on the Waterworks Committee, the Sanitation Committee, the Highways and Roads Committee and the Watch Committee (the latter responsible for employing the first-ever police constables in the country and other matters of local law and policing).

The minutes of these sub-committees, along with the main council minutes, are preserved in the Tameside Local Studies and Archives Centre, and the contributions of each councillor to final business carried out are recorded within them. These enormous tomes are nothing short of awesome in terms of their detail, embellishment, and presentation: handwritten in the most exquisite style of copperplate and produced with great pride. Of course, it takes the reader a good deal of time to adjust to each town clerk's handwriting, but it is worth the persistence because their sheer solemnity and fastidiousness provide a flavour of just how important these procedures - this new manner of British democracy - were to these new, governing municipal men. At the time of writing, however, there is unfortunately no short-cut for the reader who wants to examine Victorian town council minutes; the documents are not even held on microfiche (how I wished for a search engine facility!). Also, because there exists no secondary source list of councillors who were elected and served for each term in the borough, to find out more about Robert's level of involvement, hundreds of pages had to be examined over each year. The minutes are often an extremely dry and dull read but, from time to time, we can glimpse the odd bit of colour amidst the sepia; for example, small but amusing incidents such as when the notes included a rather embarrassing difficulty at the Stalybridge Public Baths because the council's paid attendant was found to have been using the water and detergent for her own household washing.

The town council and other committee minutes allowed me, for the first time ever, to see Robert Stanley's handwriting and signature. There are occasions too, where, when Robert was mayor, thanks to a sudden change in the style of handwriting employed, it seems likely that he took over the minute writing to dictate a letter from the council to either the Queen or to another organisation. But the local, regional, and national newspapers, too, were invaluable in seeking out the scant information available on Robert's civic life. The local newspapers - most particularly the Stalybridge and Ashton *Reporters* – provided an enhanced flavour of what really went on in those early meetings behind the town hall doors. Journalists at this time relied on taking shorthand: an excellent form of transcription. This means that real-time conversations, debates, slanging matches and the occasional hissy fit, with accompanied flouncing out of the council chambers, were reported in the weekly press. Stalybridge Town Council dialogue proved itself to be both biting and witty on many an occasion, but in relation to the minutes, sometimes what was not included in the official documentation of the meeting was more revealing than what was.

Stalybridge Town Hall in 1985, four years before demolition

Not Another Riot: Sectarianism and the Murphy Riots 1868-69

Whilst Robert began to get stuck into municipal life, the towns of Stalybridge and Ashton enjoyed five years of relative peace after the Lancashire Cotton Famine but, in 1869, a new cause for civic unrest arrived. This time the disturbances were not in relation to industrial dispute, nor issues of poverty and oppression; rather, the cause was religious differences - or, perhaps more accurately, man-made bigotry and intolerance - which was brought to the area thanks to a Mr William Murphy.

Murphy was a 33-year-old from County Mayo, Northern Ireland, and he began touring England in the late 1860s, lecturing for the Protestant Evangelical Mission & Electoral Union. He was an out-and-out rabble-rouser and was violently prejudiced against Roman Catholics. Murphy interspersed his religious rantings with political agitation and scapegoating as he travelled the country doing his best to whip up Protestant community feelings against their Catholic neighbours, who were predominantly poor Irish immigrants living in the working-class neighbourhoods of Britain. He informed his Protestant audiences that the

80

Catholics had profited in the economic recession caused by the cotton famine; they offered cheap labour and were therefore taking local jobs. Only two decades earlier, thousands of Irish immigrants had come to Manchester faced with desperation and traumatised by all that they had witnessed in the Great Famine (also known as the Potato Famine). Most became mill workers or worked as navvies within the civic construction programmes; many of these projects had been designed in order to provide employment for the poorest in society who had been hit by the 1863 Cotton Famine in the north of England.

Murphy declared that, *"every Popish priest was a murderer, a cannibal, a liar and a pickpocket."* [59] His method of inflating outrage involved putting on staged performances. Women and anyone under the age of 21 were banned from attending and he booked venues in the same areas for several nights, relying on word of mouth. The performances consisted of a dramatization of alleged sexual shenanigans between women and priests, with the confession box being a sinister place of entrapment where, Murphy told his audiences, their wives and daughters were, *"exposed to debauchery."* His claim centred on the nature of confession: that women would be prompted to think about sexual undertakings of which they were previously innocent, thereafter being cajoled into actions that were, *"contrary to the laws of nature"* at the hands of unscrupulous priests. Murphy supplemented his dramatization with a neat little handout that detailed the alleged sexual practises that these priests engaged in: highly explicit literature for its time, not to mention the fact that the sexual acts were defined as mortal sins by Catholic theologians.

Where Murphy's lecture tours had not been forbidden – many town leaders had prevented him from hiring their rooms – they were met with Catholic outrage and police presence. Hundreds of special constables had to be sworn in under the threat of considerable disorder. Disturbances occurred in Portsmouth and Wolverhampton, and in Birmingham, after Murphy railed against Catholics and called the Pope, *"a rag and bone gatherer",* there was a full-scale riot requiring the presence of police, soldiers, and cavalry.[60]

Murphy then progressed to the north west – an area with large pockets of Catholic population and already prone to deep sectarian divisions. He deliberately targeted Oldham, Rochdale and Bury and, in April and May 1868, trouble flared in Dukinfield, Stalybridge and Ashton.[61] During Easter, St Mary's Church in Dukinfield was attacked by a mob, but it was in Stalybridge and Ashton where the worst violence occurred. The populations of both towns at this time were nearly 50 percent Irish Catholic; they had already been blamed for much of the trouble relating to the Bread Riots and suffered disproportionately from poverty. Following a speech made at the Foresters Hall in Stalybridge on 13th April, Murphy ended his words by producing a gun, telling the audience that he had not requested protection from either the mayor or the magistrates but that he would protect himself and was ready to be blown up for the glory of Heaven. He then

---

[59] Diamond, M, *Victorian Sensation: Or the Spectacular, the Shocking and Scandalous in Nineteenth Century Britain*, 2003, p. 91.
[60] Arnstein, The Murphy Riots: A Victorian Dilemma, in *Victorian Studies* (1975) 1991 pp. 51–71.
[61] In 1851 in Stalybridge, there were 1,925 Anglicans, 1,645 Congregationalists, 1,757 Roman Catholics, 1,050 Wesleyan Methodists, 972 Baptists and 549 Primitive Methodists: Hill, 1987.

spoke in Ashton at the Charlestown Old Mill and disturbances also began in Stalybridge.

The seeds of a full-scale riot had been sown, and over the next few weeks trouble came to a head. In early May 1868, violence erupted in Ashton, around the Prince of Orange pub.[62] Murphy's supporters gave out Orange Order emblems to be worn around the town and fights broke out in the streets between Protestant and Catholic, 'Irish' and 'English'. Huge groups of Irish people wearing green ribbons began to assemble in Ashton's Charlestown area, outside John Stanley's mills, where the Southcottians and Christian Israelites had once met. Crowds over several thousand strong began to assemble in Bentinck Street, Old Street and Henry Square and fighting broke out, accompanied by stone-throwing. The Irish contingency used their revolvers, leading to an Orangemen retreat, but then a targeting of Irish homes began, with stone-throwing and furniture being dragged out into the streets, smashed and burned. The Orange group moved on to attack the priest's house, local catholic school and the two Roman Catholic chapels of St Mary's and St Ann's. These were defended by Irish men firing shots, but one of the churches was ransacked, with religious relics destroyed and crucifixes burned. At midnight, the magistrates read the Riot Act and the violence finally petered out. There was one fatality – a woman on Bentinck Street where, some 20 years earlier, PC Bright had been stabbed to death during the Chartist agitation, close to Robert's home. An inquest was held several days later, its verdict being that the poor woman had died of fright. In Stalybridge, people left a Murphy meeting to riot and smash windows in the town's Irish quarter and the police tried to combat the attack using cutlasses.

There was already a great deal of fear amongst the Irish people of Stalybridge; an Anglican vicar from Dukinfield who had attended one of Murphy's speeches there recorded that the man had called for the hanging of local Roman Catholic priests. The feeling of persecution and foreboding, as Murphy urged the poorest folk to turn on their fellow underprivileged, must have been overwhelming. A group of men who had been at one of the anti-Catholic lectures in Ashton were ambushed on their return home to Stalybridge by a group of Irishmen who, in preparation for the attack, had put out the streetlights and placed ropes across the road. The men were badly injured, and a counterattack took place, targeting the Roman Catholic chapel of St Peter's in Stalybridge.

Stalybridge's Catholic population had anticipated the attack, and many were there to defend against it – including the priest, who took station on the church's roof with a rifle in hand. But the building was brutally vandalised. During the commotion, the priest fired his rifle and a man was shot and killed. The Riot Act was read, and the soldiers and cavalry were called in, taking two full days to restore order in the area. The priest was tried but eventually acquitted.

Murphy himself did not last much longer than his riots. In April 1871, as he was about to give a lecture in Whitehaven, a gang of more than 200 managed to break into the hall, dragged him downstairs and beat him unconscious. He never recovered fully from his injuries and died some 13 months later.

The *Pall Mall Gazette* attempted to summarise the situation at the time:

---

62 The Prince of Orange pub in Ashton is still in existence.

Such an insignificant creature as Murphy could never have lighted such a fire as this if there had not been a vast mass of fuel ready to his hand. The ease with which he stirred up the feelings of the people both at Birmingham and in the North shows how powerful and widely spread those feelings... The overwhelming majority of Englishmen of all ranks of life do from their very hearts, and in a great variety of ways, utterly detest superstition and priestcraft... [63]

At the time of the Murphy riots, Robert had been a councillor for several years. He had sat on various town council committees including the Watch Committee, which governed local law and order. His role as a magistrate would have required him to be on-call as soon as disturbances in the town began. It is likely that he was present during the reading of the Riot Act and was present during the initial hearing of cases from these disturbances, which took place in his own ward. Through his role as councillor, he would have known the Catholic priest who stood on the roof of St Peter's - rifle in hand - and he would have known many involved in the ambushes, from both sides. As we shall see, Robert tended to divide the poor into what some commentators preferred to view as 'undesirable' and 'desirable', and by the time he was an established grocer in Stalybridge he was also a stalwart member of Old St George's Anglican church at Cocker Hill. The Reverend Jelly-Dudley, who led the congregation there, was a rather outspoken critic of the Catholic church and although Robert would not have been a stranger to anti-Irish and anti-Catholic prejudice there is no evidence from his words in the council and in the courtroom to indicate that he held such views (which, sadly, cannot be said for many of his peer group).

Whilst it is difficult to know, therefore, what his opinion would have been on the Murphy Riots, David Urquhart - one of the individuals that he admired enormously – had been very close to converting to Roman Catholicism himself, so it is likely that he would have been sympathetic to the experiences of the Irish Catholics. Like the Christian Israelites, and later as he saw with regards to Muslims, the Catholic Irish of England were a group of people who were met with ignorance and prejudice in far too many places because they dared to think differently in relation to their spiritual beliefs.

Parliamentary Witness – The Great Reform Act
Thanks to the Islamic publication *The Crescent,* not only did my family learn that Robert had converted to Islam, but we also discovered that he was a witness for the Select Committee on Parliamentary and Municipal Elections. At first glance, this event does not sound particularly enthralling, but further research has highlighted just how important Robert's participation was.

The parliamentary committee functions of British democracy tend to receive far less attention than the other Cabinet or Whitehall elements of government – largely because they occur away from the media spotlight. However, for the historian, the political analyst and anyone else concerned with the progress of legislative and social change in the UK, examining the minutes of these meetings

---

[63] See https://radicalmanchester.wordpress.com/

can prove to be more rewarding than looking at the actual statutory outcomes themselves. The minutes of the committees allow the reader to observe 'real-time' discussions and dynamics. For the family historian, they are often overlooked as a source of material because, as with my family and the case of Robert, it is almost impossible to know if your ancestor may have been called as a witness unless you were informed otherwise. And yet, the committee that Robert appeared before in Parliament turned out to provide us with the lengthiest dialogue of Robert to date. This is because the minute takers of these committees record the actual words of the questioners - the MPs and Lords - along with the responses of the witnesses, just as a stenographer in a court hearing does.

As seen in the previous chapters, the subject of universal enfranchisement continued to be a hot potato for British governments after the Peterloo Massacre in 1819 and until the date that this committee sat in 1869. Although a tiny minority of the working class had received the vote, by this point in the 1860s the vast majority were still unable to exercise their views via the ballot box. Of a population of 30 million, only 1.43 million were able to vote. It had taken a good two decades for the Establishment to realise that they would be wise to heed the Chartist demands and to widen the franchise and, by 1869, Parliament had fallen into general agreement that this should happen sooner rather than later (although not, of course, the issue of universal female suffrage). So, in 1867, the Parliamentary Reform Act was introduced by a Conservative government, and it increased the electorate to almost 2.5 million. It opened the vote to working-class 'occupiers' within boroughs (i.e., those who resided in a rented property were finally eligible) as well as to those who owned property - one of the issues that Robert himself touched upon when speaking to the committee.

The problem that the government was now faced with, however, in relation to the working-class vote was less of 'the when' and more of 'the how'. Should all working-class men (with an occupational status or not) be able to vote in both local and national elections? How should their vote be cast? Should the vote be provided openly or in private? As a nation, we have become totally blasé with regards to the right to a private ballot, so it may surprise some readers to learn that until the 1872 Act all voting was undertaken in public – meaning that anyone who happened to have a keen pair of eyes or ears would instantly know who you had voted for. And it was with this aspect in mind that Robert Stanley was called to appear before the select committee on 20th April 1869.

By the time that Robert travelled to London to be questioned by the committee he was 41 years old and had been able to vote since the age of 21, when he became a property owner and a grocer. However, very few men within the Stalybridge area would have been able to vote, and certainly no women. The findings of this committee were crucial and went on to form the backbone of the Third Reform Act 1884, shaping modern democracy as we know it today.

Thanks to the existence of the British Parliamentary Archives, it was possible to read the transcript in full, to speak to the staff about the nature of this sort of record keeping and to find out more about procedure and protocol. This select committee, for example, was an inordinately long one. It took place for several weeks throughout April and May of 1869 and Robert had to spend two days in London for the purposes of his contribution His expenses were covered; he received 2s 18d for travelling to, and staying in, London on Tuesday 20th April, and 1s 10d for 'absence from home'. The records only show the amount that he claimed for, so we don't know whether he stayed in a hotel or with a friend or family member. For a busy man, with many commitments, travelling to London marked a considerable effort on his part and we can assume that he undertook the trip and the contribution to the committee with his usual sense of gravity and with a great deal of thought. Certainly, his responses and remarks to the committee seem to be exceptionally considered, yet honest and spontaneous.

When Parliament is seeking witnesses to appear before a committee today, social media and word of mouth are often used. In the Victorian era, Parliament generally used newspaper advertisements to call for witnesses who might be experts, self-proclaimed experts or directly experienced with regards to the subject matter. Someone who knew Robert may have seen the advertisement and told him to put himself forward as a candidate or Robert could have nominated himself. If he did so, a careful reading of the transcript shows no evidence that he considered himself to be some sort of expert. On the contrary, he only mentions his work as a councillor and as a magistrate when directly questioned in relation to how he has amassed his experience about voting and the issue of bribery in Stalybridge. Unlike others who appeared before the committee for the sessions who are noted down as 'Councillor', 'Ex Councillor', 'Mayor' etc, Robert has been listed as 'Grocer, Stalybridge' and, given the fact that his other civic titles had to be more or less coaxed out of him by the committee, it is highly likely that he himself chose to be listed in this manner. Was this him demonstrating a lack of pride and wanting to give the impression that he was nothing more than a humbler grocer? Or was it because he felt that to mention his roles as councillor and magistrate would rouse the committee to feel suspicious of party-political affiliations on his part? Again, this is something that the reader will have to decide for themselves.

The names of the men who sat on the committee do not appear to be of particular interest at first glance; most of them are simply listed as 'Mr' but, on delving more into their backgrounds, the composition of this particular committee turned out to be quite spectacular, containing enormous political weight and pedigree from both the past and the future. Two men in particular that Robert would have wanted to impress his logic and views upon – although Liberals - were incumbent cabinet ministers: George Villiers, 4th Earl of Clarendon, who was the current Foreign Affairs Secretary and who had overseen the action during the Crimean War, and John Bright, Minister for the Board of Trade who was famous across the land for his pro-working-class stance. After speaking with nearly all the other men, Robert would have gone on to read their names in various national headlines during the years to come. What does seem to have been of importance to Robert is that, *"the under-secretary for Foreign Affairs left his seat on the committee and personally thanked Mr Stanley for his evidence, and it also formed matter for a discussion in Parliament."* These days it would be highly unlikely for an incumbent senior minister with the Foreign Affairs portfolio to be present on such a committee.

Throughout the questioning, Robert worked hard not to name the political party that was more guilty of attempting to unduly influence the voting preferences of the working class (this was the Liberals in most cases in Stalybridge). For example, he said that unfair practises were conducted, *"by one party almost without exception; it is very universal on one side."* He was also careful not to use the word bribery, no doubt because this was an illegal practise which required prosecution. He was clearly taking the issue of fair and transparent democracy very seriously and wanted to minimise all hints of political bias on his part, not just because he was a magistrate but probably because he prided himself on being an independently-minded person. Although he would not have known which politicians would be sitting on the committee when he agreed to appear before them, he would also have soon realised that 50 percent of the committee was made up of Liberals. Indeed, the committee was chaired by the Marquess of Hartington, Spencer Cavendish, the 8th Duke of Devonshire, a leading Liberal at this time (although he was later to switch sides several times and became the leader of the Liberals, the Liberal Unionists and the Unionists).

Thanks to the work of this committee, pressure inside Parliament – as well as outside - began to grow, culminating in the Third Reform Act 1884. This gave the same political rights for those living in counties as those in boroughs, enfranchising more men, although around 40 percent of men still did not have the vote after 1884. But this committee also led to an another, extremely important, piece of legislation. Introduced by Edward Leatham MP, a key member of the committee and brother-in-law of radical reformist John Bright (also on the committee), the Ballot Act 1875 was designed to provide the ordinary man with the protection of secrecy when voting. In combination with the Municipal Elections Act 1875 and the Parliamentary Elections Act 1875, it shaped Britain's modern electoral practices. Many people, however, such as Lord Russell (former Prime Minister) believed strongly that secret ballots were cowardly. 'Unmanly' was the word commonly used and it was felt that people should not cower behind a secret ballot; but this was all too easy for a rich man to say, as he was not at risk of losing his job over his voting allegiances. Robert's own views on the subject had been shaped by watching exactly this sort of thing occur in Stalybridge and his evidence to Parliament helped to influence another important piece of legislation: the Corrupt and Illegal Practices Prevention Act 1883, which sought to attempt to end any other form of electoral corruption.

Robert's Parliamentary Responses
The evidence that Robert gave began with him talking about how voting in Stalybridge was carried out.

Intimidation, Bribery and Anti-Screws
When asked by the Duke of Devonshire about this subject, Robert replied, *"as the elections are at present conducted, there is a great deal of intimidation, and a great deal of coercion used, and to some extent, the elections are a farce."* He went on to tell the duke that he was not aware of any specific incidents of bribery per se, but that, *"treating has been very prevalent."* The word 'treating' meant just that: providing a nice little treat to a working-class man to butter him up and gain his vote. It usually involved accompanying a chap to the pub and paying for him to become intoxicated. Robert explained further, *"Generally, for some weeks before the elections, the voters have been enticed into public houses and treated with liquor and they have been talked over; and, in consequence of their treating, it has been a very common thing for them to vote for the parties who have treated them."* When

asked further about intimidation in Stalybridge, he replied, *"The overlookers and managers of different mills have gone round to the men under them and canvassed them and told them how they must vote; told them they must vote in the way that they wished them to do."*

He was next asked whether men were sacked if they voted against the wishes of their master, *"It is a very common thing indeed. I have seen, at those municipal elections, the overlooker bringing all the men under him, like a troop marching after him, going up to the poll and watching them, and seeing them vote and taking care that they voted the right way."* He went on to tell the committee, *"In many cases, if they vote contrary to the wishes of their masters, the men are discharged and their families as well... at some mills there are very few of them that do anything else but vote as their employers wish them."* He said that this had always been the case and that it was not just the voter who suffered as a result of it, but even the children of the community, *"Since I have had anything to do with public matters in Stalybridge ... I have known cases where a clergyman and the school master has been canvassed and the clergyman has been told distinctly, he would make a mistake if he voted a certain way; he did so, and he found that the half-time factory children have been taken from his school."* Along with depriving working children of their chance at education, it seems that the town council employees also experienced this, that Robert's fellow town councillors wanted to have majority rule not only in the council chambers but throughout the executive offices, *"they have canvassed the employees of the town council, accompanied by the surveyor, and they use a considerable amount of influence over them, and in some few instances the men have been discharged since, in consequence we suppose, of their voting contrary to the wishes of the members of the council."*

Robert told the committee that differences took place in Stalybridge in relation to practises employed during municipal and during parliamentary elections, and he explained that before the very first election of an MP occurred for Stalybridge, two of the factory overlookers who had been engaging in intimidation received summonses, and that for the first national election, *"I think it entirely prevented them from using the intimidation that they had done before. I could not hear of any cases after that, because the offence is a very serious one."* Robert also explained about Stalybridge's Anti-Screw Association, where working men paid a subscription to the Association and if they were then sacked as a result of voting contrary to their master's preferences, the Association made a donation to their family in order to keep the wolf from the door until they could find another job:

> *... to some extent it did encourage a number of the men to vote as they wished to do, and the result has been that a considerable portion of them have since been discharged; not all together but one or two a week. Some little trivial circumstance has been taken advantage of, and the men have been got rid of one or two a week. The Screw Association was in existence 14 weeks after the election, because it was found necessary ... I suggested the idea of this very Association being formed to support each other, and prevent their intimidation ... [it] induced a great number of people to vote for one*

87

candidate that would not otherwise have done so, but not all; there would have been a greater number voted for our candidate if some of the millowners had done the same as others – put placards up in the mill, saying that they did not wish to influence in any way the votes of their workmen , and that no advantage would be taken of them if they voted as they thought proper.

So, it was Robert's idea to set up the Association in order to protect working men's votes. He did not pretend to the committee that he was personally politically neutral himself and made it clear that he was a supporter of the Conservatives and that he had been the acting chairman and treasurer of the Anti-Screw Association. He said that all the men serving on the committee tended to lean towards the Conservatives. However, he made it clear that he was less interested in party politics and more committed to the workings of democracy in Stalybridge, mentioning that the other members of the Association's committee – who took the decision collectively whether to financially assist a man or not – were all mill workers. The Foreign Secretary – a Liberal himself – then asked Robert what would happen if a Conservative mill owner was found to be engaged in intimidating workers so that they would vote for his candidate, with Robert replying:

We never had a case of that sort; and I do not think there is a single case in Stalybridge of that sort; I should have heard of it if it had been so... I know myself of a [Conservative] mill-owner, who was a candidate, there were two of his men on the opposite committee canvassing for the opposite candidate, without interference, and without having a single word spoken to them, and the candidate did not know of that circumstance till I told him myself...nothing followed from it.

The Secret Ballot?

Next, the committee asked Robert how many people were entitled to vote in each type of election; Robert provided the exact figures – 2,377 for the municipal elections and 5,339 for the parliamentary (the parliamentary borough of Stalybridge being much larger than the town council boundaries). He also informed them that to stand for the town council, a man had to meet a three-year residency qualification, but if he wished to stand as MP for Stalybridge the qualification was only one year. He gave his thoughts as to why there were so few voters in comparison to the large population in the area, *"the number who do not reside a sufficient length of time are generally a very low class of people; people who, some morning, the landlord comes and finds that they are gone; as a rule."* The committee then asked how the town had handled the transition to becoming a borough with municipal elections, which Robert stated had attracted, *"... a considerable amount of feeling. We have been in what I may call an excited state for a great number of years in Stalybridge."* Following this came a long line of questioning in relation to his views on whether introducing a secret ballot system would solve the problem of the intimidation of the working classes. Robert had to repeat himself and explain his views further. His fears were that if the secret ballot were introduced for both elections:

...an inferior order of Members would bid for the support of the populace, by promising them certain advantages, and appealing to their self-interest; and that in many different ways a worse class of men would be elected to Parliament than there is at present ... because in a local election you cannot promise them anything; you cannot hold out to them any hope at all, except that the rates might be a little lower; that is all that you can promise them; whereas in the Parliamentary elections you can show all the existing institutions of the country, and point out to them the wealth that exists, on the one hand, and the poverty on the other; and by so doing you can lead the working classes on to believe that they have a right to a share of the wealth... when you can make people look to their self-interest, it is very easy to frame excuses and to use plausible arguments, and so lead them to believe in the existence of a wrong.

Robert believed that whilst the secret ballot would work well at the local level – where the only issue at stake was the rates – at the national level, the stakes were much higher, and the temptation of the selfishly driven person would cause them to vote for the candidate promising them ridiculous notions in order to get elected. Robert believed that for national elections voting publicly would hold people to account and reduce the risks of 'inferior quality' MPs being elected, *"if they could do it under a system of secret voting, people would be inclined to try the experiment ... which I am afraid would come into being in case secret voting by the ballot was adopted, when there would be some chance of those men getting elected."* He told them that, so far, the proof of his statement had been borne out by the fact that in the recent general election, *"all the working men's candidates were rejected; under the ballot the House would largely be composed of men of that stamp."*

His views seem to have appeared as being somewhat contradictory to the committee. It was likely that they had only ever been faced with witnesses who were either for or against the secret ballot per se. Robert, however, was pro-secret ballot for the local elections, but anti-secret ballot for the parliamentary elections. His beliefs might be interpreted by us today as being somewhat patronising; it is as though he was saying that the common working man could not be trusted to make a good decision for the parliamentary elections and that it did not matter so much if a working-class man acted in a selfish manner when it came to the locals (as the level of the rates was far less important than national and international issues). But Robert's political context and personal experiences in Stalybridge explain his views; he saw threatening behaviour being carried out locally, the rise of communist sentiments and the 1848 revolutions on the continent - what he saw as idle talk of redistribution of wealth in order to simply win votes was something that deeply worried him. He pointed out that for national elections:

You have another class of man entirely to what you have in the municipal elections as candidates, and the question takes a far wider range .... I do look upon the Parliamentary vote more in the light of a trust, and the municipal vote I look upon as a question of self-interest only; that is about the extent of it.

But he did not believe that people should be induced to vote either one way or another, *"You cannot make them do anything of the kind; it is not right to make them do anything, only by using arguments, and trying to convince them that the other side is wrong."* For Robert, it seemed that education and reasoned logic was the way to a man's heart. He was conservative through and through – fearful of too much change too quickly and of the uneducated person exercising their vote in a foolhardy manner, *"if they could do it secretly, they might try the experiment of sending a man up to see really what he would do."*

The Intermeddler
It has been impossible to find anything negative written about Robert Stanley at the hands of the press. He seems to have been exceptionally popular, even with the political opposition in Stalybridge. However, when he spoke about prosecuting those who had been engaging in bribery over elections, he provides us with a different perspective:

> *For instance, in my case I know that I am very ill thought of by people of my own class on the other side for taking an active part in those prosecutions; people always look at it as a thing against me. For many years some of them have looked upon me as a sort of meddler interfering between master and workmen, and a sort of dangerous character.*

His next set of responses outlined a little more of his own personal motivations for taking this (unpaid) stance of advising men being bribed or treated to vote for someone:

> *Working men who are intimidated of course cannot afford to go into those things themselves, they have to be supported by some private individuals, who promise to find the money or raise the money in some way or other and those private individuals are looked upon as a sort of intermeddler.*

He explained that he had done his best to support men who were being threatened, but he lacked the money to be able to personally pay for their legal cases to be brought; hence his idea of at least creating a system of advocacy via the Anti-Screw Association. Without trying to paint himself as some sort of latter-day superhero for the intimidated working-class voters, he suggested several times that there should be a public prosecutor to support such cases. Most likely, he would have been pleased to see that legislation was pushed through some years later by members of this select committee (in the 1872 Act). And yet, he also seems to have been a realist - he conceded that even if the working man did receive such financed representation, a man might well not proceed with the prosecution anyway, because genuine fear might cause him to shrink from giving evidence, *"in a great number of cases they would."*

Although Robert's words throughout the questioning portrayed a man who referred to the 'less desirable' and 'inferior' sort of people, his views on the 'better sort' of person were not all class-based; in fact, he used this term equally for prospective MPs whom he felt might be of a more unscrupulous character. In terms of his own class, he indicated that he belonged to the tradesman class, and amongst his own kind – especially those who were strong Liberal supporters – that he was deemed to be an 'intermeddler'. We might call them a 'sticky beak' or a 'nosey parker' today. But he did not seem to mind this label too much. The fact that he chose to mention it to the committee (he did not have to, after all) demonstrates that this nickname might even have been a badge of pride: that he was going out of his way, with no financial reward, to alleviate oppression. It seems that he wanted to keep the scales of justice balanced and if it meant that he became something of an irritant, or someone 'dangerous', to those who were in the wrong – so be it.

Politics at Home

Robert was asked about the presence of trade unions in Stalybridge. He felt that they should be used with caution because, *"The members ... like all other classes of society [are] selfish, and when there are two courses to choose, they would choose the one that is the most for their own interest, sometimes when it is not a very just course. ... that which would give them more power."* Despite this, he also seemed to believe in the spirit of collectivism (as evidenced through him founding the Anti-Screw Association) and was, therefore, able to view the merits of unions, too, *"To a certain extent, I believe they ought to be supported, but they sometimes go beyond what they really ought to do, and like all other classes, they are apt to go beyond, and want greater advantages than what they really ought to have."*

The committee ended the session with the chairman asking him, *"Politics enters into everything in Stalybridge, does it not?"* Robert agreed and confirmed that at the current time, the Liberals were in the majority in Stalybridge, *"They are very much under the influence of the great mill-owners at present, that is to say, the independent class of men are not chosen, unless they will support the views of a particular party; unless they are of a particular political creed they are rejected under the present system."*

But in his usual candid manner, he also referred to the state of his own political party, the Tories:

> Some years ago, before there was a probability of the borough being made into a Parliamentary borough, we had what is called a great struggle between the popular side and the wealthy side; it was not then so much a question of party politics as it was against the intimidation and influence of the great mill-owners; and at that time what is called the Conservative side took the popular side of the question and by that means they had a majority of the town council; they then sat down and rested on their oars, and the other party gradually got a footing.

Stalybridge Conservatism

Over the years, Robert Stanley had become a loyal member of the Tory Party. By October 1874, just before his appointment as mayor, he was the vice-chair of the Stalybridge Parliamentary Reform Association (otherwise known as the local Conservative Party). This would have involved a great deal of time in terms of regular attendance, not to mention the many social gatherings and outings that the Association put on for its members (i.e. a picnic outing to Lyme Park in 1874).

In 1874, Robert took the chair for the Conservatives' annual tea party. A transcript was given in the *Reporter* and Robert's opening words were honest about past performance and yet promising; the Tories had recently seen a return to power, thanks to one of Robert's heroes, Benjamin Disraeli. Robert told the gathering:

Last year, if you will remember, ladies and gentlemen, I took rather a gloomy view of our position in Stalybridge. I thought we were going to the dogs fast. However, since then things have taken a decided change for the better. I think we may congratulate ourselves that we occupy a far better position as regards our parliamentary representation, and as regards our general interests as a party, than we did this time last year. For my own part I feel very much gratified with it and I think great credit is due to the Conservatives through the country, and in Stalybridge in particular, for the exertions they have made to change the state of things with regard to our representations in Parliament.

Robert went on to talk at length about the various ways in which they could ensure that Conservative principles spread throughout the country. The *Reporter* noted his words:

Another great mode of supporting the Conservative party was the press. He was sorry that they had not more Conservative newspapers in Lancashire. It was a strange anomaly that there should be in Lancashire two Radical newspaper to one Conservative, whilst the country including the boroughs returned 27 out of 33 members (A voice: "26") It seemed to him that the papers which had been read had been read to some purpose, but that was not the only thing which had brought them to their present position. They were indebted to a gentleman on that platform for the lectures and speeches he had delivered from time to time. He meant Mr Touchstone – (Cheers) If these lectures were to be taken as a guide and precursor of Conservative principles, he hoped they would be renewed for a good thing could not be too often spoken.

The next part of his speech reiterated something that he had mentioned to the MPs and Lords in 1869 when the select committee had asked him about the Conservative Party in Stalybridge. Robert had felt then that there was a tendency not to keep up the momentum of political activity once they were in a stronger position following an election, and again in 1874 he warned his fellow party members that they were:

...apt as a party, to settle down upon their card when they were in power. What he wanted was, that they should work as hard for their party now as when they were in opposition. If they did that, they should maintain their position, strengthen the hands of Government and be a more happy and prosperous people under Conservative than under Radical rule.

Then followed a very enlightening statement; something which I had previously suspected in relation to Robert's political and social philosophies, but which I previously had scant evidence of:

Mr Disraeli had told them that they ought to educate themselves and the people in the principles of Conservatism. They had taken up the cause and endeavoured to follow out the sayings of their leader not only in Lancashire but in the West Riding of Yorkshire and in most of the counties near to them. He believed that the more people were educated the more Conservative they became. They had always found that the Conservative party had been more favourable to the education of the people, and to their social wants and comforts than the Liberal parties. (Hear, hear). During Lord Derby's parliament, with Mr Disraeli as leader in the House of Commons, the people were given the franchise. The same party gave them the Ten Hours Bill and other Bills that had followed. It would not be right for him to attempt to pander to what were generally termed the working or the industrious classes. He hoped they should never do that, and he had faith that they would find the Conservatives did not attempt to present any questions before the people which they did not intend to carry out. The other party had paraded various questions before the people, and they had scarcely carried one which they delivered. Because they had never intended to do so. They had disrupted five Reform Bills and talked them out. But when Lord Derby took the matter in hand, he said it might be a leap in the dark, but he enacted it.

From this, we can take away that Robert placed enormous faith in self-education and education by society; using logic and rational argument, essentially, to prevent the working class from falling for the false promises given to them by the likes of the Liberals – or worse, those who promised redistribution of wealth and revolution. He used the subject of the franchise and parliamentary reform as the most important matter at hand; it seems that he was already thinking that with the enfranchisement of the working class en masse, there would soon come a day where the Tories - who had traditionally always attracted working class loyalty - would lose ground. This was precisely why he felt the Conservatives should not be content with resting on their laurels. Of course, in the event, this is precisely what did happen to voting patterns in Stalybridge, not too long after Robert's death.

Hugh Birley, the Conservative MP for Manchester, then took the stage, and soon afterwards was followed by loud cheers for Stalybridge's Conservative MP, Mr Thomas Sidebottom. The *Reporter,* however, not wanting to put too happy a spin on a Tory tea party, stated that there was "*no enthusiasm*" and that one of the main speakers, "*spoke a lot of twaddle.*" But regardless, this annual meeting would have been a very welcome introduction to Robert's next few weeks as the newly-appointed Tory mayor of Stalybridge.

Hard Work – Paying Off?
In October 1869, the Stalybridge Parliamentary Revision Court mentioned Robert Stanley's contribution towards the parliamentary reform discussions in Parliament, but other than this brief allusion and then the parliamentary select committee minutes themselves, we have no other evidence of Robert's enthusiasm

for local democracy.[64] The legislation that Robert had influenced, however, was still very much needed in Stalybridge as, on 7th November 1874, a case was reported that would have been of concern to his sense of political justice: a man was killed after being hit with a beer bottle. According to the police, it seems that he had "been taken out of his bed to forcibly vote but died soon afterwards". His wife told the court that the men who dragged him from his bed told him, *"You must go and vote for Fletcher and Ellison."* Coming so soon after the 1872 Reform Act (Secret Ballot), this case would have been a serious reminder to Robert of the need for greater enforcement of the law in this area.

His appearance at the select committee not only impressed the MPs and Lords but could not have failed to have enamoured him to the great and the good in Stalybridge. Only five years later, Robert became mayor of the town; a calm, austere and dignified man who had fast gained a reputation of trustworthiness and of doing the right thing for people. He already had a clear moral compass of what was right and wrong, but in the next chapter, we will see how his work as a magistrate further shaped his attitudes towards not just the British legal system, but perhaps also towards his fellow human beings and – ultimately – their spiritual welfare.

---

[64] The Parliamentary Revision Court for Stalybridge involved the reading out of each name of a voter who had met the qualifications of being able to cast a vote. Individuals had the opportunity to object to someone's name being held on this list if they had just cause or evidence to the contrary. More often than not, objections were more to do with political jockeying than any attempt to care about true democracy and eligibility.

CHAPTER 5

Mr Magistrate
1867 – 1876

The Magistrate System

During the Victorian era, the structure of the magistrate system in England was not hugely different to that of today. A magistrates' court was made up of the bench, meeting several times a week (three in the case of Stalybridge) and it usually involved three magistrates or justices of the peace (JPs). They could agree on and then dispense summary justice, which could carry less than 12 months' imprisonment and/or fines. Then – like now – no formal qualifications were required on the part of the magistrates and, as with town councillors, the magistrates were unpaid.

Common sense, intelligence, a good degree of literacy and integrity were deemed to be the most necessary attributes of a JP, but during the 19th century nearly all of the magistrates in a town were drawn from the extremely wealthy classes: men who invariably also had strong political affiliations and who held obvious stakes in relation to the town's business, commerce and even its church affairs. This makes Robert's appointment to the bench in 1867 even more noteworthy as an achievement; he had only been a town councillor for four years and already he was deemed to be worthy enough to 'rise above' his class status in order to dispense with justice. And business was certainly booming in terms of the throughput of bodies being hauled up before the magistrates in Stalybridge during this period. The year prior to Robert's appointment as mayor, the town council had decided to campaign for a new County Court to assist with cases that were coming too thick and fast for them to be able to effectively deal with. As the town's population increased so did the number of crimes occurring, despite the presence of the still relatively new police force. In fact, in Stalybridge the police commissioners were formed in 1828 and met in the White House pub – before Robert Peeler's 'Bobbies' were created.

The system of appointing magistrates involved 'sending the names' of the proposed men to the Chancellor of the Duchy for an area. If there were no strong objections to the appointment then shortly afterwards the recommended person could begin to sit as a magistrate.[65] Presumably some form of training was carried out, although this perhaps should not be taken as a given!

As Stalybridge Town Council became increasingly party polarised, issues began to arise in relation to the political affiliations of magistrates, and in the town council meeting reported on 8th August 1874, Councillor Adshead – a Liberal - asked Mayor Bayley - a Tory - about the appointment of a batch of new magistrates. Adshead said that it was a disgrace that these new magistrates (who happened to be members of the Conservative Party) were appointed without

---

[65] There were no female JPs in England until Stalybridge, itself, famously broke the mould when Ada Summers was appointed the first female magistrate in England in 1919.

ratification of the council and he wondered whether the business must be, *"carried out at The Feathers or at Cockerhill Chapel because there was scarcely a member of Cocker Hill Chapel who [did not hold] office in the town."* This raised plenty of laughter amongst the Liberal councillors and Adshead then referred to a motion passed in relation to council opinion on the appointment of magistrates. The town clerk pointed out to Adshead that, *"the council has no control whatever in the appointment of magistrates. The resolution says that it is not desirable that magistrates should be appointed until they have been recommended by the council."*

Adshead countered this by saying that he realised that his party, the Liberals, had been the first to ignore this resolution but he needed to state that, *"two wrongs don't make a right"* and he feared that things were being done in a, *"hole-and-corner way."* At this point, Robert rose to express his disagreement with Adshead. He said that:

> *He had not had a previous opportunity to speak on this subject. He had often thought that the resolution was a disgrace to the books of the town of Stalybridge. It was wholly inoperative, and if they noticed the date on which it was passed, they would find it was on the 1st of April – (Laughter). The Town Council never made greater April fools of themselves than when they put that resolution on the books – (Much laughter). It was a question beyond the town Council. Magistrates were appointed by an authority which gave them their charter and their power. It was a question on which the feeling of the council might be taken, and I don't think such a resolution ought to be entered on our books. It was done for a certain purpose, and it was tantamount to saying there was no right to appoint magistrates without consulting the council. I say there is the right, but at the same time I think it would be better for the council to have a vote in the matter. I beg leave to move that the resolution, which is absurd in my idea, be removed from the books.*

Although his views were supported by most of the council, it was eventually decided that the resolution would remain on the council books but would continue to be ignored unless there was – for example – some serious objection to a new magistrate's conduct or character. The *Reporter* commented on this episode as having put the Tories, *"at all 6's and 7's, and they are prepared to send forth charges broadcast against any individuals who may venture to stop between them and their aspirations."* Even though the balance of political affiliation amongst magistrates was clearly important to some of the councillors, Robert seemed to have faith that if the correct people were selected, regardless of their political views, they would not allow their views to prejudice their decisions within a courtroom. The fact that there were nearly always three magistrates hearing a case would also help to prevent an individual's personality and political persuasions from adversely affecting a judgement.

The cases that came before Robert during his time as a magistrate were many and varied. One aspect of Robert's time as a magistrate (and later as chief magistrate when he was mayor) that was rather different to the approach of the other magistrates was that, in passing sentence, he nearly always gave the person before him the choice of a fine or a prison sentence. This provided a much fairer opportunity for most people and would have caused him to be viewed in a more favourable light than the rest of his peers. Robert passed verdicts on thousands of cases during the time that he was a magistrate. Several books could be written on the cases alone so, rather than attempting to create a narrative of the typical – as well as the extraordinary - stories that Robert had to formulate a judgement on, a summary of the research undertaken into this aspect of Robert's life is listed in bullet format in Appendix 3.

Pettiness of Adults

The Petty Sessions were just that: courtroom hearings for minor acts of criminal behaviour. Although there were some nasty cases of violence between adults (particularly where women were the victims), Appendix 3 demonstrates that there were plenty of rather bizarre and sometimes even amusing ones. Others offer a stereotypical image of the relationships between 'man and wife' in a poorer Victorian household. In the *Reporter*'s 'Early Trouble In Married Life' on 16th March 1875, the newspaper reports Robert hearing a case where a young married couple were arguing fiercely. The man allegedly assaulted his wife because she would, *"not turn up her wages, which she had worked for"* and because she had allegedly insulted his mother, who had just died. In court, she told her husband, *"At dinner time, you came in and gave me your money. I said I could not get the dinner ready until I had paid for what I owed. I did not say I wished your mother would come out of her grave ... I did not push you over the table."* The husband had another story to tell, *"He gave his wife the remainder of the money and sat down to smoke his pipe. She did not offer to get dinner ready, and had not done her cleaning, although she had been at home all day ... He heard of her getting drunk and being in bed on Friday afternoon ... there was still no dinner ... she pushed him against the table and some pots were knocked off. He then just caught her with the end of his little finger."* Robert decided to let the couple off, telling them, *"The magistrates are very sorry to see you can't agree better than you are doing. We dismiss the case and hope we shall not see you here again – either of you."*

Most of the adult cases that Robert tried were in relation to petty thefts carried out by desperately poor people. I found it particularly poignant to read about the case of a woman from 31st October 1874, who was so desperate that she stuffed mackerels into her apron. She must have had a bit of a taste for all-things fishy as she was later discovered in Samuel Peeke's Tripe Shop where she was arrested.[66] She told Robert, *"I did not know where I was until the next morning, I was so drunk."*

This issue of alcohol abuse formed a large portion of the cases. Again, they ranged from the vaguely amusing, where a man was found to be drunk in charge of a horse and Robert decided to fine him, telling him, *"It is a very dangerous thing for a man to be driving around in this way"*, to the outrage of such drunken behaviour within a Christian country and Robert demonstrating his own spiritual convictions, such as in the case of a severely inebriated man on 21st November

---

[66] On several occasions, I had to suffer visiting the tripe shop in Stalybridge with my gran when I was a child. There were many of them in the town during the Victorian period and today the town has the accolade of being home to one of the oldest tripe shops in the region.

1874, where he declared, *"As it was Sunday, we shall fine you more than for any other day."*

However, it was the cases of women that received the most attention, many of which we can view today as dreadfully sad examples of extreme alcoholism. Of course, there were plenty of tales that involved inebriated men *('Where does he get the money to drink?')* but the number of cases relating to women and alcohol was so disproportionate that the self-appointed moral guardian of the area - the *Reporter* – frequently cranked out the same old headline of *'Drunken Women!'*

Indeed, this research noted that women were rarely mentioned in Stalybridge and Ashton newspapers at this time unless they happened to be in court for being drunk and disorderly. Of course, there will be many reading this today who are smiling and reflecting on the nightlife of 'Stalyvegas' and thinking,

Victorian Stalybridge Wakes - a magnet for petty crime

'Well, little's changed there, then.' But the issue of women and alcohol abuse in Stalybridge was not tied to binge drinking on a Saturday night as it is today. It was a genuine social illness and the blight of the poverty-stricken. For a woman to be inebriated was nothing short of scandalous and such a reckless and outspoken woman would have been anathema to everything that polite Victorian patriarchy stood for. However, if we consider just how restricted, oppressed and poverty-stricken the lives of so many women in Stalybridge were, we can understand that drinking must have been the only form of escape. For many it would have been the only chance for honest self-expression in a rigid, often cruel society. The *Reporter*, in its editorial 'More Drunken Women,' on 14th November 1874, offered the received judgment of the day on these women:

For the most part they present a wretched and careworn appearance which is repulsive in the extreme. They are not only the worst of drunkards, but they

98

are the breeders of thieves and pests to society. In Stalybridge we have a
circle of them. Who have lost all shame and who think nothing of being taken
before a magistrate time after time… [their] children emaciated with hunger,
and shivering with cold, and often one or more amongst the number suffering
from painful and perhaps incurable malady, [are] rendered the more
distressing and the more dangerous by the utter want of cleanliness, which
seems the invariable rule. Is not such a state of things ruinous to health,
pernicious to morals, and altogether disgraceful to any civilised community?
Can we be surprised that such a home offers no attractions which can induce
the husband to give up his absence? (see Appendix 2 for full article).

This editorial referred to the case of Rosanna Fox, who had become a
notorious problem within Stalybridge and whose 19th appearance in the court
was greeted with hilarity by the public onlookers. Rosanna had been arrested for
drunk and disorderly behaviour, as well as assaulting a policeman, and yet Robert
was remarkably generous, telling her, *"You should keep off drink. You keep saying*
that you're sorry but that is no use at all." The rest of the case went like this:

Mr Storrs [fellow magistrate]; This is her 19th appearance. - Prisoner put
herself in an amusing attitude and begged forgiveness for her conduct,
provoking the laughter of most of the people in court. Prisoner: Ye need not
be laughing – perhaps ye may have to go through it yersels. I'll sign teetotal
if ye'll give me nothing this time. The Mayor: you have been to prison eighteen
times, and that does not seem to mend you. We are going to try another
course, and we hope it will have the desired effect on your promise to sign
teetotal: we are going to let you off this time. Prisoner, throwing up her arms:
God bless ye, sir; thank ye, sir (Laughter). Don't ye laugh. O, God bless ye,
misthur Mayor. – She was then removed from the court.

Robert seemed to think that it was important to allow the woman the chance
to 'take the pledge'. This was his first action as chief magistrate after being
appointed as mayor, so perhaps he wanted to try a different course of action with
the town's most famous courtroom characters. Unfortunately, his mercy did not
produce the desired long-term effect on Mrs Fox, as she was soon back in the
courtroom, and the next magistrate who presided over her case parcelled her back
off to prison with hard labour and no choice to pay a fine instead. And then came
her 21st hearing before Robert on 12th June 1875, where he stated that she, *"had*
not bothered even turning up." The mayor had apparently now lost all patience
with her and said, *"they all knew what she was…"* so she was sent to prison without
Robert's usual option of a fine.

After reading case after case of alcohol-related crime amongst the poor that
Robert had to deal with, it is not difficult to see how years later – and perhaps as
he began to make a living as a pub landlord whilst spending more time with
Muslims in Manchester – Robert began to feel, too, that alcohol was one of the
biggest evils in society.

In addition to the more 'ordinary' cases involving violence, theft, drunkenness and
illegal gambling (tossing), there were examples that do not easily fit within these

categories but, instead, seem to demonstrate more about Victorian morality than they do about straightforward law and order.

On 5th December 1874, the *Reporter*'s editorial stated that the town council should do something about the members of the public (read 'rubberneckers') who went out of their way to attend the thrice-weekly magistrate hearings to hear all the *"disgusting details"* of the cases. Following on from this, on 3rd April 1875, the *Reporter* regaled a somewhat strange tale that involved a police constable befriending another man. They subsequently had a few drinks together and the next morning the constable found himself in the man's room, alongside a rather large joint of beef. Apparently, the constable was so alarmed by the sudden appearance of the meat carcass that he reported the crime to his superiors. A simple case of larceny, however, seems to modern ears as perhaps having had homosexual overtones. This assumption can be made because the courtroom was packed with rubberneckers - indicating the whiff of something a little bit more scandalous, perhaps, than the theft of a slab of beef! Robert sentenced the young man who had stolen the meat and thanked the constable for his vigilance whilst off-duty.

In the same newspaper edition, the editorial – not one for being sensitive towards the cause of women - criticised the magistrates for hearing cases on illegitimacy in a public courtroom. It is more likely, however, that they were less concerned about the illegitimacy case and more about the 'side of beef' tale with its 'immoral overtones'. No doubt the newspaper's proprietors felt that being exposed to such scandalous details might influence those lower working-classes to go and do the same. The *Reporter*'s editorial told its readers that public hearings of such cases, *"only happens in Lancashire and people, especially children, go there for entertainment."* It further added that at a recent case involving an illegitimate baby, *"Amongst those present were a number of boys and girls not more than 13 or 14 years of age and they repeatedly testified their delight at hearing disgusting details."* The newspaper's sentiments, along with the fact that the magistrates had a difficult time trying to keep the members of the public from laughing away merrily at the misfortunes of others, did influence a change. Some months later the magistrates were allowed to take the decision to keep the public out of the room for certain cases and where the accused (women in particular) arrived in court to, in the words of the *Reporter*, *"Tell their career of shame."*

One of the most tragic cases that Robert had to hear was on 6th February 1875 and involved an 18-year-old woman named Esther Powell who was accused of murdering her new-born baby. Esther had recently left work as a domestic servant in Ashton (citing a disagreement with her former employers) and asked to be employed at The Mechanic's Arms pub in Stalybridge. The landlady quickly grew suspicious of the girl's *"enceinte"* state and broke into her room after hearing noises. After seeing the mess that the room was in, she went over to the indoor WC where she discovered, *"A full-grown male child was found wrapped in two aprons and pushed into the soil pipe. It was taken out by Mr Lambert and found to be alive, and after being washed it was put to bed with the mother, but it died at about three o'clock."* Thanks to the work of the medical pathologist, Robert established that the girl had indeed given birth on her own that evening, but as she struggled to deliver it, she had dropped the baby on its head, and it appeared to her to be dead. In her panic, she tried to hide the body as soon as she heard movements outside her room. Robert did not feel she had committed murder, *"As the doctor says the injuries would cause the death, I see a difficulty of sustaining a charge of attempting murder ... the bench are unanimously of the opinion that it is one of those cases which they must leave to the decision of a jury, and we must commit you for trial at the next Manchester Assizes."* The Manchester jury subsequently gave the girl a harsh sentence: six months' imprisonment with hard labour.

Suffering of Children

If the stories of some of the adults that Robert had to rule on were not depressing enough, those of the children were even worse. There was certainly nothing close to a Victorian version of the UN Convention on the Rights of the Child; this was a world where children had only recently been stopped from working full days in dangerous factory jobs and crouching in horrific conditions at the bottom of a mine shaft. Beating a child for misbehaviour was endorsed both at school and at home and the legal system allowed for children as young as seven being sentenced to a flogging – or even sent to an adult prison (see below).

Robert's reactions to the cases of children seemed to be generally quite understanding, though. He frequently let 'first timers' off with a strong verbal warning designed not to encourage them. On 26th January 1865, he told a teenager, *"It is your first case, and we are sorry we can't order you a good flogging and let you go. Taking into consideration your parents are respectable people and hoping you will never appear in that box again, we shall let you go."* Like many proprietors of a small business, petty stealing roused his animosity, but he still continued to dole out the 'fine or prison' sentence for repeat offenders, in addition to telling children's parents - as he did on 20th February 1875 - that their offspring should obtain, *"...work as a half-timer than get into mischief. If there was a promise that he should go to work, the case would not be pressed against him this time, but if either of them as again brought up he would be sent to prison."*

Many of Robert's fellow magistrates, however, did not take the same meticulous approach to meting out justice. In February 1875, this led to a problem of national proportions. Robert received a telegram from the Home Secretary, addressed to him in his capacity as both chief magistrate and mayor. The telegram followed up a question in Parliament made by an MP, Mr P.A. Taylor. Whilst reading the court section of the *Manchester Guardian* (a provincial newspaper at the time that would soon became the national *Guardian*), the MP had been disturbed to hear that, in Stalybridge, James Knott, aged eight, and William Blundell, aged seven, had been arrested for pickpocketing and that the seven-year-old had been sentenced to 'prison with hard labour'. *The Manchester Guardian* copied from *The Stalybridge Reporter*'s edition of 6th February 1875, and stated:

> *The mother of Blundell was apprehended for being drunk and disorderly on New Year's Eve. Whilst she was drunk, Blundell went into Mr Davis's (butcher) shop, and was joined by his brother, Richard, aged 5 years, who was in a state of drunkenness... Mrs Fielding was purchasing some meat... soon after leaving the place she missed her money and purse... Constable Kelton visited the house, where he found the prisoners, Knott's younger*

brother, and Richard Blundell, aged 5 years, who sat drunk in a chair. The
boys had divided the money and then sent for some whisky. [67]

The telegram from the Home Office requested further information on what had happened, and that week the *Reporter* told its readers, *"A telegram from such an important office in the State has excited some interest and there has been a flutter amongst our local authorities in consequence."* After reading so many of the cases that Robert presided over, it seemed out of character, therefore, for him to have dealt the sentence of 'prison with hard labour' to such a small child. However, looking further into the court reporting, it became apparent that because the case had been a complex one – involving many children, both as the accused and as witnesses – that the bench had decided to hear it over two sessions. Robert was presiding magistrate on the first day of the hearing, but on the second day he was unable to be there, and it was, therefore, a different magistrate who decided the sentence.

In passing sentence, Robert always explicitly said whether a person being sent to prison would receive hard labour or not; and I found no examples of him meting out such a penalty for a child. On examining the cases presided over by his fellow magistrates, however, few gave the offender the chance of 'either/or' in terms of fines, and there were far more declarations of 'prison *with* hard labour'. *The Manchester Guardian* stated that the magistrate presiding on the second session (Mr Hyde) summed up the case by saying, *"We are reluctant to send such a child as Blundell to prison; but he has proved himself to be such an expert thief that we can't let him at liberty again on society without giving him some punishment. He will have to go to prison for 7 days' hard labour in each case."*

Following the outrage expressed by the MP and the Home Office, *The Stalybridge Reporter* tried to explain for its readers:

> *There seems to have been some mistake about the addition of the words 'hard labour' to the punishment ... the Stalybridge magistrates very frequently neglect to say anything about the 'labour' portion of the sentence, unless questioned on the point by their Clerk. It is so seldom that a prisoner is sent to prison 'without hard labour' that when such a thing does happen the magistrate puts special emphasis on the fact.*

The *Reporter* pointed to a case which took place the previous week: a hearing presided over by Robert, who had deliberately spoken the words 'without hard labour'. It seems, though, that the newspaper may well have been trying to cover the cracks in its own reporting and that, in fact, the *Reporter* had simply reported (wrongly) that a seven-year-old had been sentenced to prison with hard labour on top of gaol. However, the newspaper did not seem to be willing to condemn such a practise for small children. It quoted the current law which stated that: 'persons not exceeding 14 years of age ... may be summarily convicted by two justices and sentenced to imprisonment for not exceeding three calendar months, with or without hard labour' and it went on to declare that:

---

[67] *Manchester Guardian*, 5 January, 1875.

To merely confine boys in gaol has not proved beneficial so far as Stalybridge is concerned. They often get better fed and have more regular rest inside the walls of a prison than at their own homes, and they feel a delight in the journey by rail for the 'few days' holiday'. Witness the case of the notorious young KNOTT, who made himself a terror to the neighbourhood. Lest he should lure other boys into his own evil ways between the age of 7 and 11 years, he was 4 time convicted, and on each occasion, he left prison he returned home recruited in strength and a still more hardened thief. At one time he was sent to a reformatory, but the authorities would not receive him, saying they had no desire to convert their school into a nursery. What did he care about imprisonment 'without hard labour?' Imagine the home of the boy, BLUNDELL; When he was brought before the magistrates his mother was undergoing a sentence in gaol for drunkenness. The week afterwards his father was also convicted for drunkenness, and he also went to gaol. Would not that boy find more comfort and greater attractions in a prison 'without hard labour' than in a home almost void of the common necessaries for any sort of an existence? Magistrates are somewhat chary about ordering a juvenile to be whipped, and whilst they are so, there is something needed to check the impudence and hard-heartedness of a number of youths in this borough who are pests to society and a source of anxiety and trouble to the police force.

Princess/Melbourne St, Stalybridge – new St George's in background

Clearly many of the Liberals had a long way to go before they morphed into a political philosophy that we might today regard as truly liberal – although some of us might agree that the sentiments expressed by the *Reporter* in 1875 would not be out of place in some of today's tabloid newspapers. We can only imagine that

Robert was not best pleased about this situation; it would have been extremely embarrassing for his town to be singled out for attention by the Home Office and for Stalybridge to be discussed nationally as a place where brutal measures were doled out upon the heads of naughty little children. A stickler for detail, he would probably have informed both his fellow magistrates and the courtroom clerk to ensure that in future any sentence should categorically state – both in verbal and in written terms - whether hard labour was included or not and that children should under no circumstances be parcelled off to hard labour in an adult prison.

The School Board

Perhaps because of his role - and reputation - as a long-standing local magistrate, Robert Stanley was appointed to the new local Board of Education. These boards were set up as a requirement of the Education Act 1872 in areas where there was insufficient schooling provision now that the Act had made elementary education compulsory. We know that elections were required for appointment to the board (unless a position was uncontested) and that it must, therefore, have been quite a popular responsibility to undertake amongst Stalybridge's great and good.[68] One of the responsibilities of the school board was dealing with applications from parents who could not afford to pay school fees and who wanted to ask for financial assistance, but it also summoned parents to appear before them when their children were found not to be attending school. The 1907 *Municipal Yearbook* overlooked this educational aspect of Robert's contribution to civic society and I only discovered it as a result of the mention of his name during a case in 1872.

At the time of the new school board being established in Stalybridge, a national debate had broken out about the provision of state education and religion: whether it was right that a person who did not worship at the Church of England should be forced to pay taxes towards the provision of Anglican schools and whether their children should have to attend an Anglican schooling.[69] These early years of state provision and enforcement proved to be a steep learning curve for many areas of the country, and none more so than in Stalybridge. At first, the School Board slowly began to get used to its new powers to compel parents to bring their children to school and a typical example of the sorts of cases that Robert and the rest of the board dealt with was reported on 16th March 1872, where:

> The mother of one boy, who should attend St Peter's School, said her boy left home for the purpose of going to school, but went off to some other direction. The boy was very young, and both her husband and she had tried everything they could to improve him, but without effect. MR STANLEY informed the mother that she or her husband would have to make the boy go; if they did not, when he got older the magistrates and policemen would make him. The CHAIRMAN said it was a very lamentable thing for parents to lose the control over their children in this way. If the boy was not sent to school, the board

---

[68] Robert had joined the School Board prior to the 1872 'Girls and Education' affair but did not want to contest the election for 1874 and stepped down.

[69] Still a hot potato even today; many British citizens are unhappy at paying taxes towards state-provided faith-based schools.

would have to make an example of her husband. The INSPECTOR said he had
tried to frighten the boy on one occasion by taking him nearly as far as the
police station, but he went very meekly; and he believed he would sooner be
shut up than he would go to school.[70]

But in 1872, Stalybridge's school board was faced with a far more unusual case, and an onslaught of national attention, when Jonathan Schofield, a mill worker, was called before them to account for the fact of his eldest daughter's absence from school. Mr Schofield wrote extremely eloquent letters to the board, stating that his daughter's education was his concern alone; that it was his right to educate his children in whatever manner he chose, in much the same way as how he chose to feed them and clothe them was his own private business. On being summoned before them, though, and being faced with such overwhelming national interest, it seemed that Schofield decided to seek out legal advice and he changed his tactics. Rather than challenging the Education Act directly, he explained that his daughter could not attend school because she was a 'nurse girl' - she was needed to look after his other four children and elderly mother so that he and his wife could go to work in the mill. However, far from her suffering from illiteracy, he stated that he sat with his daughter every evening after work and taught her himself, to a perfectly adequate level. The magistrates ordered for the girl to be tested immediately and her scholarly standards were found to be perfectly acceptable.

Stalybridge's school board met on many occasions to discuss this case. The national press had a field day with such an interesting micro case study from the regions of what was now proving to be an enormous issue in Parliament. The Stalybridge School Board, it seemed, were doing their best to be reasonable and to listen to the family. In what was perceived by many as a victory for the 'little man' over the growing powers of the state, the board ruled that in this case the family should be left alone, and the daughter should not be forced to attend school. Some historical commentators have also viewed this case as one that highlights the issue of education for girls; the family, of course, after all, didn't expect one of their sons to stay home and look after the other children - it was always the oldest female child who took on the nurse girl role. Robert's words, too, have been perceived to demonstrate limited aims in terms of his thoughts on education for working-class girls, when he told his fellow board members:

It is not at all necessary that it should attend school. I think it can obtain
sufficient instruction from people in his [the father's] position. This is the
mistake which School Boards fall into. They think for the children belonging
to a man in this class of life that it is necessary they should attend school from
five to thirteen years of age. It is not necessary and if the School Boards look
at it in that light they will soon get into a difficulty.

With the benefit of historical hindsight, it is all too easy to criticise a man like Robert - who, to all intents and purposes, as a magistrate, school board member and later mayor would come across over a century later as a patronising,

---

[70] Stalybridge School Board Committee, 20 January 1872, p.302.

privileged, wealthy, anti-female and anti-working-class member of the Establishment. However, now that we know much more about his life and beliefs, his comments make far more sense. He would have been the only person on the board who came from the working class and who lived amongst the working class. He could never be accused of not valuing an education and he felt that the father had been providing a sound education for the child. However, he prided himself on his logical and pragmatic approach to life and he would have felt that, for this family, for this girl's education, it would be pointless to force her to attend a schooling which was simply not needed, and which would, in fact, gravely hamper the economic security of the family. It is wrong to look at this case and to portray it as a gender issue; if anything, it is a class issue. As evidenced in his appearance at the parliamentary select committee, Robert viewed the working class as consisting of different strata; he would have felt that this family were mill workers and were therefore unlikely to break out of this mould. Of course, in today's world these views would be unfashionable and hardly liberating; the words 'aspiration' and 'ambition' are incredibly important to modern society and none more so (and quite rightly) than for working class girls.

But Robert's take on the matter is entirely in keeping with his other conservative - and Conservative – values. If anything, he was displaying rather singular views, because as a Conservative and now a member of the Church of England we might expect him to want to protect the new developments of state-sanctioned education and to force a child to attend the Anglican education that he himself had been deprived of. If anything, he is perhaps guilty of being rather too practically minded, too brutally logical, and of displaying the typical values of 'laissez-faire' in relation to a family's own choices and over-interference of the state.

It would be unfair, though, to accuse Robert of having doubts about educating the working class. Over the next few years, he continued to do his best to enforce the requirements of the Act and was clearly frustrated when he heard cases where parents were not seizing every chance available to them to educate their children. So far as Robert Stanley was concerned, even lack of payment of school fees for a reformatory school was no excuse and he sternly rebuked a set of parents, informing them on 24th April 1875, *"You are getting off for very little – let this be a warning to you, don't do anything of the sort again."* On 3rd October 1874, the *Reporter* outlined the school board case of Jane Knotts, whose son was not attending school and who was known to be stealing on the streets of Stalybridge. Robert was clearly not a fan of this family, telling the rest of the board, *"No woman has ever appeared in the court as often as she did, and her children were downright naughty children."* Robert's attitude towards the Knotts family sadly seemed to have been not far off the mark when, just a few months later, the Knott boys were the very same children who caught the attention of the Home Office with the 'seven-year-old sent to prison with hard labour' case.

Robert's views on many aspects of life – education included – do not neatly fit into our 21st century version of what was an 'archaic, regressive' view and what was a 'liberal, enlightened, progressive' take on social matters. His own daughters, for example, received a good education - good enough to become teachers – and, later, his granddaughter, Marguerite, managed to get a place at Ashton Grammar School.

So, he did not try and discourage girls from having a formal education. But he obviously felt it to be silly and unhelpful to give a child, or a family, notions above their current stations in life – no matter how much his descendants disagree with his views!

CHAPTER 6

A Municipal Mayor
1874 – 1876

Becoming Mayor

Robert Stanley was the ninth mayor of Stalybridge and was 46 years old when the town council elected him to serve as mayor from November 1874-75. He agreed to be elected again for 1875-76 and in June 1875, he was elevated to the position of alderman – as opposed to councillor – of the borough. This meant that he would no longer need to stand for local elections and had a right to sit on the town council until whatever time he chose to step down.

The photograph of Robert as mayor is the earliest one that I have been able to find. It shows a man with a dignified expression, receding hairline and beard.[71] He is wearing full mayoral regalia for the photograph: the chain and the gowns. Robert was the first mayor of Stalybridge to wear chain and gowns, which proved to be the cause of some controversy (at least in the mind of *The Stalybridge Reporter's* editor – see below).

The previous mayor, Thomas Fernihough, had decided that he no longer wished to continue as mayor and Robert's appointment had been anticipated by many. The town was still

---

[71] Beards did not become fashionable for Victorian men until after the Crimean War of 1853-56 and as no photographs exist of Robert from before this period, we do not know whether he had sported one as a young man – as the Christian Israelites were required to do.

reeling from the Astley Deep Pit disaster in Dukinfield, which had occurred just a few months before, killing 54 local men and boys. Many of them would have been Robert's previous constituents, and their families would no doubt still have been shell-shocked as a result of the tragedy. The time was right for a man of compassion and of justice to become their mayor – not a rich fellow who owned the factories or the mines - and Robert's services to the borough since 1863 had been noted. The week before the municipal elections, even the *Reporter* – leading the war cry for all-things Liberal in the town - had a positive take on this, *"Such an appointment will meet with the approval of moderate politicians, and we have no doubt he will efficiently perform the duties."* [72]

Stalybridge was back in the control of the Tories again; a most unwelcome development for many of the Liberal mill owners, although others were rather more pragmatic about these developments: the rare voice of a young woman can be glimpsed in a letter to the *Reporter* of the same week, where she asked the sort of question that we might hear from young mothers today, *"Now we have a Tory Council ... Can we please have perambulator access granted in Dukinfield cemetery?"* But for the men of the town, the week of the elections had proven to be more stressful than usual – the 1872 Act would have meant rather tighter protocols and inspections of the election – and perhaps it was timely, therefore, that a man like Robert (who had actively contributed to the reforms) would be appointed mayor.

It must have been a long week for Robert and his family, waiting to see if the full council would ratify the proposal to accept him. The current set of councillors could be a volatile bunch (as we shall soon see) but by 14th November 1874, the *Reporter* noted that the following had occurred in the town council chambers. Alderman Bayley said that he:

> *... had great pleasure in proposing to their notice Councillor R Stanley as a fit and proper person to represent them as Mayor and chief magistrate ... for some years he had been looking at the movements of Mr Stanley and he thought he would make a very suitable gentleman to occupy the civic chair – (Hear, hear). He had always been very affable and kind, and if any little difference had arisen betwixt members of the council, he was always ready and willing to try to quell any difference that might arise. He was not so irritable as some men, nor yet so impulsive – but let by gones be by gones – he had come there to propose that Councillor Stanley be elected to the honourable position of Mayor and chief magistrate of the borough ... he would ask them to give Mr Stanley a unanimous vote. He thought it would only be what he deserved, for he had no doubt they would have the satisfaction, at the termination of his year of office, of knowing they had put the right man in the right place – (Hear, hear)*

Councillor Warhurst seconded the proposal, in the usual somewhat elaborate manner:

> *First of all, I am convinced we shall have in Mr Councillor Stanley a most admirable successor to our present worthy Mayor. Perfectly unostentatious*

---

[72] *Stalybridge Reporter*, 31 October, 1874.

in his character, full of candour, consideration, and kindness, I believe he will win for himself not only the respect and esteem of this council but likewise the good wishes and confidence of the ratepayers. – (Hear, hear). In Mr Stanley we have a man of large experience in municipal matters and one I am sure who will exercise the prerogative of that exalted position in an unbiased, unambiguous and impartial manner. – (Hear, hear) Mr Mayor and gentlemen, I need say no more to laud Mr Stanley. I trust he is sufficiently well known and respected by you all that you will accord to him a perfectly unanimous vote. I have a firm conviction that the prestige of the council will not be diminished by such a selection, but rather that he will add lustre to the position by preserving a dignified neutrality throughout the period of his office, that when he retires therefrom, he will hand down to his successor that chair untarnished by a single dishonourable and arbitrary act."

The motion was indeed unanimously backed by all 17 present and Robert finally took centre stage:

The MAYOR-ELECT having signed the customary declaration and shaken hands with his predecessor said: I thank you for the honour you have done me in electing me to this office. I feel that I have taken a great responsibility upon myself, and I must ask you to assist me all you possibly can in fulfilling the office to the advantage of the inhabitants of this borough – (hear hear) I only hope you will give me credit for one thing, that whatever I do will be done for the benefit of the town and I hope I shall not show any sort of party feeling (hear hear) – whilst I hold the office of mayor. I hope to conduct it in a way that will command the respect and assistance of all the gentlemen round this board. – (Hear, hear)

After having ploughed through dozens of such meetings, it should be said that most other elected mayors had not received such glowing accolades on taking up the mantle. Robert seems to have been genuinely liked, admired and respected. However, it only took a few days for the *Reporter* to slightly change its tune. The week before Robert's election, the newspaper had indicated that it felt he was the right man for the job. But then - as they say - a week is a long time in politics, particularly if you happen to be on the losing side. The outcome of the municipal elections in Stalybridge had evidently left a rather sour taste in the *Reporter's* mouth (or perhaps, rather, the Liberal owner of the newspaper felt the need for a bit of a word in the Editor's ear after the town council suddenly became a Tory majority). The newspaper, though, was forced to cast around for rather petty details in order to scribble some negatives about Robert. Their grumblings focused on his background and that of his new cohort of aldermen:

It has been aptly remarked that a curious proceeding has taken place with regards to the Town Council this week, which very seldom comes to pass in this or any other town. A grocer has been elected to the office of Mayor, and three grocers have been promoted to the office of aldermanic chair. It is said that sugar contains properties of a fattening value, if this is so, perhaps the three grocers will eat plenty of it in order that they may obtain that portly appearance that aldermen are said to possess. In this election the very opposite of 'custom' has been observed. Instead of fat men with 'hoary heads' being selected, thin men, comparatively young, have received all the honours. Alderman was derived from the word elder, one of the three degrees among the Saxons. Instead, however, the three Stalybridgers being eldermen, they are younger men, and persons of advanced age and considerable experience have been thrust aside, merely because they are Liberals, to make room for councillors who have a vast amount of information to obtain and much to learn before they can become proficient in municipal government.

Putting the somewhat humorous, yet snobbish attitude of the newspaper to one side, we should be grateful for such an observation of social attitudes; Robert had broken the mould - not just for Stalybridge but for many other towns and cities. The appointment of a 'mere tradesman' to an office which had previously been the exclusive possession of either landed gentry or the new aristocracy of millowners, would have shocked men from the middle and upper classes, and probably have delighted those from the lower end of the class strata. As we have already seen, though, Robert was proud of his profession. He had now demonstrated to the hundreds of people who had met him, worked with him and been helped by him that hard work and devotion to self-improvement would be rewarded. Robert himself was proof that England was changing, and that meritocracy might soon become the order of the day. Whilst we might think that a Liberal newspaper would surely approve of a rather anti-Establishment figure taking such a post, Robert was a Tory. So, it wouldn't have been the done thing for the *Reporter* to wave the flag for a chair of the local Conservative Association.

What would Robert have felt about the words of the local newspaper's editorial? Was he stung? Offended? Angry? Now that we know a little bit more of his character, his levels of confidence and his innate drive for justice and for civic improvements, it is more likely that his family, rather than Robert, would have been the annoyed and slighted party. It is more probable that Robert himself would have laughed it off. After all, he would have received far worse insults in the courtroom and from the factory owners, furious at him for acting against them for tampering with democracy. If anything, he would have taken the words of the *Reporter* for what they were: evidence of a bunch of sore losers.

Robert, it seemed, was no longer the intermeddler in these mill towns. He had become an interloper; there were still plenty of individuals amongst the upper echelons of British society who would have taken the attitude of 'grocer - know thy place' and who did not buy into the growing new interest in meritocratic forms of democracy.[73]

---

[73] Britain's most famous 'grocer-politician' was Margaret Thatcher, born in 1925 and prime minister from 1979-90. Robert's particular strain of Conservatism, however, seems to have been quite different to the neo-liberal philosophies developed by Thatcher. Although the individual and the family were sacred to him, he believed that protection for the workers was a good thing, that local authorities should retain independence from central government interference and that, in general, municipal delivery of services was best for local people. He believed in reform rather than penalisation for those who had broken the law and, when it came to the affairs of other countries, the less Britain involved itself the better. This is all conjecture, of course, but his political attitudes seemed to be closer to Tory 'Wets' than to those of neo-liberal Conservatives.

A New Look

Robert was the first mayor of Stalybridge who wore mayoral robe and chains. On 10th July 1875, the *Reporter* wrote:

FLATTERY IS LIKE A PAINTED ARMOUR: ONLY FOR SHOW, NOT USE! The Conservatives of Ashton are in ecstasies because they have at last got a Tory Mayor. Flattery of every description is being heaped upon him, and he is to be adorned with robes, and a chain ... The 'craze' has extended to Stalybridge, and there is a desire in certain quarters that as our Mayor led the van in the robing department, he shall not be left behind for want of jewellery. It is stated that Mr Alderman MELLOR is prepared to subscribe five guineas towards purchasing a Mayor's chain, and that if a committee is appointed to manage the business, other members of the Conservative party are prepared to follow the example thus set by the Chairman of the Market Committee. Whilst the rage for 'millinery' and 'gorgeous apparel' is at its height, would it not be as well to go in for a full set of robes for the whole of the members of the corporation? It would be a capital show to see his Worship decked out in red, and fur, and gold; the aldermen in purple, and the 'common' councillors in black. Such an exhibition would surely do what 'eloquence' has failed to do – attract the burgesses to the council chamber to hear the monthly business transacted.

This editorial seems to indicate that Robert had led the way on decking himself out in regalia. Given his propensity for austerity and aversion towards unnecessary waste, this is unlikely. However, if it were suggested to him that Stalybridge should not be outdone by Ashton and that municipal mayors across the land were doing the same, he could probably have been persuaded to dress up a bit. In fact, the action of 'robing' might have allowed him that extra bit of confidence in public in a society where disdain towards the lower classes who dared to get above themselves and take a position of authority very much existed. Robert was also now a member of the Church of England - a big fan of Queen and Country, the Establishment and the Empire – and a bit of pomp and ceremony would probably have been admired by him.[74] By the time that this article was written, he perhaps also felt that he had worked hard enough in life and in civic affairs for a visual display of it all.

It is interesting, too, to see that Stalybridge Town Council in 1874 was struggling with the same issue that local authorities battle with today – that of

---

[74] Note that in their mockery, the *Reporter* mentions the colours of 'The Establishment' – the Church of England – that are used for the clergy i.e., purple for the bishops (aldermen) and black for the common clergy (councillors.) It is also interesting to note that Robert used the term "we" a lot when he was working for the town council or as a magistrate – i.e. on a water issue he said, *"We really don't know what to say"* and on 10th April 1875, when a child threw a stone at a man working for the Town Council Sanitation Committee who was emptying ash pits in the Castle Hall area, *"We are bound to protect our servants."* This is, however, probably more of a sign of the collective 'we' of a municipal or court of law representative, rather than Robert having delusions of royal grandeur!

attracting the public to show an active interest in the day-to-day workings of municipal affairs!

Churching of the Mayor

Just minutes after Robert had been elected as mayor, the town council began their annual task of deciding which councillors would be allocated to which sub-committees. 'His Worship The Mayor,' it seems, was being added to rather too many committees because when Councillor Bayley moved that Robert be appointed to the join the Ashton, Stalybridge and Dukinfield Waterworks Committee again, the mayor tried to decline, half-joking that, *"I should like to move an amendment for I have enough to do without that."* [75] Bayley, however, was rather more long in the tooth than Robert, in terms of municipal tradition in Stalybridge Town Hall chambers, and told him that it was "customary" that the mayor had to chair all of the committees. Perhaps Robert felt his spirits slump at the prospect of all the added new workload (on top of his re-election to represent the people of Stayley ward!). However, he had plenty to look forward to the following week when his 'churching' was due to take place.

I had never heard of the tradition of churching of the mayor, probably because it no longer exists in our local area, and seems to be an extremely rare event elsewhere Britain. When I mentioned that I had discovered this my father, Brian, suddenly remembered churching, watching the procession of his grandad up to Old St George's Cocker Hill, when our Grampy Stanley – or Councillor Dean Stanley - had been elected as the mayor of Stalybridge in 1954.

I knew that Grampy (son of Robert's son, 'Unlucky Bob' Stanley) had been the mayor of Stalybridge and that he had attended Old St George's. But it was not until I found this newspaper article that we had evidence that Robert himself had become a member of the same church when he moved to Stalybridge from a Christian Israelite background. The *Reporter* gives a long description of the event, repeating every word of the impressively-named Reverend Jelly-Dudley and listing every member of the procession (including all members of the police force, all municipal officials and councillors and even the brass band - a local Masonic group, the Shepherd's Volunteer Band).

CHURCHING OF THE NEW MAYOR

The weather was very unfavourable, but nevertheless a very large crowd gathered to see the procession, which in absence of a mace, was as usual headed by Pickering, the borough porter, with a knobstick. The Mayor, having been "dressed up" in the robes recently presented to the borough by Mr. Ralph Bates ....

... [Reverend Jelly-Dudley welcomed] his Worshipful the Mayor, the aldermen, the councillors and the magistrates, and those to whom were entrusted with the administration of the affairs for the borough, and for the well-being of its inhabitants and the peace and good order of society. It was a graceful, a wise and a good old custom that the first public duty and act of the newly elected Mayor and officers should be their going together, bearing the insignia of their office, to the ancestry of the law of God to thank him for

---

[75] *SB Reporter*, 14 November, 1874.

the past mercies and to ask for His guidance and direction in the future. ....
Their church distributed the best and purest forms of Christianity that was
ever established in any country since the days of the apostles. Their prayers
breathed the spirit of the most fervent piety. They were plain, simple, and
Scriptural, and free from all forms of idolatrous rites and ceremonies. It was,
therefore, their duty to stand by and support their glorious constitution
against devices and attempts of revolutionists and ungodly men to overthrow
it ...

Rev. Jelly-Dudley went on to talk at great length about godly matters, but this extract demonstrates that he used the churching of the mayor as an opportunity to wax lyrical about the superiority of the Church of England over other denominations, clearly indulging in a bit of verbal Catholic-bashing. No doubt he was pleased that his parish church had (yet again) produced the most important member of Stalybridge's civic society. Stalybridge had suffered sectarian prejudice and violence only five years previously and, although the situation was now calmer, Jelly-Dudley's words were a painful reminder of the obvious divisions and prejudiced attitudes that remained. Here was a man who did not know the meaning of the word ecumenical. Because Robert was a member of this church, we might expect, therefore, that he would agree with its vicar. However, the mayor's speech that followed Jelly-Dudley's sermon is noteworthy. It is the one and only time where we hear him confirming that he is a practising Christian, and that he feels Christianity should be practised by others - but the reader will see that he does not necessarily agree with Jelly-Dudley's negative perceptions towards all other Christian denominations:

The Mayor said he thanked them most heartily for the honour they had done
him in accompanying him to church that morning. He hoped it would not be
a mere idle ceremony. He thought a great amount of good was done by their
processing to church. It had been a custom in many old boroughs for a long
time, and he was pleased with them for carrying out the practise. The
intention was to set a good example on the first Sunday after the new Mayor
took office, in going to some place of worship to ask for the blessing on the
work they had to do. If their procession to church had the effect of causing
the people to more regularly attend the different places of worship; to look
after their spiritual welfare more particularly than they had hitherto, great
good would be the result. As a magistrate he could confidently say that if the
people attended more regularly at some place of worship there would be
much less for both police and magistrates than there would be at present. He
had no hesitation in affirming, and he ought to do so as Mayor of the borough,
that he believed in the Christian religion. Without it they would decline in
civilisation and might sink to the position of mere savages. He hoped their
attendance at church that day would have the effect of introducing a better
attendance at the different places of worship in the borough. He begged to
announce that the collection in aid of the Infirmary amounted to between
£15 and £16. He was sorry there had not been a finer morning for there would
have been a better attendance. However, he had to thank the magistrates,
aldermen, councillors and the town clerk, the treasurer, and the other

borough officers and also the volunteers for their presence. He hoped that they would have a happy and a successful new year. They had already had a good harvest, and that would have a greater effect than anything on the success of the country. At present they were suffering from a calm which overhung the staple manufactures for the district and if anything it could tend to restore it, it was the fact that they had had such a good harvest, which would enable the people to buy cheaper food and to secure more of the money produced from their industry in the mills of the district – (Applause)

It is difficult to read this passage from 1874 and not wonder what Robert would have thought later on - in 1898, for example, when he finally said Shahadah - about his words, *"...the Christian religion. Without it they would decline in civilisation and might sink to the position of mere savages."* It is hard not to wonder, too, what Jelly-Dudley would have made of Robert's later conversion to Islam!

The Stalybridge Reporter – still bristling over the acquisition of robe and chain – carried on in their usual disparaging vein the following week, crabbing away over the fact that:

With so much 'pomp and display' the 'liberality' of those assembled is represented in the miserably small sum of £15 for a noble institution [the Infirmary]. If the Mayor, Aldermen, and Councillors had only given half a sovereign each they would have almost contributed the amount. Such a result takes all the gilt off the 'good old custom'. [76]

Robert Stanley: Socialist Similarities? Or Municipal Madness?

So far, we have concluded that Robert was a working-class Tory through and through. Modern political criticism has a tendency to distil Tory values down to the core values of traditionalism, conservatism, 'God, Queen and Country' and the supremacy of the established social order. Although he believed in taking the initiative in supporting the underdog in both a judicial and a financial sense (initiating the Anti-Screw Association, which resembled an early trade union in some respects) Robert also believed that there were 'inferior' members of the working-class. Yet most of the headline accolades that Stalybridge's *Municipal Yearbook* of 1907 credited him with would today be perceived to be examples of municipal socialism at work. It would be wrong, however, to take from this that during his work with the town council he had any socialist leanings.

Robert's final years as a councillor and then as mayor took place at a time in British history when municipal socialism was just beginning to grow in popularity. As a result of three massive waves of disease in the 1830s and 40s – cholera, influenza and typhus and typhoid – public health became a priority for Britain. The new system of local government was empowered to do more to tackle the problem of the condition of the people and there was a drive towards spending local authority money to benefit the public. These public works schemes focused on the building of better sanitation measures such as water distribution, sewers, drains, gas and baths, the demolition of slum dwellings, the erection of public libraries and the

---

[76] *SB Reporter*, 21 November, 1874.

founding of parks. They were generally instigated by Liberal councillors at the local level. But by the 1870s, there was more cross-party agreement on what these improvements could bring to the population at large.

Nationally, there are a few big names associated with municipal socialism, such as Joseph Chamberlain, mayor of Birmingham from 1873-75. His term in office ran almost concurrently with Robert's and his achievements in Britain's second city are the most famous examples of this movement. Certainly, the measures that Robert was involved with driving forward could be described as acts of municipal socialism, even if the actual motivations behind them did not necessarily spring from the same political sentiments. Mayor Stanley's efforts deserve some pause for thought: Stalybridge's moves in this direction were not emulating Birmingham's. In fact, Stalybridge's were developing at exactly the same time. It might surprise today's reader to learn, for example, that Robert pushed for the town council to take over the supply of gas; surely, pushing for corporation ownership is evidence of more socialist proclivities? But Britain's Victorian Tory attitudes were far from the neo-liberal actions of Britain's most famous Conservative politicians – such as the neo-liberal Margaret Thatcher. Robert's paramount concern was for austerity. He believed that the ratepayer should receive value for money. So, if the council could provide better value for money in terms of quality and cost, he had no qualms about pushing for municipal ownership.

Victoria Market Hall, Stalybridge

Robert was devoted to the other traditional Conservative values: independence of the household from the encroachment of central control and interference. This belief was evident when he gave his views on the school board case of 1872; a person or a family should not always be dictated to by the state when it came to what was the best economic course of action for them. Likewise, with local autonomy: one of the reasons the Bread Riots were sparked in

Stalybridge was because the setting of the Poor Relief rates and procedures had been moved across to Manchester. For Robert, these two issues of personal and local laissez-faire were of huge importance.

The concepts of liberty and privacy are usually more associated with wealthy Conservative aristocrats during this period, and we tend to overlook just how important they were to many working-class people, especially those who – as Robert did – cherished the protection of 'what little we *do* have'. The belief in hard-work, pride in the home and the desire to rise above their existing status were the antithesis of everything that he would have understood about socialism and interference of the State. David Urquhart, a man whom Robert very much admired (see Chapter 8), also shared these values; although a strong proponent of improving public health, Urquhart was often to be found opposing such measures if he felt that the detail of legislative changes would prove to be too directive. It is likely that Urquhart's philosophy on these matters was very close to Robert's; for example, in the case of his admiration for Islam and its requirements in relation to sanitation and hygiene, he would have felt that unless an individual is educated and devoted to keeping their own body clean and pure, there was little point in providing public facilities at a cost to ratepayers, as the amenities would not be used correctly. So, whilst Robert stated that he was happy to see the good that could be brought to society by the likes of trade unions, for example, he felt that improvements in society needed to focus on individual enlightenment and not create an infrastructure that presumed all men are equal. It seems fair to assume that all men were not equal in the eyes of Robert, and this makes his later conversion to Islam – with a far greater egalitarian approach to worship than mainstream Christianity – all the more remarkable.

Robert spoke confidently in 1969, that a lesser class of man would be elected to Parliament. George Brodrick, a Liberal authority on local government, seems to reflect Robert's views; in April 1884, he stated that Public Health and Education Acts were, *'founded on reasons of public utility, and not on the principle of equalising the lots of the higher and lower classes in the community.'* [77] Socialism was not a dirty word for the Liberal Joseph Chamberlain, however, who speaking a year later in Warrington said that:

> *The Poor-Law is Socialism, the Education Act is Socialism, the great part of our municipal work is Socialism; every kindly act of legislation by which the community recognises its responsibilities and obligations to its poorer members is socialistic ...Our object is the elevation of the poor of the masses of the people — a levelling up which shall do something to remove the excessive inequalities in the social condition of the people, and which is now one of the greatest dangers as well as the greatest injury to the State ...* [78]

It is likely, too, that Conservatives such as Robert, who were responsible for developing municipal socialist measures, also took a rather cannier view on things. He may have noted the change in dialogue towards a greater provision of publicly

---

[77] George Brodrick in <u>Nineteenth Century</u>, April 1884, quoted in *Town, City and Nation* by P.J Waller, OUP, 1983 p.299.

[78] J. Chamberlain, *Speeches of the Right Hon Joseph Chamberlain, M.P*, Routeldge, 1885, p.189.

owned local services, long before many of his contemporaries did. Perhaps he felt that public works were not only the right thing to do but were also a vote-catcher and a solution to any crazy communistic notions that were growing in Russia and throughout the continent. He would probably have agreed with the (later) Conservative Prime Minister, A.J. Balfour, who had said in 1895 that, *"social legislation ... is not merely to be distinguished from socialist legislation but its most direct opposite and effective antidote."* [79]

One of the few institutions that we have no evidence of Robert's involvement with – although he was probably committed to their existence - was public libraries. Free libraries had been established as a service for the working class since an Act of 1850, and by 1910 a sizeable reading public was finally in existence. Still, only a tiny number of the population were registered borrowers. This could have been, though, the result of the continued success of alternatives rather than a working-class desire to remain ignorant. In Stalybridge, a Mechanics' Institute was opened as early as 1825. It had a reading room and hosted lectures, moving between various buildings over the years and with a comparatively low take-up, but by 1860 there was sufficient interest for various philanthropically-minded local business owners (councillors Platt, Bates and Kirk, and Mr Astley, Robert's peers, who also donated the land) for its own building to be erected in the Ridge Hill area. A library, a museum, a microscope for use by its members and an events agenda packed with lectures, talks and seminars were its main features.

Stalybridge did not have its own free library until 1901, when another colleague of Robert's, Councillor (and later MP) John Cheetham, funded one. Robert was proof that if someone wanted to find the means to educate themselves, they could do so, and for this reason the provision of free public libraries may not have been particularly high up on his political agenda at this point in his life. Plus, as he claimed just minutes after being appointed as mayor, *"I have enough to deal with."*

All Gas and Air?

Lancashire 'pea-soupers' – the terrible smogs that made it impossible to see more than a few feet - were famous across the land. Little had been done to prevent them, however, because mill production was important to the economy's success. So, the arrival of gas street lighting during the 1850s was hugely popular for the vast majority, who did not have the luxury of carriage and horses to carry them about the town in the dense fogs.

In 1872, however, Stalybridge Council was faced with the problem that the gas lights did not seem to be working properly. Residents were complaining that far too many lights were dim and that the streets were as dangerous as ever. The subject of street lighting was then – as it is now – the source of great consternation, but it was thought of with rather more levity; people paid their rates and wanted to be assured that they received good value for money. The first gas companies were not owned by a town council and in Stalybridge the gas providers were not doing their job. Other boroughs were experiencing similar problems and a trend towards municipalisation of gas provision began, with nine local authorities taking control of gas before 1850, another 18 in the 1850s, 22 in

[79] P. Squires, *Anti-Social Policy*, Wheatsheaf, 1990.

the 1860s, 76 in the 1870s, 24 in the 1880s, 50 in the 1890s and 25 between 1901 and 1910. Over two-thirds of these local authorities were northern.

Two months before Robert became mayor, in September 1874 the town council discussed the gas problem, with Alderman Bayley stating that they had the worst gas provision, *"and were charged more than in any other town round Manchester,"* and that, *"the gas was so bad in Mottram Road that the people could scarcely see their way to Stalybridge."* Councillor Warhurst agreed, adding that, *"The gas was so bad in Mottram Road that the people could scarcely see to read by it,"* – certainly a cause for concern for the wealthier residents of the town who had access to books and who inhabited the grand homes of Mottram Road! But it was Councillor Robert Stanley who had taken the issue most seriously and who came to the council armed with his own facts, *"In the last week in August there were burning dimly 22 lamps, and 36 were out. On the 5th and 6th of September, all the lamps were dim. Whatever price we pay for gas it is an unsatisfactory state of things. The gas company may charge us a lower rate per lamp, but I would pay more than have it as it is."*

With cries of 'hear, hear' from his fellow councillors, he went on to read out prices from other towns and cities across the country – all of whom were paying far less than Stalybridge's 4s and 4d. He continued, *"With respect to the inspector's return as to the lighting power of the town, I have no confidence in him at all. There is some mistake in it. It is impossible for the gas to be so good, and to give such a bad light as it does. There is nothing for it but to go in for compulsory powers to purchase them. We should be able to supply cheaper gas and of better quality than we now have."*

Robert was a man who took his unpaid civic duties exceptionally seriously – making every effort himself to investigate the efficiency of each lamp in his own ward and calling for the council to consider adopting the compulsory powers needed to purchase the gas corporation. His words were received with unanimous applause but the following week, after *The Stalybridge Reporter* had printed this discussion, Napoleon Ives, gas inspector for the borough, wrote a letter to the editor and objected strongly to Robert's speech, declaring, *"Now, sir, I cannot allow this statement to go forth to the world unchallenged ..."* and following it up with a lengthy discussion on parliamentary statute with regards to lighting powers. Robert, however, had already anticipated that Ives would react in such a way, and alongside the gas inspector's letter, the *Reporter* printed Robert's own:

> *Sir – In the report of the proceedings of the Stalybridge Town Council on the 7th inst., I am reported as saying that I had no confidence in the gas inspector. My meaning was that I had no confidence in the statement that the gas was of the lighting power of 19 candles, unless rushlights are meant. It appears to me that either there is some error in reading the tables which are connected with the photometer or that there is some defect in the instrument itself. I do not think anyone who knows Mr Ives, the inspector, would believe that he would either wilfully or carelessly make a return except such as he considered a correct one. Yours truly, ROBERT STANLEY.*

I wonder if the two men bumped into each other at the town hall the next day and both declared, "Whoops!" In a small town, where party politics was becoming a greater feature of the local political landscape, Robert's response is remarkably pacifying. He did not exaggerate the misdeeds of the newspaper (perhaps keen to keep them 'on side' for the future) and he headed off Napoleon Ives's reaction at the pass. For a man who, we shall see in the future, is more than capable of strong sentiment and a rallying call, his experience within the council chambers would have provided him with the chance to hone his diplomatic skills and calm judgement. His attitude and approach as a councillor in relation to these sorts of matters undoubtedly led to cross-party popularity on his part.

The issue of overpayment of gas again raised its head in February 1875, by which time Robert was the mayor and again calling for the backing of the council to bring the supply of gas under direct control of the borough. Try as he might, though – requesting that the gas company engaged in discussions about selling their company to the town council, along with seeking advice from central government – he was met with the same answer: that if the company was not willing to sell, at the current time nothing could be done. Many years and more legislation would be needed before Stalybridge and other town councils could venture down this path.

Water. And the Muck.
The reservoir region of Greenfield lies on the west side of the Pennines, on the edge of the Saddleworth moors and is situated within the country's first national park area: the Peak District - one of the biggest attractions for visitors to the north of England. But far more than just a pretty face, for centuries this stunning and often dangerous landscape has been crucial to the survival of the towns lying east of Manchester.

It was the regular supply of rainwater from these moors which allowed for the first ever steam powered cotton mill to put Stalybridge right at the heart of the Industrial Revolution. But as population growth exploded alongside mushrooming industrialisation, ever-increasing supplies of water were needed for the towns east of Manchester. During the second half of the 19th century, whilst the country was trying to solve its issue of pandemic disease outbreaks, municipal authorities realised the need to supply towns and cities with fresh water and were subsequently granted powers by parliamentary legislation through the Water Acts. A reservoir already existed for the Ashton area when Robert became a councillor in 1863, but on the Stalybridge side of the region, extending out to Mossley and Greenfield and to the Saddleworth moors which mark the West Yorkshire border, the people were still living without a decent water supply. Water was certainly on the brain for Robert, and by the time that he joined the sanitation and the waterworks committees of Stalybridge Town Council, the issue of water preservation, cost and supply was paramount.

In the autumn of 1874, Stalybridge Town Council demonstrated just how serious the matter of water supply and preservation had become. Although conditions for the working class in Stalybridge were not as horrendous as those living in inner-city Manchester, or as bad as they had been in the 1840s, the vast majority of houses still fetched water from an outside tap, and – given that most were private renters - individual households could not afford to have the taps repaired. Stalybridge Town Council found an unusually high level of homes suffering from using taps which were faulty and leaking and, because the borough was charged for the volume of water - and this was passed on to the ratepayer - it became imperative to solve the problem.

As he did with the gas issue, Robert made it a personal mission to count how many taps were affected and then to explain the mechanical cause of the problem. This turned out to be the erosion of the leather washers (today we use rubber washers) which could simply be replaced by the borough at a minimal cost. Robert pointed out to the committee that if the pressure of the water into the tap was too high, the leather would be eroding far more quickly than it would normally. He proposed that the council – rather than the hard-pushed householder - should bear the cost of this simple replacement of eroded washers and that the issue of the water pressure should be addressed, with both proposals being accepted.

But beyond the dripping taps problem, Robert had a bigger issue to address. By the second half of the 19th century, Victorian Britain had discovered the importance of reservoir building schemes. Just a dozen or so miles away from

Yeoman Hey, Dovestones Reservoirs in Greenfield

Stalybridge, on the Yorkshire side of the moors, the wool manufacturing town of Holmfirth had suffered a catastrophic disaster in February 1852, when the Bilberry Dam burst its banks – killing 81 people, one of the worst such disasters in the world. The inquest held afterwards concluded that the reservoir was, *"defective in its original construction,"* and that, *"the Commissioners, in permitting the Bilberry reservoir to remain in a dangerous state with the full knowledge thereof, and not lowering the waste pit, have been guilty of great and culpable negligence."* Robert had been 24 years old at the time of this event and living on the other side of the hills; his shop was also at the bottom of a valley and just yards from the River Tame, which had also been prone to flooding. It was clear that existing water supplies for the growing towns of east Manchester were inadequate and potentially dangerous, so he would have been aware of the grave responsibility

121

placed upon him and his colleagues when he was appointed to oversee the design of the huge new Yeoman Reservoir in Greenfield.

To keep Stalybridge adequately supplied and to meet further demand from Ashton, the Ashton-under-Lyne, Stalybridge and Dukinfield District Waterworks Joint Committee was established in 1870. This was the first time in the country that water authorities had been grouped together on a regional basis. Robert was one of the original commissioners appointed and he welcomed this legislation, which expanded the powers of local authorities to build their own reservoirs. One of his first acts as mayor was to propose an amendment to Parliament which would allow for further time for the development of the Yeoman initiative, which turned out to be a massive scheme of works. A railway was constructed to run along the western side and Robert oversaw much of the detail involved in the tendering and commissioning of the building contract. The project was a dangerous one, too, and no doubt he would have been dismayed to have heard of the accident which occurred in November 1877, shortly after his second term as mayor had ended. Two navvies who had arrived from Liverpool that day to find work on the scheme, had embarked upon an evening of drinking and had boarded the tramway's waggons against the advice of the brakeman. The waggons tipped them out and down into the valley where they were instantly killed.

The construction of the reservoir took years to complete, and Stalybridge's 1907 Yearbook noted Robert's valuable contribution to the scheme, referring in particular to his financial acumen and sharp eye:

> *During his term on the Council, the Joint Waterworks scheme made great progress, and it became necessary that the values of the various Waterworks be ascertained so that each of the townships concerned should know the exact value of the properties acquired. Mr. Stanley strongly supported the proposal of saving the great expense of Arbitration by coming to a friendly agreement as to values, and he submitted figures which were discussed by the various representatives, but which were rejected by one of the corporations as not being favourable to their interest. So, an arbitration was held in 1879, Sir F. Bramwell being appointed Arbitrator, the proceedings costing about £20,000. The decision of the Arbitrator was within a comparatively small margin of that named in Mr. Stanley's valuation.*

Here was a man yet again doing his utmost to provide a practical solution to a problem, eager to save money and time for the ratepayers.

On 8th August 1874, the mayor discussed an appeal from Ashton town councillors requesting that Stalybridge share the cost with their larger neighbour for "a new instrument that measures temperature and humidity." Under the steer of Robert, the councillors decided against a contribution, feeling that there were more pressing concerns in relation to the public environment, as opposed to splashing out on fancy new gadgets.

On 6th February 1875, the *Reporter* noted again that the mayor had his eye on wastage of water within the town and on 6th March Robert had been patrolling the streets, this time counting 65 trapped gullies. On May 8th, the *Reporter* noted an exchange between Robert and Councillor Storrs in council, over the level of pollution in the River Tame, with Storrs blaming ashes from bonfires and Robert stating that it was the fault of pollution being flushed into the water from the towns lying above Stalybridge. But water was still being wasted and Robert informed the council that Stalybridge was using 40 per cent more than Ashton, even with a considerably smaller population, and there was insufficient water available to last a hot summer. The *Reporter*, however, was cynical about the mayor's directives to reduce the amount of water consumption on behalf of households and industry, instead arguing that sewers and gullies needed to be flushed. The newspaper pushed for the Yeoman reservoir scheme to be sped up, *"There is something unexplained somewhere and the public have the right to know."* In its 12th June 1875 edition, the *Reporter* noted that the mayor and town clerk had been down to London along with Mr Buckley and Alderman Bayley to meet the solicitor-general in relation to the Waterworks amendment, which was duly proposed and accepted by the government.

Alongside the issue of adequate provision of water came the growing awareness of the need to improve sanitation in Stalybridge. Various government inquiries, along with the discoveries of medical science and more knowledge of infection, had led to municipal measures for improved sanitation. In February 1875, Councillor Dickinson had carried out an extremely detailed sanitation report for the town and was thanked by Robert for his efforts.

During his previous eleven years as a councillor, Robert would have seen huge strides in the level of sanitation available in the town from just three decades prior, when Friedrich Engels had visited this "repulsive" town. The Stalybridge Public Baths was opened in May 1870 - the same year as Ashton opened its own baths - and were a gift to the town by local philanthropists Robert and Margaret Platt, costing £7,000. As with all the big names in town, Robert knew Platt - who served alongside him on the town council - and Margaret Platt herself was born in Salford, no doubt being familiar with the Turkish baths built in that town at the urging of David Urquhart.

The design of Stalybridge's public baths was quite advanced for its time; the smoke-shaft of the enormous chimney was constructed with a hollow chamber around the central smoke flue, which ventilated the baths and swimming pools for those using the baths. Inside were two large swimming pools which would soon have been the centre of socialising and exercise for many of the town's residents. By a bizarre chance reading of an edition of the *Reporter* for 15th August 1874, I stumbled across the name of Thomas Stanley, Robert's fourth son, who had been competing in the Stalybridge Swimming Contest. But perhaps more important than the ability to have fun and to exercise was the chance to get clean; the building also housed 20 private individual tubs, and soap could be purchased – far preferable to the usual but onerous task of heating up water at home in order to use a tin bath, which was the fact of life for nearly every Stalybridge resident at this time.

Progress with public health occurred slowly but by April 1875, the mayor noted his "satisfaction" with the town's annual medical inspections which declared that only two to five per 1,000 deaths were the result of preventable diseases. Despite this, there were still plenty of cases of hardship and unhygienic conditions, and the sanitary officer had found alarming levels of overcrowding –

one of the most appalling being a two-roomed house in the town where two elderly women, two grown adult women and eight children were all living together.

Robert's own perspective on the sanitation issue reflected the views of one of the men he most admired: David Urquhart (see Chapter 8). Urquhart had campaigned for the Turkish bath system to be introduced across Britain. He had noted that the Islamic faith placed an enormous emphasis on personal cleanliness, that the practise known as 'wudu' – washing specific parts of the body before praying, five times a day – had the effect of greatly reducing disease and contagion. The link, for him, between personal cleanliness and a reduced mortality rate was obvious.

In May 1875, the town council again discussed the problem of "smoke nuisance" as a result of the hundreds of chimneys belching out thick, noxious, black smoke. Robert redirected the debate; not because he was trying to defend the factory owners, but because he said that the council, *"Should start by tackling our own [smoke from the public baths] before we start going for the masters."* He followed this up by saying that if the council were now on a path to accost the culprits of pollution, *"Then the Sanitary Committee would first indict the Mayor, Aldermen and Councillors of this borough of Stalybridge."* His comments caused much mirth, but he had a point - Stalybridge might like to bask in the glow of having provided a most progressive public baths building which ensured that none of its service users suffered from smoke inhalation whilst inside – but at what cost to the vast majority outside of it?

A Place to Perambulate: Stamford Park
Today, Stamford Park is one of the North's finest examples of an early Victorian public park, thanks to its boating lake, paddling fountains, bowling green, aviary and crazy golf.

The idea for a public park was first mooted in JR Coulthart's Report on the Sanitary Condition of Ashton-under-Lyne in 1844. The report had recognised the poor health of the cotton mill workers and the lack of attractive leisurely activities available to them. In 1856, a local campaign began in order raise funds for such a park, the feeling being that it would be good for the towns not to be reliant solely on the goodwill of donations from mill owners. By 1872, a location was chosen – the former home of cotton industrialist Abel Harrison. The Earl of Stamford agreed to sell the land for the price of £15,000 to the 'Trustees of the Public Park for Ashton-under-Lyne and Neighbourhood,' one of which happened to be Robert Stanley.

The park marked another joint venture between Ashton and Stalybridge town councils, as the land chosen was situated on the historic boundary between the two towns – also the dividing line between Lancashire and Cheshire. The founding of Stamford Park was another example of municipal socialism, seeking to provide beautiful public spaces for both the wealthier classes (who immediately claimed the land adjacent to such parks and built their luxurious homes there) and for the working classes, who could breathe fresh air, learn about science and nature, exercise and appreciate musical concerts. Local supporters had initially wanted to employ Joseph Paxton (who had created Birkenhead Park, Chatsworth and the People's Park, Halifax) as designer but one of the trustees suggested that the best approach would be that of competitive tender. The contract was awarded to a Mr Lindley but was then retracted and instead given to a local man, Mr Gregory Gill of Stalybridge, because his designs were deemed to be more, *'practicable, especially on the grounds of expense.'*

The original Stamford Park must have been a captivating treat for all. It included a menagerie, bowling green, flower gardens, museum and a conservatory which housed exotic plants. 'The Dingle' encapsulated the Cock Brook valley, complete with stream and rocks for children to scramble over. The grand opening of the park took place on 12th July 1873, when Lord and Lady Stamford attended

as VIPs and the towns of Ashton, Stalybridge and Dukinfield decked themselves out with bunting. Between 60-80,000 people watched the processions of the local great and good from Ashton and from Stalybridge, as they were regaled with trumpet fanfares and the firing of cannons. Later, the local dignitaries enjoyed a sumptuous banquet at the Drill Hall and the new committee of trustees was presented with a special badge made of black leather.

According to the *Stalybridge Yearbook* of 1907, even before he was mayor, Robert Stanley was, *"One of the original Trustees of Stamford Park before it was taken under municipal control"* in 1891. This would have involved taking responsibility for raising funds for the upkeep and development of the park, given that no local authority had oversight of it at this point. As various newspaper articles of the time illustrate, fundraising consisted chiefly of holding bazaars. The Stamford Park Bazaar of 1875 proved to be the one and only time we hear the name of Emma Stanley, the 'Lady Mayor', in the newspapers, because she was holding a stall to raise money - although the report does not mention what her stall was selling. It may have been that Emma was roped into doing this; perhaps there was a tradition of the Lady Mayor being expected to contribute some sort of role at a high-profile fundraising affair. But it is equally likely that she would have seized the opportunity herself, given that the park would have been a joy for anyone to spend time in.

Victoria Market Hall

The 1907 *Stalybridge Yearbook* states that Robert Stanley was the chairman of the building committee for the market hall. Before the town council had decided to build an actual market hall, a market ground existed in the area and the town hall itself housed an inside market. There was also an old fish market, popular with Stalybridge's (largely Irish) Roman Catholic community who were required to abstain from eating meat on a Friday. The fish market, however, was certainly no place for the religiously inclined during the evenings. Time and again the *Reporter* tells of fighting within the market - which was located right next to several pubs and was a haven for thuggery of all kinds after last orders. The tradition of post-pub munchies would have been just as prevalent then as it is now, with hunters heading off for fish and chips and black or mushy peas as opposed to a kebab or curry. On 3rd April 1875, the *Reporter*, as per usual, pulled no punches, describing how the public flocked there to get, *"Mussels, cockles and oysters consumed in a beastly and unseemly manner."*

The decision to build a market hall, with a new fish market opposite, would have been a welcome relief to many and especially good news for Stalybridge's jailbird-drunks, who were forced to linger in the adjacent cells. On 19th July 1875, the *Reporter* noted *"the stench"* and remarked that it was, *"...a disgrace to put anyone into the cells that were near to it ... they ought not to be poisoned for getting drunk."*

The building of the Victoria Market Hall was led by Robert, after he had been a councillor for only three years. This project was one where Councillor Stanley's skills would have been superbly employed. Unlike the other councillors – all born of wealthy local families - his experience in setting up a small business, his knowledge of running a shop, along with his understanding of Stalybridge's customer base – was both unique and invaluable. Named after Robert's (possibly) greatest female hero, the Victoria Market was opened on 18th July 1866, by Mayor James Kirk, only a year after the splendid Victoria Bridge on Trinity Street was built. It cost the town £8,969, was designed to supplement the provision of an outside markets area and is one of the era's few buildings still standing in Stalybridge that Robert had strong connections with. Not too long afterwards (much to the relief of the prisoners in the cells) the new fish market was built opposite the Victoria Market in 1881, at a cost of £1,600. Sadly, during the 1990s, trading ceased in the market hall and the people of Stalybridge – perhaps still in shock over the demolition of the once-glorious 1831 town hall building – rallied themselves and opposed local authority plans to close it to the public. Victoria Market is now known as the Civic Hall and is, for many, the central point of Stalybridge. Although the days of bustling shoppers and the exchange of coins have long gone, Robert would probably have been pleased that it now houses community events and the constituency offices of the local MP (although it has to be said that a long-term future for such a building is, unfortunately, never guaranteed in an age where Property is King).

CHAPTER 7

His Worship (It's all in the detail)
1874 – 1876

The previous chapter covered the more significant achievements that Robert was remembered for, as listed in the 1907 *Municipal Yearbook*. Other aspects of Robert's time as mayor may not have been quite as glamorous as the huge schemes that municipal socialism brought forth but, in many ways, they are far more telling of his personality and character.

Transport: Treasures and Troubles

As the creation of canal networks across the north of England brought increasing money and trade to the mill towns, so did the dawn of the railways. Robert may have spent his childhood and early adulthood treasuring the rudimentary skeletal infrastructure of railways serving the country, but by the time that his business was flourishing in Stalybridge, rapid expansion of the network had occurred and was transforming the lives of people, massively contributing to the economy of the British Empire.

Stalybridge Council's letter to the railway companies, following another death at the station in 1874

Stalybridge's main railway station was built in 1845, just before Robert and Emma's marriage. It was established by the Sheffield, Ashton and Manchester Railway, though a station already existed adjacent to it: the Lancashire and Yorkshire railway station, which served as a terminus from Manchester Victoria. The main function of the 1845 station was to link the area to the South and ultimately to London, because it provided a network to Stockport where passengers could then travel straight down to the

127

nation's capital. This new line also opened up the chance to travel over the Pennines via Huddersfield to Leeds and beyond. In 1848, just as Robert and Emma moved over from Ashton, the awesome Standedge Tunnel – just a few minutes' ride from Stalybridge - was built to carry passengers the five miles under the Pennines. A second railway tunnel was built in 1871 in order to cope with the increasing volume of passenger travel.

Anyone who has experienced the joys of travelling on the Leeds to Manchester railway line and embarking from Stalybridge station during rush hour will be all too familiar with the overcrowding problem. In the north west of England there is rarely a week that goes by where the regional media is not tackling the issue of this line, with too many commuters, not enough trains and the various train operators' failures to address the problem. Unfortunately, 150 years ago the very same problems existed for Stalybridge.

On 10th February 1874, Robert was reported as discussing the fact that a new railway bridge was needed along with a new station in order to serve the growing population. There had been many injuries and several deaths from train accidents at the station, all attributed to overcrowding and 'insufficient facilities'. Robert lamented the neglect by the Manchester, Sheffield and Lincolnshire Railway Company (MSLRC) (which was responsible for most trains on this route) over the previous years, and noted that the state of affairs would shortly become worse when the two other major train companies in the north of England amalgamated, *"No doubt the excuse will be ... that the other companies will build a station ... they [MSLRC] have always thrown the blame onto the Lancashire and North West and the Lancashire and Yorkshire Railways Companies..."* He then added – tongue firmly in cheek - that he was sorry that his fellow members of the council were not actually shareholders in the MSLRC and that until they were, *"he was afraid they would not get a new station."*

By 8th August 1874, Robert was telling his fellow councillors that they must oppose the increase of the powers of railway companies in Stalybridge until station access and suitability had been improved. However, on 7th November 1874, his worst fears were realised when the *Reporter* informed its readers that at 6am, on her way to Ashton, Ann Hague, described by the *Reporter* as, *"a respectable connected woman,"* was, *"cut to pieces,"* by a train travelling from Huddersfield and heading for London via Stockport. This case was an example where the Victorian press came into its own for gruesome details. The *Reporter* went on to inform its genteel readers, *"One of her legs and a quantity of flesh was found and placed in a bucket. The rails and also the wheels of the engine were smeared with blood [it was] sickening to behold."*

This happened just weeks before Robert was elected as mayor, and one of his first actions as leader of the council was to chair a special emergency meeting – open to all townspeople – on this horrific accident. The account of this meeting in the *Reporter* marked the first time that I saw confirmation that Robert did know Joseph Rayner Stephens personally and enjoyed a good relationship with him. Stephens – still the darling of the people and champion of the oppressed, following his prison sentence - was invited by Robert to speak. Robert opened the meeting:

The room was crowded with adults and on the platform, there were several members of the borough bench and also of the Town Council. Robert Stanley Esq. the newly elected Mayor took the chair amidst loud cheers ... The question before them was one on which the whole of the inhabitants of Stalybridge were agreed. There was not a single individual that did not sympathise with the object of the meeting. The time had come when, in consequence of the deaths that had occurred at the Stalybridge station, the public of Stalybridge should show in some unmistakable manner that they were disgusted at the manner in which the railway company had provided for the safety and accommodation of the inhabitants of this borough. He believed that they were unanimous, and it ought to go forth to the world that the public of Stalybridge were in a state of indignation at the numerous deaths, which were clearly susceptible to the want of proper accommodation (Cheers).

Stephens then took centre stage and, for a man who rarely praised those in elected office, he began by saying:

We live in times when believe me, comparatively few public officers are doing their duty [but Robert is] the wisest Mayor and Alderman ... I rather think that a Mayor with a borough, that is the wisest man of the borough (Loud laughter) ... I rather think that a borough like Stalybridge and all the other boroughs in the country can deal with the London and North-Western or the Manchester, Sheffield and Lincolnshire, or any other company that is a public nuisance (Hear, hear). Anyway, I for one obeying the call of the Mayor to come here, mean to do one man's share in it along with the rest of my fellow burgesses (Hear hear).

Robert closed the meeting by saying, *"I thank you and trust the meeting will cause a remedy to be applied to the disgraceful state of affairs at the railway station. I think it is horrible – the amount of deaths there is past all bearing, and I do hope something will be brought about to alter the present state of things."* The *Reporter*, though, took issue with this meeting, declaring that Rayner Stephens's speech was, *"not worth the paper it was written on"* and then (perhaps clutching at straws for something negative to say) that his, *"interpretation of the mosaic law"* was flawed.

Prior to the public meeting, the *Reporter* told its readers, on 14th November 1874, that Robert had presided over the dictation of a letter which was to be sent to the Home Office, declaring the town council's horror at the accident. Robert had also dictated a letter to the MSLRC, stating that the company needed to shoulder the blame and make the necessary changes at the station. It seems that the railway company had already been considering expansion in the area and wanted to open an entirely new railway line. In January 1875, the council received a reply from the company which was met with great dissatisfaction by the councillors when they saw that the company had simply referred to a parliamentary bill which would assist in station improvements across the country. Robert took special umbrage at their response, adding his political knowledge on such matters and saying that the company should not have presumed that the recommendations of a bill would necessarily occur, and they should have, *"...taken the precaution to read the proposed bill ... their first bill was but a draft through which they got to know their opponents."*

By 12th June 1875, plans were looking more concrete for railway line expansion, but not for providing a better station. The mayor called a meeting, inviting local people to look at the railway company's plans, *"thereby connecting Stalybridge with the other important Lancashire towns."* Robert was vehement that the state of existing services at Stalybridge station needed to be improved before any new work was commenced, stating that:

> *People came through the town from Leeds or Liverpool or London and they took away the opinion that Stalybridge was a poverty-stricken place, and not worthy of a good station. If they looked at the traffic which went through it, they would say it was simply an insult to them as commercial men. It was disgraceful that such a building should continue year after year, and it was not only an insult to them as a Corporation, but it was a standing insult to the inhabitants of the borough. (Hear, hear).*

A new committee was set up which included Robert and, although for the rest of his time in office there were no more fatalities reported at the station, he continued to call for improved facilities and engaged in frequently embittered communications with the MSLRC. Eventually, the 1880s saw Stalybridge receiving a much more suitable station, one which is still preserved admirably well today, with its best feature being the old Stalybridge Buffet Bar: a central stopping off point for all who like to try out the North's 'Real Ale Trail'.

Tram Troubles

In January 1872, two years before Robert became mayor, there was an issue surrounding 'Mr Summers's Tram' within the town. The Tramways Act 1870 had mainly licensed private enterprises and although local authorities could build and lease tram systems, they were not allowed to operate them. Summers was a wealthy industrialist who owned ironworks throughout the town. He had put down tram tracks on Russell Street, linking his workplaces to the railway station in order to assist with the arrival and departure of heavy materials used in his business. This marked a precedent in Stalybridge: should he be allowed to use a road in this way i.e., in order to profit his business, even though the specific road in question was not owned by the Corporation? Robert disagreed with most members of his own political party and some accused him of having too much sympathy with a businessman who wanted to take advantage of the public purse. His words in the council chambers, however, seemed to reflect more that he believed this new mode of transport could ultimately be used by the public throughout the town. The *Reporter* seemed to be impressed with his take on things:

> *It is, however, satisfactory to know that Mr Stanley, Dr Hopwood, and one or two others are not so blind to the interests of the town as to sacrifice commercial prosperity for political spleen. We congratulate those gentlemen ... this was the first division that has taken place in the new council – the leader of the party has now discovered that he cannot pull the strings of*

intelligent men with too authoritative a hand ... all honour then, we say, to Mr STANLEY for throwing off his political allegiance when an attempt to cripple the advancement of trade was being made. That gentleman came forward boldly and unflinchingly, and he told the council in language that could not be mistaken, that he would promote the prosperity and foster the progress of commerce at any cost. He was immediately attacked for his independence by the MAYOR who seemed almost thunderstruck that one of his pet sixteen should dare, before his eyes, to throw off the shackles of political despotism, and come to the rescue of the Liberal eight who were fighting for a just cause.... The amendment moved by Mr STANLEY, which was in effect that the Highway Committee should consider 'the error of their ways' was carried by twelve to seven. [80]

Allowing Mr Summers to use his tramway began the first moves towards adopting public use of trams for the people of the town, reducing reliance on the railway lines to Ashton and to other towns and moving the population away from the use of stagecoaches.

The Miscellany of Mayordom

The town council's minute books provide illustrations of the day-to-day situations that Robert presided over during his two years as mayor. In addition to chairing all of the sub-committees, there were more mundane aspects required of the mayor, such as approving the mortgages of local people (working class people could not borrow from a bank; instead, a local authority could issue loans to those with a good credit record) along with setting the rates to be paid by householders. But it is in the more miscellaneous aspects of being involved in leading a community that the more interesting flavours of Robert's life as mayor can be encountered.

Bells and Technology
On 6th February 1875, *The Stalybridge Reporter* noted that the mayor said:

It was proposed that a large bell should be fixed at the Town Hall, so that in case of fire it might be heard by the policemen all over the town, and so bring them quickly to the office. He wished to ask whether it was advisable that they put themselves in communications with the Ashton Town Council, for the purpose of connecting the two towns by means of a telegraph wire, so that in case of fire they might soon get the Ashton brigade to assist them, and in the case of fire in Ashton they might have the help of the Stalybridge brigade which would very likely result in a deal of property being saved. In case of riots, it was also desirable that there should be instant communication with Mr Chadwick and the Chief Constable of Ashton. Also, with respect to the escape of thieves – there were many occasions on which the telegraph would be of great use to them.

---

[80] *SB Reporter*, 13 January 1874.

Robert had instantly made the connection between a new alarm bell for the fire engine service and the benefits that a telegraph system could bring to the people of the borough. As someone who had witnessed many and varied forms of social disturbances during his lifetime, he was keen to make use of any new technology that would immediately bring the forces of law and order into the town. The arrival of the telegraph must have been as important for municipal management as the development of the fax machine in the 1970s and then email in the 1990s were. [81]

As Mad as a Dog

In the 1870s, a fear of dogs was often not to do with any lack of training on the part of an owner, or of an overly aggressive animal; rather, it was because of the very real threat of 'canine madness' – or 'hydrophobia' (rabies). There were several such cases in and around the towns close to Stalybridge during this decade and an outbreak occurred in July 1875. The *Reporter* provided a terribly sad and detailed account of one such case in Hyde, where a man was bitten after adopting a stray dog. He locked himself in his house after his wife fled, attacked anyone who tried to enter and slowly went mad, then died. Rabies was then – and still is now, in some parts of the developing world – a horrific way to meet your end.

Because cases of rabies had been found in Ashton and in Hyde in 1875, Robert had to decide how to prevent any possible outbreak in Stalybridge. Robert ruled that for the period of a month all dogs in the boundary of Stalybridge must be kept indoors and those that were found outside of a property and unattended would be taken by the police and destroyed. This inevitably irked some people, with one 'anonymous' writing to the *Reporter* to complain that, as chief magistrate, Robert's interpretation of the Dogs Act had failed to explain adequately the concept of a dog being 'found outside and to be in charge of a person'. Whatever the technicalities of the law, there were precious few incidents of any townspeople flouting his ruling, although the *Reporter* complained that the confinement was unnecessary, that rabies was rarely seen and that Robert would have been better concentrating his efforts on dealing with, *"the screeching of cats"* in Stalybridge, which was apparently a greater problem for the people of the town!

Councillor Meller Gets Silly

On 6th March 1875, the *Reporter* related a fracas between Alderman Meller and the rest of the town council. Meller had taken umbrage over inspections that had been made of privately let houses by two other councillors who were members of the Sanitary Committee. In the middle of council proceedings Meller rose to his feet, asked exactly who had appointed these two councillors to go around inspecting dwellings and stated that one of the occupants had said one of the inspectors had claimed to be a doctor. Meller stated, *"I pause for an answer,"* in the middle of the meeting – effectively demanding an adequate response from Robert. The mayor told him that this was not the time to discuss the matter and that by doing so he would compromise colleagues. He repeatedly asked Meller to sit back down, but

---

[81] As someone who is old enough to remember the typing pool and the thrill of the fax machine, I can imagine the excitement that the arrival of the telegraph system must have generated for Robert and his peers.

the man refused and repeated over a dozen times, *"I pause for an answer."* Meller was a Tory and so, for the Liberal councillors, this situation was an absolute delight as Robert struggled to reason with him and to move the business of the meeting on.

Meller became increasingly agitated, telling the council, *"I am not like some of you men – I am a fighter!"* and with Robert's appeals of, *'Come now,"* *"You had better sit down,"* and, *"There is nothing in order in this, I cannot answer the question,"* he eventually began to lose patience as Meller, *"hurled defiance across the table,"* according to the *Reporter*. After Councillor Storrs (a wealthy local builder) had intervened, reminding the council that as a municipal authority they had a duty to ensure that private landlords were not letting properties to the poor that were unfit for human habitation, Meller finally appealed to Robert, asking him, *"Are you going to let men go round in this way?",* but by now Robert had lost all patience with his comrade and replied, *"Certainly!"* [82]

The *Reporter* pointed out that if Mellor had gone about his objections in the right way, he might have received more sympathy. Mellor was probably either a private landlord himself or his friends were, and he was objecting to this state-sponsored 'snooping'. Inspections, in general, were on the increase and despite the positives of municipal socialism many people were incensed by the greater levels of bureaucracy accompanying it. It seems most likely that the two councillors told the householder that they were inspecting on behalf of the Sanitary Committee and that there were statutory obligations for medical inspection in relation to privately-let dwellings. The householder probably read this as them claiming to be medical doctors. Ultimately, though, Meller had the sympathy of the Liberal press, which disagreed with Storrs and his colleagues about the overriding need for inspection for sanitation purposes, *"It may be praiseworthy on their part when they display so much zeal in promoting the public welfare; but there can be no doubt they are guilty of trespassing when they enter 'an Englishman's castle' without being invited to do so."*

Councillor Ives Gets Silly

Our next 'silly-scene' from Robert's council meetings involves the newly elected Councillor Napoleon Ives, formerly the gas inspector for the borough but now wanting to try his hand at local politics. From his earlier breakdown in communication with Robert over the price of gas, Ives had already revealed that he was a little bit too quick to react and was somewhat pedantic in his approach. By 30th January 1875, Ives had only been a councillor for two months and was causing ripples of discontent. The problem, according to the *Reporter*, dripping

---

[82] This is how *The SB Reporter* related the situation to its readers; *"It is seldom we are treated to a 'scene' like the one enacted in the Council Chamber on Monday evening. Alderman MELLER, who appeared to have worked himself into an unnatural state of excitement previous to the opening of the evening, waxed wroth ... Appeals from the Mayor; snubs from his own political friends; and the laugher of his opponents had no effect upon him. There he stood for about twenty minutes, and his declamations and his attitudes created a considerable amount of confusion. He had at length to give way without being satisfied and he gave way to a pressure on the brain by relaxing into a state of somnolency whilst the 'leader of the Conservative party' aired his eloquence on the question of trapping sewer grids."*

with sarcasm, was that, *"a luminary from the gas inspector's office"* had felt that the local Tories were lacking a leader – not even, *"the Mayor, with all his good sense"* was deemed to be the leader that they needed, *"and consequently [Ives] felt that a grave responsibility had suddenly, through a heated imagination, been cast upon himself."*

Ives sent a circular to the other 17 Tory members of the council, inviting them to a meeting where they would discuss his proposition to become their leader. But, apparently, none of them turned up. Not content with upsetting the conventions of his own political party, Ives's somewhat abrasive personality, his propensity to pick over minor points and to make long, deliberate speeches within the council chambers did nothing to win over the good feeling of the Liberals towards him, either.

On 10th April 1875, the *Reporter* recounted an incident during the town council meeting. Ives had asked for an agenda item on whether The People's School (which Ives had an involvement with) could be allowed to, *"have free use of the Town Hall and cloakroom"* in order to raise money for Stamford Park. This in itself was not the slightest bit controversial, but a rather unusual reaction took place as Robert prepared to introduce Ives's address on the matter:

> *Whilst the Mayor was reading the above, there was a general rising in the Council, several members looking at their watches and saying their 'train was due', the remark being accompanied by a titter of laughter. They proceeded to march out of the chamber in Indian file, and whilst they were doing so, Councillor Ives, who appeared somewhat astonished and annoyed, said "...the question should have to come before the Council – (interruption caused by members looking for their hats and umbrellas) ... I am not asking for a precedent ... but it seemed to me that the opposite party might get up and move ...*

Ives's speech on the matter then set out to be as laborious as he had now become accustomed to, but suddenly Councillor Storrs interrupted and asked the mayor if the meeting was quorate for the subject. Robert, having counted:

> *... said there were only seven members present, consequently Mr Ives was out of order, and could not proceed. Thereupon Councillor Ives looked flushed and indignant, but suddenly recovering himself he said: I must bow to the decision of the Mayor, and I thank you for the kind manner in which you have listened to me so patiently up to now in reference to the motion. I move that the best thanks of the Council be given to the Mayor.*

Ives's motion was somewhat 'crawling' to say the least; perhaps he had finally realised that he had very much annoyed the entire council as a result of his previous behaviour and attitude. Either way, the six remaining councillors passed the motion and Robert told Ives, *"I am very much obliged to you."* Then the *Reporter* noted the involvement of its own journalist:

> *Councillor Ives, walking up to the reporter desk with a vexed look, said: '" What train is due? They say their train is due". It was suggested that it was*

"an express to shut him up, and the journey has been performed very effectively". Amidst much laughter the proceedings thus abruptly closed, and Mr Ives left the room saying he should have to spend three hours in putting on paper his opinions on the conduct of his 'friends'.

So, perhaps Napoleon didn't learn his lesson after all.[83]

Another Upstart: Rigby the Pork Butcher

Although Robert broke the mould for tradesmen wanting to enter the Victorian local political arena, not every shop owner was welcome there. To the horror of the *Reporter* in November 1875, Mr Rigby - a local pork butcher – put himself forward to be elected as councillor. The *Reporter* gleefully noted in detail every flaw in Rigby's character: that the man was barely literate (he kept misspelling his own name) that Rigby was *"henpecked"* by his wife and that his wife exclaimed in public that her husband was, *"making himself a laughing stock."* Indeed, Mrs Rigby apparently attended a meeting her husband had called with his potential supporters so that she could, *"point out the errors of his way."* Napoleon Ives happened to be standing against Rigby for the same ward – with Rigby not declaring which party he supported - and in the end Ives won the vote.

It is difficult not to feel sympathy for poor Rigby; not only was he torn to shreds by the *Reporter*, whose snobbery towards the butcher was quite vociferous, but his misery must have been deepened further when one of his supporters told him that the election had been rigged and that Rigby had actually won. Subsequently, the man began to celebrate his 'victory' but was then informed by the town hall that, no, sorry, he had lost – fair and square. No doubt many of the wealthier men in town felt that it was bad enough to have a few grocers bossing them about now – the last thing that they needed was an illiterate, henpecked butcher on board.

Fun and Games

Life as the mayor was not always a constant treadmill of meetings, cantankerous councillors, and courtroom scandal; Robert often had the cheery prospect of attending many funerals, such as that of the Reverend Floyd of Holy Trinity on 17th April 1875: a rather grand affair because the vicar had also been a leading Freemason, from the Moira Lodge. But there were occasions of less levity, where Robert was required to act as a chairman of some debate or another, or simply as the local VIP at an event. There were various high points scattered throughout the year: the bazaars to raise money for Stamford Park, the Stalybridge agricultural show (where, in September 1874, Robert had found time to squeeze in a stint as a steward running the cheese stall) and the time of year that every working-class

---

[83] It seems, however, that Napoleon Ives must have mended his ways and begun to play a more diplomatic political game because he succeeded in becoming mayor from 1884-85. He did not forget Robert's kindnesses to him – publicly standing up for Robert during the Bulgarian Crisis.

person looked forward to - the Stalybridge Wakes, which is still marked out in today's calendars of the town.

The Wakes

The Wakes were an occasion where families finally got to down their tools, spend time together and scoff delicacies such as black peas, gingerbread, ice-cream, mussels and oysters. In Stalybridge, there was always a travelling circus in the markets area, promising a host of attractions which the Reporter described on 25th July 1874 had: including: swing boats, hobby horses, rifle galleries, models, paintings, coconut shies, marionettes, a camera obscura, gymnastics, and goats. The performers included *"Daniel in the Lions' Den"* and if the tragedy of having to gawp at *"the wonderfullest dwarf alive"* doesn't make you cringe enough, then you may be even more dismayed by the *Reporter's* next words, *"Misses Jane and Margaret Smith – the Yorkshire Twins were exhibited to the admirers of fat women."*

OAPs for Tea

One of the most popular events of the year was the Old Folks Annual Tea Party. In comparison to modern society where, sadly, there seems to be a tendency of side-lining, ridiculing or ignoring the eldest of our population, 1870s Stalybridge honoured their oldest community members. On 26th June 1875, the *Reporter* gave a full account of the 15th annual tea party. Robert was asked to the party as chairman. The guest of honour and opening speaker was a certain Mr Joseph Rayner Stephens, who – for the first time – now qualified in the age stakes (threescore and ten) to officially be counted as an 'Old Folk' himself. Stephens told his fellow 'Old Folk' that he was pleased that he had finally earned his rights to a free cup of tea and he then entertained them with a speech expressing his love for Stalybridge. The *Reporter* – not exactly a fan of this man of the people – described how he quite readily offered others *"a pinch of snuff"* and how he sat listening to Robert, *"in a cloud of tobacco smoke."*

Robert told his audience:

... that this was the fifteenth annual tea party of the old folks, and he hoped he would live to see one or two more fifteen annual tea parties. (Laughter). At all events it would be that time, before he would be at the age to entitle him to attend the party as one of the old folks. No one attending could not feel a pleasure in doing so when they saw so many old people enjoying themselves and talking over old times. It was a source of great gratification to him to come there. He had been several times, and he hoped to be spared to meet them for a number of years yet. Their numbers had been thinned through death, and of course it was only to be expected at their extreme age some of them would go, but he trusted that during the next year they would be more fortunate. There were several speakers who would address them, and he would not occupy their time because he knew some of them were anxious to have a dance. That was a very pleasant thing to have, and it was a nice thing for the old folks to talk of the years gone by and bring them back to their old courting days. These matters would be to them a source of pleasure for some time to come after that evening was over. (Cheers).

The Reverend Jelly-Dudley then gave those present a semi-sermon, after which, *"the Mayor descended from his perch"* and enjoyed a dance to the tune of 'I Loved Him' with the oldest residents of the town, Mary Plummer, aged 96, and 'old Maggie Haslam'. The women were described by the *Reporter*'s journalist as, *"jovial, friendly and clear in intellect ... as half as nimble of foot as many women are who have not seen thirty summers."* Mary Haslam had, *"another new dress which had been presented to her by a lady resident. As usual she presented the Mayor with a handsome bouquet of flowers specially made up for her at Belle Vue Gardens."*

But the most wonderful surprise, for my family, on discovering this article about the tea party was the sudden arrival of a Mr William Stanley! Thanks to the *Reporter*, William got a special mention:

> *Then the Mayor's father, now 89 years of age, had made his annual journey from Cardiff, a distance of 200 miles, to see his son and join in the frolic of the old folks' tea party, as he had done for several years past. He is a noble old soul – happy in the evening tide of his life.*

It is difficult to read the account of this and not to feel rather impressed. Even today, it would be no mean feat for an 89-year-old travelling some 200 miles alone; but to imagine this occurring when travel was so much less comfortable makes William's sudden reappearance in our story even more special. From what the *Reporter* said, the tea party had become an important part of William's year, but it sounds as though this particular trip was a rare treat for him: the chance to see his son having become the mayor of Stalybridge, holding court and treating the old folk of Stalybridge with grace and good humour as they, *"for a time, bathe their wrinkles in the sunshine of social enjoyment."*

Council Chuckles – and Warm Words

Robert may have looked every inch the serious, civically-minded Victorian mayor and then the deeply religious, contemplative Muslim in the three photographs that we have of him, but through reading many pages of town council minutes it becomes clear that he possessed a rather impish sense of humour, something that seems to have been passed down through the generations. The love of laughter was also of huge importance to Abdullah Quilliam – but this side of his personality has been somewhat overlooked by scholars. It seems that when the two men finally met, as well as having much in common politically and religiously, they would have enjoyed many light-hearted moments, too. What was hilarious to most Victorian men may not translate easily into our own modern language of humour (and, quite frankly, some of the jokes that Quilliam published in *The Crescent* could easily have been used by a dodgy, sexist 1970s comedian).

Despite this, there were plenty of moments where the modern reader can also see the funny side of a situation, such as on 8th August 1874, when Robert had the whole council in fits of laughter over the fact that only he had noticed that the particularly bothersome resolution they were discussing had been made on April Fools' Day, saying, *"The Town Council never made greater April fools of themselves when they put that resolution on the books. [Much laughter]."*

In the courtroom, too, it was not unknown for him to say something humorous, such as during a case which involved a couple who lived together but who were not married. They were arguing over money. Robert had to try and fathom out the nature of the relationship and told the man that, of course, *"you are the housekeeper!"* much to the laughter of those in the courtroom.[84]

There are plenty of other examples where Robert came back with a witty retort or two, although his humour never appeared to be caustic or cruel towards an individual (which is something that cannot be said for many others on the council). But my favourite example of his sense of humour is reported on 10th April 1875, when Robert - as the mayor - was discussing with the council the safety of travelling in 'cabs' (horse drawn vehicles) within the town. Robert mentioned that the borough employed a man whose responsibility it was to check the cabs in operation. Councillor Dickinson asked Robert, *"Is he a good Inspector?"* The Mayor replied, to much laughter; *"I think he is pretty fair. I heard him recommend a man, one day, to get his horse a new leg."*

As well as coming across as a kind and warm human being to all that he encountered (even the annoying Napoleon Ives), Robert also gave heartfelt tributes to colleagues who had passed away, such as Councillor Burnley. On 10th April 1875, the *Reporter* noted Robert's words on the life of his fellow councillor:

> *The Mayor said he should like someone of the opposite side of politics to second the resolution, and he would do so himself. He had known Mr Burnley for twenty years, and a more genial, truthful and straight-forward man he never knew in his life – (Hear, hear). Mr Storrs had said all that could be said on the subject, and he cordially agreed with every word he had uttered. They would miss him.... He always liked to see him, and he was a man esteemed by every person sitting around that board. (Hear, hear).*

A Crisis - Of Bulgaria

Until September 1876, Robert's mayoral track record had largely consisted of the ups – as opposed to the downs. He had proven himself to be a fair and kind mayor who gained the support of both Conservatives and Liberals. However, thanks to a specific incident overseas, this was all set to change. In Bulgaria, the mainly Christian population was determined to gain independence from the Ottoman Muslims and, as the Turks sought to stave off nationalist elements, around 15,000 people were said to have been massacred at Philippopoli. Gladstone was still the leader of the Liberals and used this news to rail against the foreign policy of Disraeli, who preferred the presence of the Ottoman Empire in the region, in order to act as a buffer against Russian encroachment. Christian sentiment in Britain was outraged, and across the land both national and local leaders held gatherings in order to officially declare against the action of the Ottomans. Not in Stalybridge, however, where Robert refused to call a meeting. Until now, this book has focussed almost exclusively on Robert's attitudes and beliefs in relation to British domestic and civic policy but from this point on, the narrative will attempt to explain more fully the development of his interest in international affairs.

---

[84] *SB Reporter*, 19 July, 1875.

STALYBRIDGE, REFUSAL OF THE MAYOR TO CALL A MEETING

A requisition was on Thursday afternoon presented to the mayor of Stalybridge, asking him to call a public meeting for the purpose of passing resolutions respecting the Turkish atrocities in Bulgaria. The requisition was signed by about 170 influential persons, manufacturers, clergymen, etc. comprising men of both political parties. The mayor, who is a Conservative, yesterday sent the following reply:-

[To: Robert Platt, Esq. Dunham.]
Dear sir, -

I have carefully considered the request contained in the document handed to me yesterday, and find that it is my duty to refuse to call a meeting. I cannot see that any good purpose would be served by it, as the occurrences to which the document refers took place in May last, and the Turkish Government have taken the proper means to prevent their repetition. The meetings now being held in other towns similar to the one proposed by you, can only have the effect of weakening the influence of the Government in the councils of Europe, by conveying the impression that the conduct of our Government is not in accordance with the opinions of the country, and encouraging the Servians to continue their unjust war, and also tempting the Russians to interfere in the affairs of Turkey in such a manner as to bring about a general war, in which we would be obliged to take part. I consider the whole agitation on this matter to be the work of Russian agents, and am sorry to see so many of my countrymen allowing themselves, through their feelings and prejudices, to be catspaws of to serve another State, and against the interests of their own country. Yours Truly, Robert Stanley, Mayor.
(Manchester Guardian, 9th September 1876).

It should be noted that Robert was not in denial of the fact that many Bulgarians had been killed; rather, his reasons for not calling the meeting were because he felt that they would be pointless, that the situation was now in the past, that matters had been put in place in order to ensure that they would not take place again, that the majority of British people were behind the existence of the Ottoman Empire and that - most importantly – calling such meetings was a ploy designed to create 'cats paws' of the British people who were playing directly into the hands of 'Russian agents'.

The same edition of the *Guardian* is filled with accounts of meetings across the land where horrified politicians and churchmen gathered in order to condemn what had occurred; in Manchester, a fundraising appeal was set up to assist those affected and £150 was donated by Hugh Mason of Ashton - a rich industrialist and philanthropist who was a peer of John Stanley and who would have known Robert, too. A fledgling suffragette, a certain Emmeline Pankhurst of Manchester was also part of the collective cry against the Turks and became caught up in the many demonstrations which did eventually culminate in Gladstone winning the general election of 1880.

Robert's refusal to call the Stalybridge meeting was addressed to Robert Platt, who had directly asked the mayor to call the meeting. Platt was one of Stalybridge's wealthiest residents and also a former mayor and councillor of

Stalybridge. He was friendly with Gladstone and had invited him to Stalybridge in the aftermath of the Bread Riots. Platt would have been a strong supporter of Gladstone's declaration against the Ottomans in Bulgaria. Did Platt already know Robert's views on the Ottoman Empire? Was he deliberately – publicly - trying to force his hand? Or were his intentions less manipulative; simply following what other borough mayors were doing in response to what had occurred in Bulgaria?

Robert's action would have shocked and disgusted thousands of British people; his letter of refusal was reported on in newspapers across the country and even in Parliament. Given the fact that Robert had only ever publicly commented on local and national politics and affairs before, his thoughts on the Bulgarian atrocities would no doubt have baffled and stunned many. Evidently, many felt that Robert was getting 'above himself.' So, in Stalybridge, a meeting was called anyway. During the same week that Robert had refused to organise the event, the *Stalybridge Reporter* produced a blistering editorial on 16th September, hinting that Robert had deliberately left the list of men who had signed the requisition at his Manchester office so that people could not see how popular the request for a meeting was:

The unwarrantable conduct of ... the mayor in refusing to call a town meeting ... has created a widespread feeling of indignation that he should thus have endeavoured to stifle free speech in the borough and the feeling has been mingled with shame, at the position which Stalybridge has then been made to assume in the eyes of the country - by his insulting reply to the gentlemen who signed the requisition. That requisition was one that ought to have commanded the respect, at the very least, of the mayor ... the feeling was strongly expressed that although the mayor had, in his letter, taken a purely party view of the matter and had endeavoured to stir up party feeling and party prejudice ... Alderman Stanley made an excuse that he had 'left the requisition in Manchester' and promised to bring it on Wednesday but then had been unable to go into Manchester.

The editorial did its best to reproduce a list of those who had signed the request. In the same edition of the newspaper, an angry letter, signed 'SB' appeared. Given that the initials 'SB' stand for 'Stalybridge' and that the language is practically the same as that employed by the *Reporter's* editorials, it is likely that the newspaper decided to employ a commonly used tactic of the media – to write a letter to itself about the terrible actions of the mayor in order to influence the thinking of others:

Sir, - Stalybridge has once more exhibited itself as the one place in the country where blind prejudice reigns supreme, as the one place in the country where the common feelings of humanity are to be stifled by officialism in order to save the credit of the party.... The Mayor of Stalybridge is above all this, he is beyond the common feeling of humanity; he says that such expressions of opinion 'will do no good' will 'do harm rather than good' and with such reasoning he has snubbed the most respectable list of memorialists that was ever presented to a mayor of this borough ... Leave public questions of importance to be settled by your Mayor Robert Stanley Esquire, JP. You should not imagine you can understand questions of high state policy. You should not presume to think yourselves capable of criticising the conduct of great men. You are not qualified to judge impartially upon these things – your small minds cannot form just conceptions of the most important issues involved in them. When such as you meddle in these matters, you only become tools of crafty and designing men 'cat's paws in the hands of Russia'. 'Go home and be peaceable, my children, and thank your stars you have me to sit over you'. The people of Stalybridge are in effect, rudely told they are a set of fools who don't know what's what ... but if the Burgesses of this borough have any manhood in them, they will let this Mayor know that it is not his place to judge for them ... And he who would thus attempt to stifle free speech is only wanting the power and not the inclination for greater acts of tyranny. Yours etc. 'SB'

In the *Ashton Reporter*, owned by the same proprietor, an uncannily similar editorial was produced on 23rd September:

Men of all sorts and conditions signed a memorial to His Worship saying in effect with regards to the aforesaid matter 'On Stanley On', but Stanley did not appear to see it ... Mr Robert Stanley Mayor of Stalybridge, declares emphatically and ex cathedra that the ... government have 'taken the proper measures' ... if the mayor had been Stanley Pasha he would have adopted precisely the same means for addressing the raping, the pillaging and the firing ... 'the proper means' ... whilst they may, according to the rule of thumb, be 'very proper', are, nevertheless singularly ineffective ... Mr Robert Stanley, Mayor of Stalybridge like all expert controversialists, keeps his best arguments to finish up with ... for he deliberately expresses his opinions as follows; 'I consider the whole agitation on this matter to be the work of Russian agents'. Shades of David Urquhart and Chisholm Anstey - what are we coming to? What Russophobia has burst out in SB? Has the Mayor used the eye of an eagle or the lens of a microscope in order to arrive at this startling conclusion? Is it really true that we have - all of us - been stuffed full of Russian caviar and that our newspaper editors have generally been got at by artful Muscovite intrigues? Presumably, if you scratch Lord Hartington you will find a Cossack skin underneath .... A network of spies exists and has been cast over England - which is no longer in its right mind - and all except the mayor of SB has been blind to its abduction.

After the meeting had taken place, the *Stalybridge Reporter* gave a long and detailed account of the 'great meeting' on 23rd September, but its sub-header stated: 'Attempt To Upset The Meeting – Disgraceful Conduct Of A Few Conservatives'. One of the speakers had begun by saying that it had been said that Britain was becoming a nation of shopkeepers, and the irony of this was that, despite this, *"At Stalybridge, the population would be heard, not withstanding that a shopkeeper there had thought fit in the exercise of his right to say that a meeting should not be held (Laughter and Cheers) under his patronage."* Mr Summer, whose tramway Robert had so boldly defended previously, was one of the biggest critics of the Ottoman Empire and read aloud from a treatise that Gladstone had written, which stated, *"The Koran says that every Mohammedan shall slay ever Christian dog which crosses his path."*

Platt, a good friend of Gladstone, was one of the main speakers and gave a long treatise himself, using the occasion to provide the audience with his own views on Muslims:

Mahometans and Christians could live together in equality in a country, but never so long as the Mahometan was the ruler. It had been said that they [the British] must be just to the Turks. Well, he supposed the gentleman who had made that statement had in his mind the good old law, that they must 'Give the devil his due'. Now, if they were to give those Turkish devils their due, it would be to kick them all over the Bosphorus.

He went on to inform the crowd of some of the horrors that government ministers had been told of that had occurred in Bulgaria, *"Some of these poor Christians had been compelled to see some of their children roasted, and then to eat part of the children's flesh."* At these words, the 'disgraceful conduct' of Conservatives apparently erupted within the meeting, caused by a man named Joseph Leach, who attended the meeting with his supporters and decided to take his place – uninvited - on the platform. Clearly, Leach held similar views to those of Robert on the Bulgarian Affair and he kept trying to interrupt speakers in order to offer an amendment to the proposed motion condemning the actions of the Turks. A scuffle broke out, with Leach's supporters leaping across the desk of the newspaper reporters, and punches were thrown. Leach had to defend himself using his own crutches and one of the vicars received a kicking. The police had to physically break up the fracas, but whilst it seemed that many people were outraged at Robert's take on the matter, he still had a good degree of respect amongst some, such as Leach and his supporters. Councillor Ives, too, – even though he had wanted a meeting called – asked the meeting to add Robert's name onto a local committee to raise funds for those affected in Bulgaria, and he then asked for support for the mayor as a person, requesting three cheers from the crowd for Robert.

We cannot know, of course how any backlash might have affected Robert personally. It is likely, though, that the anger at his views caused him to decide not to continue as mayor, given that he stepped down just two months later when he could have been re-elected. However, it does seem that Robert Stanley was made of stern stuff; he was used to taking on corrupt mill owners and dodgy courtroom characters, not to mention obstreperous councillors and top politicians who had given him a grilling in 1869. So, it is probable that he was confident of his perspective on the matter and would not be swayed by what he clearly saw as sentiments that would, in all likelihood, drag Britain into a general war. Plus, as Robert's interview in *The Crescent* mentions, other mayors from Belfast, Cork and Wolverhampton followed his example.

CHAPTER 8

Pub Life. And the Ottomans
1877 – 1897

Most of this book has been written in chronological order but this chapter marks a slight departure from that approach, mainly because this is one of the most unknown portions of Robert's life but one that would probably have been a time of reflection, mingled with new discoveries, for him. Perhaps, too, it would have involved new concerns for his family as – albeit slowly – Robert's life began to take a turn in a rather different direction. For this reason, this chapter begins with his new life post-mayor but will thread back through a few decades to when his interest in foreign affairs first began.

The Move to the Pub

Robert's term as mayor ended in 1877 but he continued to be an alderman for Stalybridge and a magistrate until 1898. He was only 49 years old when he stepped down as mayor but, for a man of his skills and activity levels, he was clearly not ready to retire just yet.

It seems that Robert's family had been thinking about what we today would call their future 'work-life balance' and that someone (probably Robert) decided that taking over a pub might be an interesting business option for them. The pub that they acquired was the New Inn. Unlike most of the buildings that Robert was associated with, the New Inn is still in existence today and has not fallen foul of becoming a theme-pub; it is still a classic, working-man's pub. It lies at a main crossroads in the Hurst area of Ashton-under-Lyne, practically on the border with Stalybridge, and on the key thoroughfare to Mossley, towards the Saddleworth moors and West Yorkshire. The pub was only a few hundred yards from the local infirmary, today known as Tameside General Hospital, and the Ladysmith Barracks (which was established primarily as a result of the Bread Riots during the Cotton Famine year). Right outside of the hospital and opposite the barracks is The Odd Whim pub; Robert Stanley may have been aware of the irony of serving up pints in such proximity to Prophet Wroe's gatehouse for his New Jerusalem.

At the current time, we cannot be entirely sure if Robert continued with his grocer's business on Princess Street, Stalybridge, during the period 1877-98, but in 1896 there was an R. Stanley listed in the trade directory as owning a grocers, but this time at 61 Stamford Street in Stalybridge. During this time, he continued to have his tea trade business address in Manchester and most of his sons were listed in the censuses as commercial travellers. It would be likely that they were travelling salesmen, perhaps working for and with their father in selling tea and other goods to grocers.

Emma and Robert had been running their grocer's business for 30 years by the time that they took over the New Inn, with Robert having notched up some 40 years 'on the shop floor'. It would have been somewhat of a leap in the dark for this middle-aged couple. However, it seems that the plans for this new enterprise would have been for the entire family and not just for Robert and Emma. From consulting the list of owners of the New Inn, we can see that a Thomas Stanley took over the pub in 1878 until 1879. Thomas was the second son of Robert and he would have been 27 in 1878. There was then a gap of two years with no proprietor, and then Robert Stanley is listed by the brewery as being the next landlord in 1881.

This gap provokes some comment, because in the long list of the history of the ownership of the New Inn there are no other gaps. It might well be that the non-ownership represented a renovation period, an issue with the deeds or that Thomas had been acting as landlord during this time and had taken some sort of leave of absence. The latter theory might very well back up the information that our Auntie Gay received from distant relatives in the USA recently, who had heard that Thomas was a bit of an 'independent' soul! It could also have been that Thomas had not made a great success of the pub on his own and that his good old dad decided to step in and turn the business around for his son. Either way, we know that Robert and Emma and some of their (now mostly adult) children had made the New Inn their family home by 1881.

By the time that Robert and Emma had come to live at the New Inn, they had brought up ten children (baby George had died aged only a year old at a time when Robert had been a councillor for 18 years). In 1881, just shortly after the family had moved into the pub, the family consisted of: Thomas (27), Mary-Jane (25), Robert 'Unlucky Bob' (23), Emma junior (22), Sarah (20), John (15) and Alice (10). And then in the 1891 census everyone was ten years older, with Unlucky Bob, Emma junior and John all having left home.

The living quarters of the pub were sizeable and certainly big enough for a servant, which the family was employing by 1891, to live with them - a Mary Donald, who had been born in Stafford. Having a live-in servant was not necessarily a sign of being affluent; many working-class women employed 'live-in girls' or 'nurse girls' to help them manage their many children, especially if they had to go to work at the mill. Certainly, the occupation of being a publican was not an easy one during Victorian times. Although the working day might have felt less frantic to the couple, with slower starts to the day, after lunchtime the day and the evenings were no longer their own. Still, if any evening rowdiness with the customers did occur, the couple would have had grown-up sons on hand to help with the occasional eviction of inebriated punters.

Perhaps for Emma, an added attraction of moving to the pub would have been that of removing Robert from customers who had spent too much time in the shop chattering away or complaining about town council matters. The New Inn was still only some 20 – 25 minutes' walk away from the town hall but that extra bit of distance could have brought relief from local politics being immediately on their doorstep. The lack of historical evidence on Emma herself is frustrating but it is fair to say that she probably would not have been a particularly shy person. As wife of a councillor, and then a mayor, she would have been used to having many people visiting her home with various municipal and personal problems. Later on, as a landlord's wife – even if she was not comfortable herself in working behind the bar – she would have had to cope with regular society, general rowdiness and appearances as the partner to the man with his name 'over the door'.

Robert would still have played a big role in managing the pub, but the freedom from the shop floor and the endless meetings involved with being the mayor would also have permitted him to spend more time in Manchester at the Old Corn Exchange, meeting new and varied people from different backgrounds. It seems likely that it was at this point in his life when he finally had a little bit more time to look to the outside world for a different way of living and perhaps, ironically, he met and became friends with the first Muslims in his life whilst he was landlord of a pub.

The Booze Question

For many Muslims who have heard our family tell the story of Robert, this part of his life might seem to be a little bit puzzling. How could a Muslim have reconciled owning a pub with the fact that the Qur'an forbids the consumption of alcohol? However, we know for a fact that Robert was not a Muslim when he took over the New Inn; it was some 17 years later that he said Shahada. Christianity does not prohibit alcohol and many Christians support its consumption by quoting Bible verses such as 'a little wine is good for the stomach'. The question of Robert's views on alcohol is also a difficult one to answer. Shortly before her death, we asked our Granny Edith what she knew about her great-grandad, Robert. The only information that she could give us was, *"Nothing really – other than that people said he was a Rechabite."* No-one in my family had ever heard of this term before, but we soon discovered that it means someone who practises temperance. Of course, in relation to his later life and his conversion to Islam, this description makes perfect sense and, with hindsight, knowing that the family clearly wanted to either cover-up or forget that he had converted to Islam, this might have been the version that they preferred to use - their way of explaining that Robert was a little bit 'different' to the average man from the area. It is quite easy to imagine a Stalybridge accent saying, "Well, ol' Robert, 'ee's gone a bit religious-like, an' he dun't drink noremore." This would have been a preferable tale for the family to spin just prior to the outbreak of the First World War and increasing levels of Islamophobia in the UK.

Of course, it could have been that Robert did not drink alcohol himself, anyway. There were many Christian groups and sects that forbade the use of alcohol at this time – and many that still do. The Christian Israelites themselves were prohibited from its consumption by John Wroe, and the temperance movement in the West received enormous support throughout the 19th century and into the first few decades of the 20th century. 'Taking the pledge' – as agreeing to swear off alcohol was referred to - was a way of life for many. It was more than the dietary or lifestyle choice it often is today – it was a campaign, an absolute passion, and it was not just the prerogative of the religious. Many secularists were also horrified at the effect that drink was having on the population and so, although the temperance movement found its strongest support in the Dissenting churches, it also included champions from the Church of England and those who were concerned with the health, social and economic wellbeing of the population – particularly that of the working class.

The odds are, though, that Robert did regularly drink alcohol before becoming a Muslim, even if he had been close to the Christian Israelite church in his younger years. In all the temperance-related meetings that were examined during this research, there is no mention of any member of the Stanley family. Added to this is the fact that it is difficult to believe anyone who belonged to the temperance movement would buy a pub and run it themselves as a business investment. But also, 'male culture' in these south-east Lancashire towns very much revolved around pub life. Stalybridge itself was home to a famous brewery – Heginbotham's – and the production and sale of alcohol

The New Inn today

was a key component of the local and national economy. For example, the town council discussion in August 1874, when Councillor Adshead said that most of the council, *"business must be carried out at either The Feathers or at Cockerhill Chapel … there was scarcely a member of Cockerhill Chapel who did not hold some office in the town."*

Adshead was only half joking, because Stalybridge's oldest parish church was Old St George's at Cocker Hill. On moving to Stalybridge with his new bride, Robert's home and grocer's shop was located very close to the church and if he – as presumably he had - drifted away from any form of involvement with the Christian Israelites it would have made good sense to start attending Old St Georges. For one thing, the church was deemed to be more 'low church' than the nearby 'high church' of New St George's, but it also had a large congregation and an enormously loyal following of the great and good wealthy Conservative families of the town. If anything, the Conservative party tended towards the laissez-faire attitude in all respects – and this included the consumption of alcohol, whereas more adherents of temperance would be found throwing their lot in with the Liberals.

Joseph Rayner Stephens - a man whom we now know had a strong admiration for Robert - was also a Tory radical, but a famous Dissenter, too, and was frequently wheeled out by the brewery lobby in order to sing of the joys of

146

booze. The Licensing Act 1872 had responded to concerns by the temperance movement, and pub hours had been restricted, with a subsequent backlash by the brewery industry and fans of public houses. *The Stalybridge Reporter* described Stephens as being, *'famed for the protection of the fair and honest trade,'* which was otherwise known as the brewery trade. It printed a lengthy speech made by him at the North Cheshire Licensed Beer and Wine Retail Association annual dinner, which was held in Stalybridge and reported on in their 9th March 1874 edition. There he spoke strongly in favour of the odd tipple, *"When men, women, and children are 12 ½ hours in the mill – will you tell me that they are not liable to the temptation of wanting something to sup? Are they not very dry, and do they not feel dull and heavy? Do they not want some excitement and stimulant?"*

Reverend Stephens did not condone drunkenness and the ruinous path that alcohol could lead to for some. He explicitly stated that any problem of over-reliance on alcohol amongst the working class was always to do with their unhappiness at the terrible conditions that they were forced to live under, thanks to the exploitative middle and upper classes.

It seems, therefore, that there would never have been a moral dilemma for Robert owning and managing a pub before he became a Muslim. As a magistrate he - more than most - had been witness to the misery, poverty and despair that alcohol addiction brought to the lives of those that it blighted. On taking over the New Inn he probably thought that the average working man could control his consumption and simply use pub life as a chance to improve sociability and enjoy their much-needed leisure time.

The Pub as a Hub

Pub life was of huge importance in the area, with dozens of pubs in Ashton alone. The public houses and hotels provided entertainment, social life, cultural life and employment for many, not to mention a bit of warmth from the cold and much-needed escape from the crowded chaos of family life. It goes without saying that a pub was not somewhere you would find a 'lady' on her own, other than those that may have worked behind the bar. Working class women did go to pubs but would very rarely do so without their husband and, even then, the vast majority of 'respectable working class' women tended to look down on those that did so. Pubs were – like nearly all other public spheres at this period – the exclusive domain of men.

For a small number of people, the path to the pub was one of rack and ruin – but Robert Stanley, as a magistrate, would not have laid the problems of society at the doorstep of the pub; he had seen far too many people access drink outside of the pubs in order to blame the businesses themselves for that. His view would probably have been that the pub was not to blame – the person was.

The Stanleys' concerns in relation to prestige, respectability and decent behaviour would not have allowed the 'hoi-polloi' to frequent the New Inn. From newspaper cuttings obtained from the time we can see that, in addition to providing the usual place to drink and socialise, the New Inn acted as an important place for local functions – entertaining parties, for example from the Hurst Village Brass Band and the Stayley Hunt. It seems that the borough coroners from both Stalybridge and Ashton also felt the pub to be a worthy place to meet, choosing the venue as a base to hold their formal inquests. Although there exists no comprehensive list of inquests held at the New Inn, quite remarkably a few newspaper cuttings from the time exist and show us a selection of the sort of inquests that were held at Robert and Emma's home: the death of a man on the railway line at Ashton's Park Parade station, the fatal burning of a worker at Stalybridge's Copley Mill, the deaths of several toddlers due to fire in the family home (all in relation to being too close to the fire and their clothes catching alight) and an accident in the enamel works that killed a bobbin-carrier.

The New Inn was probably chosen as a venue for inquests because it lay close to the boundary line between both towns and/or because of its proximity to the local infirmary, whose doctors may have needed summoning to attend. But it also points to the fact that the venue was deemed to be a respectable one and perhaps had a sense of impartiality, thanks to the ownership of Robert Stanley, who was still serving as a magistrate at this time.

Robert and Emma would probably have enjoyed the fact that their establishment was chosen as a place where such important legal proceedings took place, but it is quite likely that, after the initial novelty in relation to the change of lifestyle and occupation had worn off, the day-to-day running of a pub might have seemed somewhat mundane after the constant ups and downs of civic life in Stalybridge. There were still incidents and excitements in the area during this period and, in 1890, a particularly protracted spinners' strike occurred, which lasted for seven months and required some 50 extra constables being sworn in to deal with the disturbances. But in general, the social context throughout the 16 years that the Stanley family lived at the pub were quiet in comparison to their previous home and work life in Stalybridge.

The Tea Road to Manchester: and Beyond
It is likely that this was a point in Robert's life where he met an increasing number of both foreign and locally-based Muslims. In fact, Robert's younger cousin – Deane Stanley, son of Uncle John Stanley – ran a Turkish towel company based just down the road from the New Inn, in Ashton, which would have inevitably involved discussions about Turkish matters, as would Robert's own tea-trading links with countries that were predominantly Muslim.

Coffee was first consumed on a large scale by Yemeni Sufi Muslims during the 15th century. As Islam spread, so did the liking for coffee, becoming an important component in creating and consolidating the Ottoman Empire during the 16th century. The key ingredient of coffee that we now know as caffeine was deemed to be more acceptable to the Islamic religion than alcohol. Unlike alcohol, it was not generally deemed to be 'sukr' (an intoxicant) whereas alcohol, according to Hanafi law, left the drinker, *"incapable of distinguishing a man from a woman or the earth from the heavens."* Coffee houses were particularly popular in Cairo and Constantinople, but this was soon set to change. During the 18th century, religious rulers tightened restrictions on the use of coffee and, after the British landed at Tangiers in 1718, Morocco was suddenly flooded with green tea, which had lost market share in Britain due to the ever-increasing problem of contamination.

Tea took off enormously in this part of the world; as a result of the Crimean War, British traders had lost access to the Russian market, meaning that exports from Morocco and Turkey massively increased. Soon tea began to be consumed in higher quantities in Britain. It was a lucrative business in many ways and Robert's trade was both very common and extremely competitive. By the time of Victoria's reign, tea "had become the symbol of British oppression" for many working on the tea plantations overseas. [85]

Because tea was such big business, it was also an industry that was susceptible – literally – to corruption. Adulterated tea was a huge problem during this era and when Robert was first elected mayor in 1874 the government had recently taken efforts to address it through passing an Adulteration Act. As with other moves towards better public health, the 1870s saw a crackdown on the 'filling' of food items such as tea, where it was all too easy to place unpalatable extras into a blend in order to bulk out the leaves. As a tea trader himself, Robert must have been very aware of the ease with which this sort of practise

Manchester's Old Corn Exchange, 1895

could occur. On 25th July 1874, the *Reporter* recounted a case where William Pickering, a Stalybridge shopkeeper was found by the local police inspector, Captain Arrowsmith, to have adulterated blends of Caper Tea and Gunpowder Tea. As inspector of local foods, Arrowsmith regularly undertook the practise of buying samples from local shops and examining them; he had always advised shopkeepers to send him samples to test before they bought them out of bond. The batch sold by Pickering to Arrowsmith contained 2oz each of steel filings and other white mineral powders. Robert was the presiding magistrate who heard this case at Stalybridge Petty Sessions. Pickering's business was based not far from Robert's own shop, but Robert decided to let him off with just a fine as opposed to a prison sentence. Perhaps he realised just how vulnerable a hurried local shop owner could be when purchasing batches from an unknown supply chain source.

Throughout his tea-trading life, the fact that (China aside) the biggest tea-trading countries were primarily Muslim (Indonesia, Turkey, Iran, Bangladesh and Lebanon) would have meant that Robert - far more than the average person from Stalybridge - would have been exposed to face-to-face interaction with those who had previously lived overseas. During the second half of the 19th century, Victorian society began to develop a much greater interest in the Middle East and

[85] Wild, J. *Black Gold*, Harper, 2005, p. 134.

in Orientalism. Even *the Stalybridge Reporter* happily ran series such as 'At Home With The Shah Of Persia' on a regular basis but for most locals living in these towns there would be no chance to ever meet 'a foreigner'. Robert, however, would have personally known tea and coffee merchants who came from the Ottoman Empire. His great knowledge about Britain's actions abroad - gleaned from reading the newspapers and engaging in discussions in Urquhart's Foreign Affairs Committees – would have found an outlet to be shared with the very people who had far more personal experience of these matters than he had. Tea would have been another cornerstone of Robert's self-directed and informal education.[86] And it may well have been these trading networks that led him to hearing about a new convert to Islam, a man some 28 years younger than himself who went by the name of William – now Abdullah – Quilliam.

As mentioned in the previous chapter, by the time that Robert became mayor he had begun to take a great deal of interest in Britain's affairs overseas. Robert's refusal to call a meeting about the Bulgarian Atrocities was the one and only time that he risked being pilloried in public as an unpopular man and jeopardising his standing as mayor. But why was he so interested in these issues? Understanding this aspect of his life helps to further explain the path that he eventually took in becoming a Muslim. Thanks to *The Crescent*, it becomes more obvious that his concerns lay not solely on the issue of Bulgaria but on many more international questions.

When most people change their religion and begin to grow their learning in relation to places with strong links to that religion, they often become more politicised in relation to contemporary issues affecting those regions. The UK's 'New Muslim' community is an excellent example of this; meet the average British Muslim convert and you cannot fail to be impressed by their knowledge of other countries where Islam predominates.

However, Robert Stanley did not become a Muslim until 1898 and yet, during the last few months of his mayoral term in 1876, he felt strongly enough about what was being said about Ottoman Muslim actions in Bulgaria that he was willing to risk ruffling feathers both locally and in the corridors of Westminster. Just two years previously, Robert had declared very publicly that he was a Christian when he took part in the churching of the mayor parade. And yet in 1876 he was refusing to align himself with national Christian outrage at what seemed to have been occurring in the region.

We have learned by now that Robert was a rather unique personality, thinking for himself, being willing to be impartial and to support the underdog. But just how and why did Robert come about his opinions on the affairs of Bulgaria and other foreign countries? In order to answer this question, we need to spend some time looking at the role of Britain and its entanglements with the Ottoman Empire and then relate it back to his own life.

---

[86] Another strange twist of family fate: after Robert's death, no-one seemed to stay involved in the tea trade. However – like Islam – tea and coffee resurrected themselves in our lives when our family co-founded 'Dark Woods Coffee', an ethical, high-end roastery and importer based in West Yorkshire.

Ottoman Growth and Decline

The Ottoman Empire receives very little attention in British school history lessons today, but in the 19th century the Turks, their customs and their presence in the world generated a great deal of discussion. The Ottoman period – the name coming from Osman I, circa 1300 - lasted for more than 600 years, and at the height of its phenomenal influence its largely Islamic empire spanned most of south-eastern Europe, taking in Hungary, the Balkans, Greece, sections of Ukraine, and parts of the Middle East, North Africa and the Arabian Peninsula. During the 17th century, these Muslim rulers governed the waters of the Mediterranean and their traders had a massive presence across the region. The ruler of the Ottoman Empire was based in Constantinople (now Istanbul) and was known as the Sultan (or Caliph). This leadership was based on that of a monarchy, with heirs apparent.

Prior to the First World War, the Ottoman Empire was in a state of transition and decline. A failed invasion of Austria drove Turkish presence from Central Europe and by the 1850s the Turks were faced with rising nationalism and fragmented ethnic groups that were increasingly demanding self-governance and separation. As the Ottomans were eventually routed from North Africa, their economy began to fail – being overtaken by the stronger French, British and other European systems to which the Ottomans owed hundreds of millions of pounds. The Tsar of Russia, Nicholas I, himself summed it up when he described the Empire as 'the sick man of Europe'.

However, the leading powers of Europe were not pleased to see the vast might and power of the Ottomans wilting. Turkey controlled areas of enormous strategic importance in the region, such as the Bosporus Straits – and there was rising concern at the territorial ambitions of Austria-Hungary and Russia. Keeping the Ottoman Empire together was crucial in order to keep the existing buffer zone. As the 20th century approached, Turkey began to feel increasing pressure as to which European power it should ally itself with. For the Sultan, a partnership with France was out of the question, France being a close ally of the despised Russia. So, when the First World War broke out, it transpired that the Ottomans had chosen Germany, a power equally fiercely opposed to all-things Russian.

There has been a recent revival in British films, books and media in relation to the Victorians' fascination with all-things Ottoman and with all-things Islamic. At this time in history, there was a huge interest amongst European writers and painters with the more poetic and supposedly sensualist Muslim societies. Western Orientalists embraced learning Arabic and other languages spoken by Muslims; archaeological focus on the region flourished and even the military across Europe and the USA adopted the fashion of the Zouaves (first used by Berber tribesmen). For many people, the Islamic religion was proving to be fascinating - even a young Winston Churchill's family had to beg him not to ever consider converting to Islam as he was spending so much time in the company of Muslims.

Russian Fear and Loathing

The Russians have always captivated both the interests and the deep concerns of many in the West. But even before the paranoia of the Cold War and the more recent spats with Putin, such concerns and even loathing of Russia has existed for two millennia. A Russophobic narrative has not been a product of even the past two hundred years; much longer-held beliefs have ensured that there was an almost unbridgeable clash of civilisations between the West and Russia.

For those who supported the Ottoman Empire this deep mistrust was only natural given that, under Catherine the Great in the 18th century, the Russians had made it clear that their ultimate ambition was to reclaim Constantinople. The Russian Empire wished to seize Turkey's capital from what they perceived to be an Islamic stranglehold and to turn it into the centre of Christian Orthodoxy. At this point in history, the Holy Land itself relied very much on the stability being provided by the presence of the Turks who had control of the region. Jerusalem in the 19th century continued to be a flashpoint for violence and witnessed aggression as a result of street battles between Christian sects, which the Ottomans who governed the region were forced to try and police.

This situation - and continuous Russian Orthodox proselytizing of Catholics in Poland – only served, for many in the West, to cast the Ottoman Empire as a more stable example of civilisation. For many Westerners, even though the Ottoman Empire followed Islam as opposed to Christianity, the history of their actions and approach to governance of their Empire continued to offer preferable tactics to those of the Russians. The aggression of many Christian sects such as the Maronites and Druze in the Levant and the non-stop fighting that seemed to occur between the Greek Orthodox and the Armenians proved for many to be poor examples of Christian behaviour and something that they did not wish to be associated with, at the expense of Muslim lives.

This could well have been the attitude of Robert Stanley in 1876 when he refused to call a meeting about the Bulgarian Atrocities. Although there is nothing in the primary sources to indicate his views on the Russian Empire, or on the actions of Christianity as it manifested itself in Bulgaria and in similar regions, we can find out more thanks to his letters in *The Crescent* – both before and after he became a Muslim. Robert's letters, as published by Quilliam, clearly illustrate the fact that he saw the hand of Russian agents in many affairs and incidents within the region. Did Robert become a fan of the Ottoman Empire as a result of his views on the Russian government? Did his interest in the antics of the Russians lead to his fascination with the Ottomans? Or did something else happen that led to his growing disillusionment with the actions of so-called Christians in the Balkans – and perhaps at home?

These are impossible questions to answer accurately, given the lack of a diary written by Robert, but there are various theories that we might want to consider. To begin with, his association with the Christian Israelites and this group's natural sympathies with the Jewish race and religion may have influenced Robert from a very young age to perceive any nations that persecuted Jews as a threat to others. During the period 1791-1835, the Russian Empire began acquiring large amounts of territory from the-then Polish-Lithuanian Commonwealth, areas that had considerable Jewish populations. The Russian government allowed (reluctant) Jewish communities to continue to live in these areas and forbade most of them from moving elsewhere unless they were prepared to convert to Russian Orthodoxy. The first pogroms against Jews during this period occurred in 1821 in Greece (also a long-standing enemy of the Turks) and soon spread throughout the new Russian territories. Interestingly, this year was significant in the growth of the Christian Israelite church in Ashton-under-Lyne, too, and John Wroe himself frequently referred to underhand Russian antics and agents.

In 1881, shortly after Robert's mayoral term had ended, Tsar Alexander II was assassinated. Some, urged on by the Russian press, blamed Jewish agents for the murder, given that one of the perpetrators was of Jewish origin. Consequently, from 1881-84, waves of anti-Jewish riots swept across south-western Russia (modern day Poland and Ukraine) with more than 200 accompanying incidents within the Russian Empire. Certainly, the horrors that many Jews in the region had to face during this period would have been cause for concern for Robert. However, it does seem that his interest in the region pre-dated the later wave of pogroms and would probably have extended beyond the atrocities committed against the Jews.

Travelling (Vicariously) with Urquhart

Thanks to Quilliam's interview with Robert published in *The Crescent*, we know that any views on overseas issues that he had developed as a young man would have been further influenced by the famous diplomat, traveller and campaigner – David Urquhart.

Urquhart was born in 1805 and was some 23 years senior to Robert Stanley. Oxbridge educated and from a privileged upbringing, he travelled to the East and fought in the 1827-28 Greek War of Independence – just at the time that Robert was born. His reports from the region – championing the Greek cause - earned him the attention of the British government, who saw him as a source of talent and great intelligence. He was despatched to Constantinople as a diplomat for British interests to Turkey from 1831-34, with the mission of trying to agree the border between Turkey and Greece and attempting to obtain the support of Sultan Mahmud II. However, instead of remaining neutral, he became enamoured with Turkish culture and was appalled at increasing Russian interventions in the area. He wrote *Turkey and its Resources,* which campaigned for British support of the Sultan, and even designed the national flag for Circassia, but he soon came into conflict with others due to this anti-Moscow pamphlet.

In 1835 he was appointed as secretary of the British Embassy at Constantinople but was recalled to Britain when British attempts to halt Russian aggression in Circassia failed. He left the diplomatic service but continued with his writing and campaigning and became the Conservative MP for Stafford from 1847-52, just at the time that Robert would have been making his grocer's and tea trading businesses a success. Determined to draw public attention to foreign policy issues at a time when Chartism seemed to be garnering most of the British headlines, he created his own 'Foreign Affairs Committees' (FACs) to promote his causes and to stimulate discussion in relation to the Government's actions abroad. A network of these FACs was set up across the country and became known as 'Urquhartite' groups. Interestingly, three of these committees appeared in Robert's locality; one in Ashton-under-Lyne, one in Gamesley (part of Glossop, just a few miles from Robert's home), but most significantly of all, one in Stalybridge itself. In 1856, Urquhart became owner of *The Free Press* (later renamed *The Diplomatic Review*) which included contributions from Karl Marx. In 1860, his ever-widening interests on the impact of British foreign policy spurred him to write a book on Lebanon.

Balliol College at Oxford University holds papers on Urquhart's FACs and it is important to note that there are various communications between Lord Stanley of Alderley and Urquhart. Lord Stanley is a fascinating character himself and one of the earliest recorded converts to Islam. Although my family has been told previously that there was some sort of genealogical link between our branch and the Stanleys of Alderley, we have been unable to prove it to date. Robert, however, would have been aware of this famous man who shared his name, lived not far away and who lived life as a British Muslim, along with being a peer of the realm and a diplomatic representative of the Government overseas. It is more or less certain that the two men met, and this may well – at first - have been a result of involvement in Urquhart's FACs, and then later on at the Liverpool Muslim Institute, with Quilliam (see Chapter 9).

David Urquhart

Although we have no evidence of correspondence between Urquhart and Robert himself, and have no proof that Robert was a member of the Stalybridge FAC, and although there is very little information in existence on these FACs in his local areas, a chance 'find' was stumbled across in the *Reporter*. The letter was written by a rather disgruntled reader in June 1863 – the very year that Robert was first elected councillor:

Sir – I was not aware until the other day that we had a 'Foreign Affairs Committee' in Stalybridge. In looking over the London Times I noticed a statement to the effect that petition had been presented to parliament from the Stalybridge Foreign Affairs Committee, praying that government would restore the Prince Aseem to his lawful rights … Now who Prince Aseem is, I do not know, neither do I know who the Individuals are who sit in solemn secrecy … There is no doubt that these men are in possession of information which, if made public, would convulse all Europe. They are well up, no doubt, in all matters foreign; and if I knew these individuals I would certainly be led to regard them with a kind of superstitious awe. … If Englishmen would organise 'Home Affairs Committees' and attend to their own business instead of groping after Prince Aseem Jah, it would be much better … there are many people in Stalybridge who, no doubt, prefer looking after other people's business to minding their own …But it does not follow that these people are wise in their own generation. Indeed, an individual whose business is to meddle with 'foreign affairs' will be blind to the wants and requirements of their own homes…But there is one matter that I would like to bring before the notice of the Foreign Affairs Committee and if they succeed in putting it down, I venture to promise them a glorious immortality. It is the American war. Can they do nothing in this matter ..? Yours respectfully, 'Exotic', Stalybridge 24th June, 1863.

It seems that the 'charity begins at home' sentiment was as common then as it is today! Robert, who seems highly likely to have been involved in this committee, was perhaps seen as an intermeddler not only because of his involvement with trying to prevent voting malpractices but also because he had strong interest in international issues.

It is interesting, too, that 'Exotic' pointed to the American Civil War issue. Given that the war and the stoppage of cotton had resulted in such dire consequences for local people, the correspondent felt that it was hypocritical for local men to be so outwardly focused on all-things Oriental. However, we should also note that this letter was written the day after Robert chaired the debate in the town hall on 'The American War'. This fact could just be a coincidence, but it is also likely that the disgruntled reader had attended the debate and come away feeling rather more fired-up about the subject. Ironic, then, that the chairperson of the debate on the USA was probably part of the group being accused of neglecting the issue!

Islamic Ambassador?

Urquhart had become an ambassador for Islam and for the Ottomans, even though his own personal beliefs were creeping closer to that of Roman Catholicism.[87] He had learned through his own first-hand experience to have an enormous respect for Islam and its practices, in comparison to what he saw as the hypocritical actions of many Christians. Orlando Figes, in his 'History of the Crimean War', quoted Urquhart when he declared Islam under the Ottomans to be a uniquely, *"tolerant, moderating force"* and:

> *What traveller has not observed the fanaticism, the antipathy of all these [Christian] sects – their hostility to each other? Who has traced their actual repose to the toleration of Islamism? Islamism, calm, absorbed, without spirit of dogma, or views of proselytism, imposes at present on the other creeds the reserve and silence which characterize itself. But let this moderator be removed, and the humble professions now confined to the sanctuary would be proclaimed in the court and the military camp; political power and political enmity would combine with religious domination and religious animosity; the empire would be deluged in blood, until a nervous arm – the arm of Russia – appears to restore harmony, by despotism. [88]*

Robert Stanley would have been 25 years old at the start of the Crimean War. In 1853, following Russia's decision to seize Crimea from the Turks (Crimea until this point had always served as a vassal to the Ottomans), the Sultan declared war on Russia. The Russians were feeling an increased need to take control of the

---

[87] At a time when the Catholic Church declared the Doctrine of Papal Infallibility, Urquhart became a proponent of 'theological dimension' (a world-wide canon law enforced by the agency of the papacy).

[88] D. Urquhart, *Russia and Turkey*, Ridgway, 1835, p 87.

Bosporus Straits and Greece complied with them, looking to Russia to defend their own interests in the region. Britain's mistrust of Russia's interests had led to them trying to improve relations with the Ottomans but it needed both Greece and Turkey to be 'on the side' of Britain. It therefore started out at the beginning of the conflict attempting to be as neutral as possible. And yet, the most immediate reason for the outbreak of war was the issue of the Holy Land; the French were concerned that Christian minorities who followed Roman Catholicism were yet again being forced towards the Russian Eastern Orthodox church.

As an avid reader and one who delighted in absorbing facts, Robert would have anticipated that this war was going to culminate in a new balance of power within Europe and the Balkans. It inevitably did - resulting in the creation of Austria-Hungary and the affiliation of this new state with the Russian Empire. Robert told Quilliam in *The Crescent* that he had met Urquhart some 30 years previously – this would have placed their meeting just after the end of the Crimean War. Urquhart, like many others, had declared Great Britain's role in the war to be wrongful. He felt that Turkey was still in a place to be able to fight her own battles without the assistance of the likes of Britain, which was clearly using the war in order to consolidate its own regional interests.

In relation to domestic policy, Urquhart was caught up in the issue of public sanitation. He opposed government legislation on sanitary reform on several occasions – arguing that statutory-imposed action was wrong: a sentiment that might have gained some sympathy from the Conservative-supporting Robert. He did his best to try and convince others that state-imposed decrees were not the answer to solving the actual causes of disease. Instead, he pointed towards the lifestyle that Muslim Turks had adopted as a far better way of living, *"If London were [Muslim],"* he wrote, *"the population would bathe regularly, have a better-dressed dinner for [its] money, and prefer water to wine or brandy, gin or beer."* Urquhart lived on the Continent from 1864 until his death and his own observations from his life overseas caused him to become an advocate of the virtues of Turkish baths. He declared that Muslims and their adherence to cleanliness rituals and facilities, such as the baths, were literally lifesavers for these populations. He was directly involved in establishing various Turkish baths in Britain, including the one in Salford, an area of Manchester afflicted terribly by disease and poor sanitation in the early to mid-19th century.

Urquhart himself died in 1877, around the time that Robert said that he had met him and when Robert was still mayor. The meeting between the two men, which was mentioned by Robert in *The Crescent,* may have taken place at a lecture by Urquhart in Manchester or at one of the branches of his FACs, but wherever it was, it had a profound impact on Robert.

The Influence of Urquhart

Born with an inquisitive mind and a yearning for justice, the influence of both John Stanley and John Wroe's interests in international issues may have set a blueprint for Robert that was strongly stimulated by David Urquhart both in terms of British foreign policy and in terms of a growing interest in Islam. Even some of the titles of books written about Urquhart or including important sections on him, such as Robinson's *David Urquhart: Some Chapters in the Life of a Victorian Knight-Errant of Justice and Liberty* and AJP Taylor's *The Trouble Makers: Dissent over Foreign*

Policy 1792-1939 sound uncannily like the sort of man – or the sort of approach – that Robert ended up adopting in his public years from 1863 onwards.

It is somewhat ironic that a non-Muslim, who was closer to conversion to Roman Catholicism than to Islam, had such a profound effect on Robert and that Urquhart was the first person mentioned in Quilliam's life story of Robert Stanley. But this could have meant that his conversion was even more heartfelt, logical and conclusive.

In many ways, Urquhart might be seen as the natural precursor to Quilliam in terms of his being a consolidating influencer in matters of both faith and politics for Robert. Urquhart would certainly have been viewed by many in Britain as being somewhat of an eccentric, and not just in relation to his outspokenness with regards to British injustice overseas - he also had the habit of dressing in Turkish robes. Yet despite the words and the garb, Urquhart was also accepted as part of the British Establishment – evidence for Robert, perhaps, that his respectability might be able to be preserved if he ever made such a strident decision in his own life. Urquhart's life and influence no doubt had sowed some seeds for Robert. They took a long time to grow but were rooted deeply.

A Tea Threat?

It would, however, be wrong to conclude that Robert's journey towards Islam was simply a matter of falling in love with the faith and with the people that he had met. There may well have been economic reasons behind why Robert – at least initially – became fascinated with the Ottoman Empire.

A huge part of his family's livelihood relied on the tea trade, and this factor would have been even more important to him as he stepped down from the day-to-day running of a pub and of a grocer's shop. It sounds cynical to suggest that Robert wanted to preserve the Ottoman Empire so that he could keep his existing supply lines of tea open, but it should be considered. After all, it would be very unusual for any small businessman not to express concern over the fact that their ongoing sources might be interrupted or tampered with. Even if Robert's protectionist attitudes towards the Ottoman Empire were not prejudiced in such a way (because, after all, we do not know for certain just how reliant Robert's profits were on batches of tea brought from Ottoman lands), his interaction with Turkish tea traders on the floor of the Old Corn Exchange would have been highly coloured by these traders' own concerns for their economic futures and the need to keep their own supply chains and links with Britain open.

The Failings of Christianity

We have seen that Robert publicly affirmed his Christianity at the outset of his mayoral period in 1874. However, some 28 years later, he chose to abandon Christianity: indeed, to publicly criticise the Church and its followers. The path to Islam seems to have been an extremely long one for this man. To convert to another religion at the age of 69 is unusual at any rate in modern-day society and even more so during the Victorian era - and in a place of great conservative tradition. Because we can never know why he took such a long time to change his faith, and because he never stated a sole reason for his decision, we can only guess that his growing disaffection for the ways that British Christians were meting out their foreign policies overseas – in particular with regards to the Ottoman Empire and the treatment of Muslims - were key in nudging him closer to Islam. And, of course, without access to copies of *The Crescent* which contain his letters we would not know that this gradual change had occurred in his mindset whilst he was living at the New Inn.

Quilliam and the other converts frequently levelled the word 'hypocrisy' at the conduct of the 'Christian' British Empire and of Christian factions overseas. But like Liverpool, the town of Stalybridge had provided some sterling examples of un-Christian behaviour on the very part of those who were meant to be its ambassadors. Sectarian conflict and divisions were frequent, not only between Catholics and Protestants but even within the same church denomination. Robert may have only just turned 21 when he came to live in Stalybridge, but his own church – Old St George's – had been the centre of a national furore. It seems that the persecution of the Christian Israelites, the trouble between the two St George's, the Murphy Riots and the ongoing sectarian rows at home and abroad, along with the influence of Urquhart, were the key ingredients that set the stage for Robert becoming seriously interested in Islam.

And then he met his final influencer: Mr William 'Abdullah' Quilliam.

CHAPTER 9

Quilliam and the Liverpool Converts
1887 – 1898

"...An age where if you didn't conform, your picture was turned to the wall for all time." Patricia Gordon, commenting on the life and times of her grandfather, Abdullah Quilliam.[89]

Introducing Quilliam

Quilliam's name has been mentioned in previous chapters. Some readers will already know much about him. Others will have never heard his name before. Whatever the case, in trying to understand what this man would have signified to Robert Stanley, we need to explore some of Quilliam's own biographical detail.

William Quilliam was born on the Isle of Man in 1856. His family was wealthy, middle-class and well-known amongst the Manx population. Quilliam was raised as a Wesleyan Methodist and from a young age campaigned alongside his parents against the evils of alcohol. But in addition to being strong teetotal activists, the Quilliam family had outspoken opinions on other social issues. They were firmly against the horrors of slavery, for example, and the brutality of capital punishment. Because Quilliam came from a Non-Conformist church-going family, which in the main usually tended towards the Liberals, many scholars have presumed that he was a Liberal. Others have pointed to the fact that because Quilliam was pro-trade union, he would have had socialist inclinations.

William 'Abdullah' Quilliam

However, whilst researching the life and times of Robert, there seemed to me to be similarities of views on class and politics

---

[89] R. Geaves, *Islam in Victorian Britain – the Life and Times of Abdullah Quilliam*, Kube, 2010 p.283.

between all the key figures in Robert's life: John Wroe, John Stanley, Joseph Rayner Stephens, David Urquhart and Quilliam. It seemed to me that Quilliam had rather more in common with these 'Tory Radicals' than he did with either Liberals or socialists. Yahya Birt's latest research on Quilliam's political affiliations have now demonstrated that this was indeed the case and that Quilliam even put himself forward as a Conservative parliamentary candidate in 1882.[90] Both Robert and Quilliam, therefore, would have shared a similar outlook on life before the issue of Islam even came into play.

Quilliam's Liverpool

The port of Liverpool is only a short ferry ride across the North Sea from the Isle of Man, and the Quilliam family had a strong connection with the city. Quilliam was educated at the Liverpool Institute and, although the Quilliams retained a family home and remained on the Isle of Man, Quilliam settled down in the city in order to build up a legal business.

During the second half of the 19th century, Liverpool outshone London in many ways. Whilst Manchester was the UK's capital in terms of King Cotton, Liverpool was riding the waves thanks to the Manchester Ship Canal, the Leeds to Liverpool canal network and the new railway infrastructure. As the Leeds to Liverpool route was created and carved out the main artery of trade and riches across the north of England, the frenetic pace of capitalism increased in intensity. Liverpool was the centre of the modern world for commodities, for an influx of immigrants and for the outpouring of emigrants to the Americas, not to mention the shameful slave trade on which the port had built its riches during the 18th century.

Like its rival, Manchester, Liverpool experienced a dismal economic gap between rich and poor. Being born into a philanthropist family, the young Quilliam wanted to use his legal skills to help others less fortunate than he was. Even before his conversion to Islam, he had already made a name for himself by championing the sort of causes that many other solicitors would simply not touch. He was a fiery and passionate advocate for Liverpool's most destitute, forgoing payment where the individual could not afford it. He gained a reputation for being an exceptionally honest and principled man, even though in later life he was thought of as somewhat eccentric, appearing at ceremonies in his Turkish robes with a pet monkey perched on his shoulder. In many respects, Quilliam was not dissimilar in attitude to the great northern social philanthropists of the time: the Rowntrees and Cadburys in Yorkshire, Hugh Mason in Ashton and the Lever Brothers in Port Sunlight. However, rather than being an employer who provided decent housing and fair pay, Quilliam instead did his bit for suffering people through the donation of his legal expertise.

Like Robert, Quilliam's interests embraced civic affairs and local and international politics. Unlike him, though, young Quilliam had received a top-quality formal education, one that took him to university and equipped him with a professional qualification. He also had wealthy parents who could back him as he set up his own business and – crucially - who would bankroll his desire to travel

---

[90] Y.Birt, *The Quilliams, Popular Conservatism and the New Trade Unionism in Liverpool,* Islamic Review Special Edition, 2019.

overseas and to experience first-hand the British Empire and other cultures. This opportunity to travel was a key factor in Quilliam's own path to Islam, which occurred in 1887 after visiting Morocco (although in one account of his life, he stated that it occurred at the age of 26 when he visited France, Algeria and Tunisia). At the time of his conversion, he was 32 years old; Robert was 28 years his senior and old enough to be his father. But despite his comparative youth, Quilliam is famed for building an astonishing Muslim convert community in the UK.

Contemporary Quilliam

Today, Quilliam's name is by far the most well-known of all white British-born converts, eclipsing those of Yusuf Islam (Cat Stevens) and Sinead O'Connor. However, his journey towards Islam was nowhere near as lengthy as the 70-year-old Robert's was. Making comparisons between Robert's life and the background of the other well-known converts such as Lord Headley, Marmaduke Pickthall, Lord Stanley and with Quilliam himself, underscores the incredible achievements of Robert and perhaps renders the obstacles that this Stalybridge man had to overcome even more impressive.

When my family first learned about Robert's association with Quilliam, my brother had already been a Muslim for nine years and was very familiar with the name of Abdullah Quilliam. For academics and students with a background in Islamic Studies, the word 'Quilliam' is an extremely well known one – indeed, a friend taking Islamic Studies at SOAS in London confided in me that whenever the name of Quilliam was mentioned in class the general reaction was a groan of 'oh, not him again'. But the fame of Abdullah Quilliam has not always been so amongst British Muslim society.

Ron Geaves was one of the first academics to thoroughly research Quilliam's life, and the new interest in this man and his achievements has been continued by a host of dedicated academics such as Jamie Gilham, Yahya Birt and Siddique Seddon, to name but a few. Birt has pointed out how the life of Quilliam had to be 'rediscovered', and the main community activists responsible for this were the educationalist M. Akram Khan-Cheema and electrical engineer M. Akbar Ali.[91] The research into Quilliam's life began in the 1970s but did not really take off until the late 1990s, when a Muslim convert couple set up the Abdullah Quilliam Society (AQS) in Liverpool. Thanks largely to the efforts of these hard-working individuals, today's British Muslims can feel a strong affinity and connection with the practise of their faith in the UK. Britain's first mosque is now being painstakingly restored to exactly how it was when Quilliam was Sheikh al-Islam. A new generation of Muslims and non-Muslims are enjoying worship, education, and study at Brougham Terrace in Liverpool.

Quilliam's story reassures many British Muslims that their faith is not something 'foreign' or something inevitably associated with the immigrant influx of post-war Britain. There have, of course, always been Muslims living in Britain, particularly in port areas or larger cities thanks to trade and imports, but these communities were tiny (in comparison to Jewish groups, for example) and very

---

[91] Y.Birt Preachers, Patriots and Islamists in *Victorian Muslim – Abdullah Quilliam and Islam in the West*, ed. R.Geaves and J.Gilham, Hurst and Co. 2017, p.138.

little was recorded about them. Quilliam's community was something completely different; rather than being born into Islam overseas and then bringing their faith to these shores, this group was the first ever wave of white converts who continued to live within British society. They were ready and willing to pledge allegiance to Britain, even though (as will be seen) they were often critical of international government policy and actions.

However, for some British Muslims today, and even more so for non-Muslims, the name of Quilliam brings confusion. This is largely due to The Quilliam Foundation, a think-tank which named their organisation after him because they believe Quilliam to be a positive and moderate example of what 'being a Muslim in Britain' should be. The Quilliam Foundation, however, tends towards a more secular version of British Islam. It also partners with the British Government on counter-terrorist measures such as the Prevent programme, an action which has invariably resulted in suspicion on the part of many Muslims who deeply distrust Prevent.[92] Confusion, therefore, exists over the difference between the Quilliam Foundation and the Abdullah Quilliam Society (AQS), but the latter is a completely different entity. The AQS is based in the Brougham Terrace mosque of Liverpool and focuses on celebrating Quilliam's historical achievements, renovating the original building and on outreach and education to the local community. The AQS is not an organisation that attracts any form of controversy or affiliates itself with any government or political group. It should be said, however, that many involved with The Quilliam Foundation feel that they have received undue criticism of their work and that a more secular version of Islam and co-operation with the Government is very much needed.

Despite modern-day arguments over the use of Quilliam's name, the astonishing achievements of Abdullah Quilliam's life cannot be doubted. His association and strong friendship, therefore, with a working-class elderly man from Stalybridge are made even more remarkable. Rediscovering Robert's life, however, has shed light on the fact that Quilliam may have actually needed Robert Stanley 'in the fold' rather more than Robert himself needed Quilliam.

Abdullah's Achievements

Quilliam's mind, range of interests and energy levels were nothing short of astonishing and in many ways his personality seemed to have been very similar to Robert Stanley's.

The Editor

Quilliam was evangelical in his zeal and was unashamedly keen to gain converts to Islam. He made every effort to demonstrate to Victorian society that the Islamic faith transcended race and place of birth. His main method of doing this was through his publications. As well as writing books and tracts, Quilliam produced

---

[92] Prevent was introduced to deal with radicalisation and extremism that the British Government felt was leading to terrorism. Under Prevent, public sector employees are encouraged to report people that are deemed to be at risk of radicalisation. Prevent supporters say that other forms of extremist tendencies are included (such as far right racists), but critics believe the programme is a thinly-veiled excuse to target Muslims and to attempt to force them to be less critical of government initiatives – particularly foreign policy.

two international magazines: *The Crescent,* which billed itself as 'A weekly record of Islam in England', and *The Islamic World,* which was a monthly periodical. Both magazines were subscription-based and taken out by individuals living in Britain and across the world. Reliance on the printed word was vital for Britain's convert community in an age without TV, radio or the internet. As the Christian Israelites had found, having ownership of, or access to, printing machinery was all-important for religious groups.

The content, influence and reach of Quilliam's publications was formidable. He chose every advert and article that appeared, unashamedly doling out his own opinions in lengthy sermons and features. Editorial licence both began and ended with Quilliam and yet he was also generous to his readers and allowed views different to his own to be printed – although he always reserved the right to reply.

Whatever the religious convictions (or not) of the reader of this book are, *The Crescent* and *The Islamic Review* prove to be a fascinating read.[93] The publications reflected Quilliam's own interests and passion for secular pastimes: geology, travel, history and poetry as well as the sort of articles we might expect from a magazine written for converts (abstinence from alcohol, the Principles of Islam, actions of the British Government overseas, polygamy, the errors of the Christian church, the beliefs of other faith groups, the progress of the Ottoman Empire, etc). But the articles in the magazine were well-researched and professionally written. Quilliam crammed both magazines with facts and viewpoints and at times some of the letters to the magazines venerating his good works tend towards bordering on the sycophantic; in some ways, no different to any faith group's publications today. But the adverts – for kosher soap, for brass band instruments, carbon batteries, fruit, deaf aids and Urdu instruction – are somewhat eclectic and make for a colourful read. If it is easy today, for a non-Muslim, to be mesmerised by Quilliam's formidable intelligence and observations, how much more captivating a read, then, would *The Crescent* have been for someone like Robert Stanley, a man who, by 1893, was searching for a publication that met his growing intellectual and spiritual needs?

Sheikh al-Islam

In 1890, *The Crescent* tells us that the Sultan (or Caliph) of the Ottoman Empire, Abdul Hamid II, proclaimed that Quilliam had been appointed as the leader of Islam in the British Isles – or as Sheikh al-Islam. This honour was also said to be endorsed by the Emir of Afghanistan, a close friend to Ottoman Islam. In 1891, Quilliam and his son, Robert 'Ahmed', undertook the long journey from Liverpool to visit the Sultan, with the 12-year-old boy being appointed with the honourable title of Bey and recognised as Bim-Bashi of the Turkish army.

From this point onwards, 'brand Quilliam' became gargantuan. His activities seemed to increase tenfold, with various accolades and titles bestowed and regaled regularly in *The Crescent* and *The Islamic World.* He embarked on many trips abroad and received visits from foreign dignitaries, but his attention was not only on Britain and the Ottoman Empire. In 1895, he travelled throughout West

[93] Thanks to the Abdullah Quilliam Society in Liverpool and the British Library, nearly all of the copies produced by Quilliam of *The Crescent* (*TC*) and *The Islamic World* can be accessed at www.abdullahquilliam.org

Africa - a region that he greatly admired due to the existence of states free of the slave trade – and in Sierra Leone he was asked to open a mosque on the Sultan's behalf, thereby creating a lifelong connection with the country. During the same year, Prince Nasrullah Khan, the Shahzade of Afghanistan, visited Quilliam in Liverpool and handed over a donation of £2,500 from his father, the Emir Abdur Rahman Khan (this would be around £310,000 in today's prices). It was thanks to this donation that Quilliam was able to purchase Nos. 11 and 12 Brougham Terrace in addition to No. 8, and it meant that in 1895 the Liverpool Muslim Institute (LMI) was formally opened.

The Liverpool Mosque - during Quilliam's era

The First Mosque (and another one)
The mosque established by Quilliam in Liverpool in 1887 lays claim to being Britain's first mosque. However, this title should really be jointly owned with the Shah Jahan Mosque in Woking, Surrey. The Woking mosque was built by Dr Gottleib Wilhelm Leitner in 1889. He was not a Muslim, but as a child he lived in Istanbul and studied at a madrasa (an Islamic religious school). He felt strongly that a purpose-built mosque should be created for Muslims in Britain. Quilliam's Liverpool mosque was based within the properties already standing at Brougham Terrace and was not purpose-built.[94]

The Muslim communities in Woking and Liverpool grew in parallel to each other, but the congregation in Woking was slower to be created whereas, under Quilliam's direction, the community at the LMI instantly flourished. After Quilliam left the UK, and the community in Liverpool stagnated, the congregation in Woking

---

[94] Both mosques have generously welcomed our family and supported our work. Readers are recommended to visit both mosques.

became the centre of Islam in Britain and, when he returned to England, he also spent much time in Woking, where he was eventually buried.

Today, both mosques are thriving, and both are passionate about opening their doors to non-Muslims who are interested in finding out about their history and what it means to be a Muslim in 21st century Britain.

Caring for the Children – School and Orphanage

Because the LMI was to be a centre of education for both Muslims and non-Muslims, Quilliam decided to open a boys' school in 1891. Requests were made for donations, and it was hoped that the school would provide an Islamic education for children from all classes of society. In 1896, an orphanage for both boys and girls, and a girls' school, was established. During these years, the plight of Liverpool's disadvantaged children had become an increasing cause for concern for Quilliam. He regularly began to appeal for funds, using *The Crescent* to justify the need for such an orphanage. Quilliam declared that the streets of Liverpool were soaked in sinfulness, not just in terms of alcohol abuse and various forms of criminality but also in relation to sexual immorality. He was no prude in relation to sexual matters, however. Quilliam said that double standards were operating in British society when it came to the subject of sex outside the sanctity of marriage and that the Christian church was doing little to address the hypocrisy prevalent:

> *While society forgives the man any transgressions of this nature, it remembers for ever a woman's slip ... those who cruelly hound down the weaker sex for the slightest deviation from the strictest morality appear to have entirely forgotten the teaching of Christ upon the subject ... 'Neither do I condemn you'.*

Putting the 'weaker sex' comment to one side as an anachronism of language, Quilliam's desire to support women and their children was quite progressive an attitude for its time; he had believed the new initiative to be not just for the children but for their mothers, too, *"It will give the mothers of the children an opportunity to retrieve their character, and once more return to the path of virtue and respectability."* [95]

At the time that the orphanage was established, there were over two thousand illegitimate births in Liverpool; baby-farming was being conducted on a large-scale across the country and infanticide was all too common. In comparison to many of the other achievements attributed to Quilliam, the orphanages have received little attention, which is a shame as the level of thought, work and dedication put into them was most impressive.

The orphanage was known as the Medina Home and was based at 4 Shields Road, after Quilliam purchased the building. He told people that the original inspiration for the scheme came from a Jewish woman who had asked him to look after her child. Perhaps she believed that Quilliam's pro bono donations to the poor, and his dedication to an Abrahamic faith, meant that the child would be safer

---

[95] *TC,* 21 June 1899 (note – Quilliam's article on the purpose behind the Medina Home is repeated frequently in editions of TC).

with him than growing up on the streets or placed within a Christian institution. Quilliam took the liberty of re-naming the boy Ishmael. [96]

Some of the children were accepted from off the streets with full orphan status but others were effectively orphans because the adults in their lives could not look after them. Adults who had placed them in the orphanage were asked to contribute five shillings a week towards the cost of care. In addition to bed, board and supervision, all orphans received a high-quality education involving the usual 'Three R's but they were also exposed to a wide range of subjects including ethics, science, religion and debating skills (adult versions of these lessons at the school were also open to any non-Muslims who wanted to improve their learning). In return for a place within the orphanage, any adult who placed a child there had to agree to the child following the Islamic faith. There were no outright objections to this in the press at the time, even though Quilliam often came in for the usual snipes from an ever-cynical press. It is difficult not to think of what sort of a reaction such an initiative would garner from the more xenophobic elements of the press today.

The orphans soon became a quirky feature of Liverpool civic society. The boys wore a fez and performed recitations for visiting VIPs and royalty to the LMI; they were present at Muslim funerals, too, handing out copies of *The Crescent* to curious non-Muslim onlookers, an interesting proselytising strategy at an event that often attracted negative reactions from members of the public. Quilliam's insistence that the orphanage should be Muslim is not so surprising when we consider that his own children (from both his families) were raised as Muslims and that even his own mother converted later in life. Undoubtedly, too, his royal sponsors from overseas would have insisted on a strong Islamic element to any such initiative.

A Christian Blend

Quilliam could be ferocious in his criticism of the Christian church for spreading negative views about Muslims. He spent much time railing against Christian duplicity versus what he saw as the openness, transparency and egalitarian nature of Islam. He was not opposed to Christianity per se, though; indeed, as 'people of the book', Christians were always welcome at the LMI and Quilliam himself was happy to spend time with clergymen and ordinary Christians. One of his wives, Mary Lyon, remained a Christian and never converted to Islam.

Compared with the practises of British Muslims today, Quilliam's version of Islamic worship also incorporated strong elements of Christian tradition. For example, the presence of an organ in a British mosque today would be unheard of. But the usual method of worship at the mosque would involve Quilliam as imam (leading the prayers and giving a sermon) with the congregation singing together, accompanied by the organ. He was always quick to declare the multi-racial appeal of Islam, but most of his congregation were white British converts. However, he saw no harm in adapting the words of well-known hymns so that reference to the

---

[96] Many Muslim converts decide to take on a Muslim name when they accept Islam. This is not a requirement, however. Most of the British converts at the time of Quilliam chose a Muslim name with a similarity or the same initial as their original name i.e. Bilal for William, Djem for James, Hanifa for Hannah, Reschid for Robert etc.

deification of Christ or the Trinity were excluded or amended. This was an act of ingenuity on the part of Quilliam as he sought to cultivate a feeling of familiarity amidst what would have initially been a new and unfamiliar approach to worship for any convert. He would have been aware, too, that singing sessions provide a sense of camaraderie and of unity that rouses the spirits. Although Quilliam liked to focus on science and logic as a method of attracting new converts, he was also fond of the British arts and his efforts had gained two highly acclaimed converts: the poet John Yehya-en Nasr Parkinson and the artist Walid F. Preston.

Christian seasonal enjoyment was also a feature of the LMI. From 1888, Quilliam had begun putting on a Christmas breakfast for the poorest children of Liverpool. These Christmas parties were held every year until 1908, with 200-400 children being fed in the morning. When the event became too popular, crowd control had to be introduced, with a further evening session being added. The party-goers in the evenings numbered 400-600 and, like those in the morning, would be fortified with beef sandwiches, fruit buns and cups of tea. Entertainment was provided by the female Muslim converts who regaled the children with songs and musical recitations. One of the arguments that today's right-wing extremists in Britain aim at the Islamic faith is that it views expressions of the Christian faith and tradition as anathema, that Muslims somehow want to stamp out all signs of Christmas. It may be true that in a very few places where extremist Islamist thinking is prevalent such an attitude can exist, but the average British Muslim today is perfectly at ease with the celebration of Christmas as a religious festival. Indeed, the recent unearthing of Quilliam and the LMI's legacy has done much to promote the sharing of Christmas as a seasonal and national celebration for Muslims and non-Muslims, as with other religious festivals observed in the UK.

Quilliam might have wanted to use the LMI's Christmas celebrations as some sort of Islamic evangelism, as a Victorian version of modern-day 'spin,' or perhaps to show that Muslims also honoured the birth of Jesus of Nazareth – a revered prophet of their own. However, after analysing many copies of *The Crescent*, it was interesting to note that Quilliam never sought to pitch Muslim celebrations against the Christian events of the year. Indeed, Quilliam's readers would be hard pressed to have even known that Muslims were observing the fast of Ramadan or the celebrations of Eid al-Fitr and Eid al-Adha. During Ramadan, The *Crescent* mentions that fasting, iftar and special prayers occurred but, in comparison to the awareness that these celebrations now receive in British society, Quilliam's early convert community were remarkably quiet. Was this because Quilliam wanted less attention to be drawn to Islamic celebrations? Did he feel that the talk of fasting for a month might put British people off the Islamic faith? Or is it simply a fact that we hear more nowadays in Britain about Ramadan and Eid celebrations because British Muslims are reacting to the rising tide of Islamophobia and want to assert their identity and devotions? It could also be that Quilliam and his congregation shared similar sentiments to the Quakers, that important dates in the religious calendar, and sacrifices such as those carried out in Ramadan, should be done so with genuine humility and with as little fuss as possible.

Visitors to Quilliam's LMI were often Muslim sailors docking at the port – men from the Indian subcontinent, from the Middle East and from Africa - who had heard about this rare haven of Islamic worship in Britain. However, there was also a growing number of Muslim-born inhabitants of the city who chose to settle in

Liverpool and a small group of resident Yemenis – as in Manchester – who would have enjoyed spending time in the mosque. Quilliam was vigilant about recording the nationalities of visitors and, in addition to the many Ottoman businessmen, officials and sailors, there were travellers representing the Indian subcontinent and many students who came to study in Britain.

Robert: Discovering Quilliam

In the feature on 'Brother Reschid' in *The Crescent*, we unfortunately do not learn how and when Robert first encountered Quilliam, so we can only make guesses at this. As previously mentioned, Urquhart was one of the people who had signposted him towards Islam, and Quilliam himself noted the honour that this man had bestowed upon the religion, quoting Urquhart's words within Quilliam's own treatise *Faith in Islam*:

> '*Islam, as a religion, teaches no new dogmas; establishes no new revelation, no new precepts; has no priesthood, and no church government. It gives a code to the people, and a constitution to the state, enforced by the sanction of religion'. That Urquhart was right has been admitted by many. Palgrave, Vambery, Rawlinson, Layard, Rolland, Stanley of Alderley, De Chonski and others.*

Robert – a keen reader and follower of the news – could have heard about Quilliam and his work from the newspapers. *The Manchester Guardian* repeated items from publications such as *The Liverpool Mercury* or *The Liverpool Evening Express*, and even the very local newspapers such as *The Stalybridge Reporter* would often feel fit to mention affairs in Liverpool from time to time. But Robert could also have learned about the existence of this rather interesting convert from people in Manchester – Muslims, perhaps - when he made his visits to the Old Corn Exchange.

By the time that he had converted, Robert had been working in the tea trade for over 50 years. The tea and coffee trade in Victorian Britain then were as important and as valuable as they are now in the 21st century. Today, however, the supply chain involved, from farmer growing the crop to the beverage reaching our kitchen cupboards, is a great deal longer than it was 100 years ago. Dozens of actors are involved in the chain: millers, processors, packagers, sellers, buyers, importers and carriers are stationed in the country where the tea or coffee is grown, and in other countries too. And then more links are added in the UK, along with quality control and food hygiene standards.

Trade was rather more direct when Robert Stanley worked on the floor of the Old Corn Exchange. He would have bought his tea from either trusted agents or those who would have brought the tea into the country themselves and who could well have been familiar with each estate or would know the smallholder farmer who had grown the actual leaves. He would have met Muslims from the Indian subcontinent and from the Middle East and Ottoman-dominated regions and would have purchased tea from them. For a man as well-read and as inquisitive as Robert was, the opportunity to test the views and reports as provided in the British newspapers, and to find out the truth of what might be occurring in these countries, would have been irresistible. These days, one of the biggest causes for concern in relation to Islamist radicalisation is that of the internet. Back in the 19th century, if any form of British counter-extremist agency had existed it might have focused its attentions on the trade routes.

At the current time, we have no evidence that Robert ever left Britain, either for work purposes or for investigative tourism. Although a homeowner, his financial resources would have been tied up in property, his home and work commitments were very great and – unlike the middle class – there was no trend amongst the working class for overseas tourist travel. Robert's curiosity about Islam, though, may have been stimulated when he began to hear the stories of extremely well-connected dignitaries converting to the religion. Men such as Lord Henry Stanley of Alderley, whose Alderley Park estate in Cheshire was some 18 miles from Manchester.

Henry Stanley was a government diplomat in the East, and he converted to Islam in 1862. To date, my family has not managed to prove a connection with these Stanleys, so, despite the name, proximity and Islamic coincidence, it would not be wise to presume that Robert Stanley was brought to Islam thanks to distant-cousin Lord Stanley! It is almost certain that the two men would have met, given Robert's appointment as vice-president of the LMI. Quilliam was friends with Henry Stanley and in 1903, at his invitation, Quilliam was introduced to Prime Minister Arthur Balfour. So, whether these two Stanley men were related by bloodline or not, they were no doubt asked on many occasions if they were distant relatives and it is easy to imagine that after Robert's conversion, they may have joked together about being 'Brothers in Islam'.

Striking Up a Correspondence – Towards Conversion

Robert struck up a correspondence with *The Crescent* (i.e. Quilliam) at least three years before his conversion in 1898. The first mention of him is in the 23rd October 1895 edition of *The Crescent* - two years after the first edition of *The Crescent,* which was first published in 1893. In this October 1895 edition Robert had one of his letters published, entitled 'The Armenian Question'. However, it then took two and a half years before we see – in a small and unassuming column - that 'Robert Stanley, Esq. Justice of the Peace for Stalybridge' is named as one of the latest converts to Islam. Quilliam was meticulous in recording all those who chose to adopt the faith, not just for the sake of keeping accurate records but because evidencing the regular trickle of those who had chosen Islam was good publicity for the faith and showed that his claim to be Sheikh al-Islam of the British Isles had legitimacy.

In Robert's first letter to *The Crescent* on Armenia, he states that he is sending an article which appeared in *The Manchester Guardian* in relation to the Madame Novikoff affair. This, he felt, was evidence of Russian double-dealing. The letter is the first time that we ever see his own written views on foreign affairs and, typically, he employs language that aims to address fairness:

> *Taking a judicial view of the reports of what has taken place in the treatment of the Armenians by the Turks, nothing has been done different to what would take place if the people of Ireland or Poland had allowed themselves to be*

deluded and incited to rob and murder their neighbours at the instigation of foreign emissaries.

With respect to Lord Salisbury's apparent policy at Constantinople, let us bring the case home. Supposing Italy and France were to demand that Ireland should be placed under European control on the grounds that the majority of the people being Roman Catholics, they could not expect justice from a Protestant nation. No English Government would dare to give up the right to govern Ireland without a fight for it. The Turks are in that position. They are asked to give up the right to govern that portion of their country in which the bulk of the Armenians live at the dictation of a foreign power. ... the apparent policy of England in sending the fleet to the Dardanelles is simply playing with fire... Those who have been nudging this course should read up on the consequences of the disturbances of the expulsion of the Moors from Europe, and they will find that in consequence of the disturbance of the balance of power which followed, the nations of Europe were at war for two hundred years to the immense destruction of human life and property.

On reading history, it would seem that the spirit of evil stirs up the fanatical feelings of the nation and their rulers are driven to acts which their descendants look upon as their madness. Let us hope that Lord Salisbury so far understands the position, that he will bring us through this crisis without either bloodshed or injustice. Yours truly, ROBERT STANLEY, Mossley road, Ashton-under-Lyne.

Quilliam's biography on Robert in *The Crescent* in 1908 does not explicitly detail the reasons behind his conversion, so we are left with trying to piece together the journey. In order to establish his encounters with Quilliam, therefore, it was necessary to read every edition of the magazine and to scan them manually for Robert's name (no search facility was available at that point in time). Thanks, once again, to Quilliam's desire to record information, we found that after Robert's initial letter to him as a non-Muslim that Quilliam had been sending copies of *The Crescent* to the Robert, probably requested by him in the letter he sent in October 1895. In the 20th November 1895 edition, in his 'Answers to Correspondents', Quilliam stated, *"R. Stanley (Ashton- under-Lyne)- Have sent you all the back editions you asked for. Hope you received them all safe."*

After this, it seems that the men had taken up some sort of regular correspondence, because in the 4th December 1895 edition, in the same column, Quilliam noted, *"R.S (Ashton-under-Lyne) – Thanks for letter and enclosure. Always glad to hear from you."* Quilliam subsequently publishes the following, in the same edition:

To the Editor of 'The Crescent',
DEAR SIR – I have sent the enclosed letter to the Marquis of Salisbury. If you think it is suitable for The Crescent, it is at your service. Yours truly, ROBERT STANLEY.

THE MOST NOBLE THE MARQUIS OF SALISBURY
By this post I send you a copy of The Crescent in which is published a letter signed by Hajdee Muhammed Dollie. If the statement of the manner in

which our Mahommadan subjects are treated is correct, it is clear that some of our public men are either fools or fanatics, because they do not look at the subject with both eyes, or else being aware of the facts in condemning the Sultan in the language they do, they are both hypocrites and imposters. Yours, ROBERT STANLEY

The letter that he is referring to was written by Dollie, a South African Muslim who spearheaded Anjuman-Islamia in London.[97] Robert was obviously feeling angry about the treatment of Muslims in Britain to produce such a pithy but obviously incensed letter and send it to the Prime Minister, and to wish for Quilliam to publish it. Again, in the 11th December edition, Quilliam informed Robert that he had sent further issues of *The Crescent* and that Robert's next letter would appear in the 18th December edition. Dripping with sarcasm, Robert again returned to the subject of Armenia and wrote for this edition:

A Warm Letter to the Chairman of the Anglo-Armenian Association.
To – Mr Stevenson MP (Chairman of the Anglo-Armenian Society)
DEAR SIR – Your rearrangement of the provinces of the Turkish Empire is a masterpiece. In the event of the division taking place, I hope you will remember me, as I think I have as much right to a slice as any of the rest. Perhaps the following will be of interest to you: -
DEAR SIR – In answer to your request re. division of the Turkish Empire, after due consideration we have concluded that the administration of the Turkish Province would be best conducted by the Sultan and his advisers.   GERMANY, ITALY, RUSSIA, AUSTRIA, FRANCE, ENGLAND. However, as you seem to think that the decision of this matter does not rest with the Sovereign and Statesman of Europe, but with yourself and a few poor creatures, who make a business of buying all the gossip they can and read it out in penny-worths, perhaps the thing will go on in accordance with your programme. If not, the Anglo-Armenian Society had better resolve itself into a Mutual Improvement Society. Your truly ROBERT STANLEY.

In the 19th February 1896 edition of *The Crescent*, Quilliam communicated with Robert in the notes section of the magazine, noting 'Received and entered,' – although what this refers to, we cannot be sure. A year after his first letter was printed, on 30th September 1896 another of Robert's letters is published, with Quilliam giving it the title of 'A Manly Protest':

To the Right Honourable the Lord Mayor of Manchester
As a ratepayer of the City of Manchester I attended a meeting called by you on the Turkish Question. I must protest to its being called a meeting representing the opinions of the citizens of Manchester. The meeting

---

[97] Dollie was a keen supporter of the Sultan and Quilliam reported that the Anjumani-Islamia had opened a temporary mosque in London in December 1895, near Regent's park. Quilliam quoted from the opening speech, "As Christianity has adapted itself to the modern era, so should Islam." Geaves, p.210.

was mainly composed of women, curates, dissenting ministers and idlers. The men who have made Manchester what it is were absent – minding their own business. Yours truly, ROBERT STANLEY.

Although I would have preferred for Robert not to have clustered women, curates and dissenting ministers in with idlers, we do need to view this letter as an example of Robert's life and times. Quilliam, too, seemed to agree with Robert on the lack of 'manliness' involved in discussing the Turkish question in Manchester. It is worth commenting on the fact that, again, Robert chose not to describe himself as ex-mayor of Stalybridge in his correspondence.

On 21ˢᵗ October 1895, Robert had again been sending newspaper extracts for Quilliam to print and on 3ʳᵈ February 1897, a note for the attention of Robert appears, stating that, *'The Turkish Consul is at present away from Liverpool'*. Quilliam and his son, Robert 'Ahmed', had been appointed (although not officially by Britain) to various consulate posts on behalf of friendly Muslim countries and this communication indicates that Robert had perhaps been intending to visit Quilliam at Brougham Terrace.

In the 17ᵗʰ March 1897 edition, *The Crescent* published a letter to its editor from Robert, addressing the issue of Greece – ancient enemy of Turkey. I have included it in its full length here, due to the fact that it raises not just foreign issues but is evidence of Robert's views on the domestic political front (and I apologise in advance for any offence caused by my great grandfather's comments in relation to Greeks and 'Oscar Wildes"!)

DEAR SIR – What is the meaning of the conduct of Greece in setting the world at defiance? Is it the encouragement she receives from a portion of the English press, or is she secretly supported by the leaders of the Liberal Party? If so, England as represented by them is playing a dangerous game which will sooner or later recoil upon ourselves.

Why so many of the English people should sympathise with the Greeks it is difficult to understand by anyone who looks at the subject with both eyes. A people who may be looked upon as the most degraded of any of the so-called civilised nations; a people that contain within its member more brigands and Oscar Wildes than any other known community; a people so unruly and unreliable that monied men fight shy of lending them money. So that its funds are lower in price than any other, in fact they are on the verge of national bankruptcy; a people that for the last 70 years England has taken under its wing and given every assistance and encouragement.

We have given them the Ionian Islands with their rich productions. We have admitted their produce free from duty, while we have compelled the Turks to pay a heavy duty for the same produce. What pettifogging statesmanship is this! To outside nations this line of conduct is utterly contemptible, and the time seems to be approaching that the advent of a Bismarck will be looked upon as a political necessity, and he will be hailed as a national saviour. Since the passing of the Reform Bill of 1832 the Government of the country has for the most part of the time been in the hands of men who have made politics a business, and their names are synonymous with hypocrisy, corruption and selfishness. Office by any means has been their motto. They have hampered the country with engagements in its foreign relations that in the intervals when honest men have been in power it has not been possible for them to counteract, hence the confusion that appears in the minds of honest men in regard to our foreign affairs. Since the passing of the Ballot Act a still lower class have aspired to office, men who look upon outrages and the use of dynamite as legitimate means of gratifying their ambition, hence the necessity arises for the advent of a strong man who will rule with an iron hand, otherwise the country will drift into a state of anarchy, only to recover itself under a dictator.

The ancients had a saying that those whom the gods would destroy, they first made mad. In the eyes of the civilised world the English people seem to have gone mad on this Turkish Question. Yours truly, ROBERT STANLEY.

Robert was still very much part of the 'Queen and Country' brigade, though, and he headed up a formal procession in honour of Victoria at Stalybridge's Diamond Jubilee celebrations on 23rd June 1897, when the entire country was flooded with parties, processions and celebrations. Over in Liverpool, Quilliam and the Muslims at the LMI also held celebrations and in Robert's hometown, the *Reporter* described the events as including:

A large demonstration of school children, numbering over 10,000 and of friendly society representatives. Jubilee medals were distributed in their thousands, and in the evening the Corporation provided various treats for the children. After dusk the town was brilliantly illuminated and there were fireworks displays and balloon ascents.

Around this time, we know, thanks to *The Crescent*, that Robert and his family had moved to Manchester by 18th August 1897. This was at least eight months before his conversion and he had evidently been spending his time reading and researching, as in a letter named 'Turkish Diplomacy', he states:

TO SHEIKH ABDULLAH QUILLIAM

DEAR SIR – On looking over some old numbers of Temple Bar, I came across a letter from Constantinople in which the following quotation appears:

'The Turks must be admirable diplomatists. Not a European nation can be compared to them; they merely let the dangerous meddler knock his head against stone walls till he loses his wits. Thus, they are quit of him, and immediately strengthen their position to be ready for the next assault'.

The quotation seems perfectly true to-day. The Powers have meddled in Crete, and find they have been knocking their heads against a stone wall, to the amusement of the Turks and of all cool-headed thinkers.

Let us hope that the Sultan will find himself strong enough to get rid of the meddlers in Crete, and to hold Thessaly for the sake of the happiness and prosperity of its people.

But there is another aspect of the question. Is it possible that the powers have meddled in Crete for the twofold purposes of preventing bloodshed and throwing dust in the eyes of the fanatical parties in their respective countries? If so, then, though we may admire their diplomacy, we cannot but despise their hypocrisy. Yours truly, ROBERT STANLEY, 278, Upper Brook Street, Manchester.

In addition to writing to Quilliam, it seems that during this same period Robert had taken it upon himself to write to the Caliph. He told Quilliam in his 1908 interview in *The Crescent* that he had advised Caliph Ghazi Abdul Hamid Khan on three important issues. Firstly, he had sent him a copy of Ville's work on agricultural chemistry, informing him that by sending Turkish subjects to study this system of agricultural improvements, the Ottoman army could be increased, *"...probably to the extent of at least fifty thousand persons, and had this policy been carried out, say, for a quarter of a century prior to that date, at least fifty thousand soldiers could have been added to the army and the treaty of peace would probably have been signed on the other side of the banks of the Danube instead of at St. Stefano."* Quilliam noted too that, *"Our brother received a letter of acknowledgement from the Imperial Chancellery, and, [shortly after] ... young Turks [were] be selected from the Imperial civil school and sent to study in the agricultural schools of Germany in order to qualify them for the posts of inspectors of agriculture in the Ottoman Empire."* Next, Robert explained that:

> *In order to become more fully acquainted with the tenets of the Islamic faith [he] read and re-read Sale's Translation of the Koran-Shareef, and was much impressed by the same [but was] struck by the doctrine set forth in that holy work and with the manner in which Christians persistently misrepresented the teachings thereof" and so he wrote to the Caliph requesting that he assist with producing a new translation of the Qur'an which was not carried out by a Christian as this: "would do much to remove the misunderstanding unfortunately so prevalent at the present time amongst English speaking people as to the life and teaching of our holy Prophet."*

Finally, he wrote to the Caliph, informing him:

> *...that existing treaties with foreign Powers prevented the Ottoman Government from increasing certain imported duties on articles manufactured by some of the European nations; but he pointed out that there was nothing in these treaties to prevent the Ottoman Government giving bounties to their own people to encourage a greater production of home-made goods; and our brother felt that if a few young men were sent from the Imperial Civil School at Constantinople over to England, particularly in the Lancashire and Yorkshire districts, to study the manufacture of cotton and woollen goods in Technical schools in this country, that ... their own Empire would become independent of foreign manufactures, and thus employment be found for a large number of inhabitants of that country.* (See Appendix 1 for more on Robert's letters to the Caliph)

It is fascinating that this advice for the Caliph occurred before Robert even converted. He had clearly become deeply convinced that the Ottoman Empire needed all the help and support that it could get. It must have impressed Quilliam considerably to find such a ferociously intelligent elderly man who was not a Muslim but was going out of his way to assist the cause of Ottoman Islam. If Robert was not already under suspicion as being a potential 'traitor' to the British Government by doing all that he could to help a foreign power, he very soon would be. Robert had also been purchasing additional copies of *The Crescent* in September 1897, indicating that he was deeply impressed with the publication and that he wanted others to read it. By 2nd February 1898, he had taken out a subscription.

Illustration of Quilliam in The Porcupine magazine

Of course, we have no way of knowing the actual first meeting with Quilliam, or when he first visited the mosque at Brougham Terrace; it might even have been during Ramadan or the Eid al-Fitr celebrations in February 1898, which received enormous press coverage due to the attendance of the mayor of Liverpool, but we can be certain that on 22nd April Robert eventually professed to the Islamic faith at the LMI:

> *The Sheikh had the pleasure of adding another name to the roll of the Faithful on Friday evening before he left. This last addition to the membership of the Liverpool Muslim Institute is Robert Stanley, Esq., Justice of the Peace for Stalybridge.*

The Big Attraction?
Spending more time in Liverpool would have reminded Robert of some of the Christian hypocrisy that occurred in his hometowns of Ashton and Stalybridge,

175

albeit on a much larger scale. These places suffered with sporadic outbursts of sectarian animosity, prejudice and violence and, in addition to his exposure to the Christian Israelites' theology, it might have been that as he moved into retirement Robert began to think more about the way that these groups differed in their attitude towards concepts such as atonement, the virgin birth, original sin and the incarnation. Perhaps his time spent talking to Muslims at the Old Corn Exchange, or in reading various publications, most notably Quilliam's *Faith of Islam* and *Fanaticism*, could have provided answers towards his ever-increasing doctrinal doubts.

Thanks largely to the works of Geaves, Gilham, Birt and several enthusiastic scholars, there now exist some fascinating narratives of Quilliam's life, but his fellow convert community has received far less attention, although those from the middle and upper classes have been far easier to trace: Lord Headley, Lord Stanley, Henri de Leon and Marmaduke Pickthall, for example.

There was an enormous surge of interest in the religion of 'the Mohammedans' during the last quarter of the 19th century, with even Queen Victoria and Winston Churchill being held in thrall by the faith and practises of Muslims. But Robert's personality seemed to have been far too conservative (with both a capital and a small 'C') to follow fashionable trends of the period. He was an elderly man by the time he met Quilliam, and just a few months short of turning 70 when he converted in 1898. He had been studying the situation of the Ottomans – and, by association, the religion of Islam – for at least four decades from a small and ferociously traditional northern town, and perhaps even for much longer, if his depth of understanding demonstrated through his letter is anything to go by.

Given that Quilliam would have been something of a celebrity in the north west of England, could this be why Robert sought out a friendship with him? Was Robert somehow motivated by the dazzling star that was Quilliam's fame? The fact that the Caliph and the Emir were friends with Quilliam and regarded him highly, along with funding his initiatives, would have deeply impressed anyone who was aware of international politics and foreign relations. However, from getting to know more of Robert's background and personality, it does seem unlikely that so late on in life he would have been chasing famous friends – and certainly not at the risk of upsetting his reputation and family. Rather, his gravitation towards Quilliam and towards Islam presents itself as being genuine and natural for the ever-logically minded Robert. He seemed to have been a man with an inquisitive mind, who sought out people who he could learn more from.

Yahya Birt and Ron Geaves have pointed out that Quilliam always took great pains in presenting an egalitarian and racially diverse image of the Liverpool congregation.[98] Although most of the white converts that we hear about from this period were middle class and well-off, there were plenty of poorer worshippers. There were several male clerical employees from the maritime industry who would have found the more equal relationships within the mosque to be a refreshing change from the snobbery and rigid class system at work and in church. Joining the LMI also provided working class people with access to a free education on many different topics.

---

[98] See Birt.

Would the egalitarianism of Islam have been an attraction for Robert? Until this point in his life, his philosophy had been that a stratum of better educated and better brought up people tended to hold the landed wealth and the reins of power. He believed that there was a 'decent' working class who wanted to improve their lot and that there was an 'underclass' who all too often displayed fecklessness and who were happy to remain ignorant. It is unlikely, therefore, that Robert was motivated by the lack of hierarchy present in Islam, but perhaps once he had experienced the benefits and camaraderie of a flatter structure within spiritual association, he came to enjoy it and to believe in it as an ideal.

In modern-day Britain, most of the conversion experiences that mainstream media tells us about are those of younger people (usually men) converting to Islam at a young age. Whilst it is patronising to state that youth who become Muslim are gullible or easily brainwashed, it is a truism that as a person ages, they become more conservative and are less likely to change a facet of their life such as their faith. This makes the decision by an already deeply conservative, elderly man to change his faith, to risk his reputation and his relationship with his family, even more remarkable. There were elements in Islam, of course, that Robert would have already found to be quite familiar – for example, the Christian Israelites and many dissenters also frowned upon the use of images, plus the familiarity with Old Testament stories which were also shared in the Islamic faith. And yet it was still a striking change of faith to make for someone at the age of 69.

Neither did Robert seem to be suffering (yet another) patronising age-related stereotype: early onset dementia or delusional behaviour. Right up until the publication of *The Crescent* ceased, his letters were startlingly eloquent and sharp in their observations. There is no notation of any frailty on his part, either in Quilliam's write-up of him or in *The Stalybridge Reporter*. His death certificate simply states 'senile decay' – but this terminology does not mean that a form of dementia was present (see final chapter).

A Meeting of Two Minds?

Socially, Quilliam and Robert Stanley came from very different places in the world. Quilliam was born into a highly educated middle-class family, received an excellent college education and was funded by his parents to become a lawyer. He was financially capable enough to be able to provide many hours of pro bono work for the city's poor, not to mention being able to own two homes and to buy the first property that housed the LMI. Robert, on the other hand, had to contend with the issue of how his own parents' relationship began in a somewhat scandalous manner, given that the couple had needed to relocate to Cardiff. Born into lowly terraced housing in a Cardiff market area, there was no legal obligation to send Robert to school and although he did have the advantage of possessing a wealthy uncle in the north of England, John Stanley had his own family to provide for. The young Robert had done a hard day's graft from the age of ten and made great strides in civic life as a result of his own achievements rather than any sort of privileged upbringing.

Quilliam was some 28 years younger than Robert Stanley and the same age as Robert's sons. In Victorian society, the younger person was expected to respect their elders and betters. In the main, Robert would probably not have been easily impressed by a much younger man unless there was concrete evidence for its need. The social circles that Robert moved in were those of an unquestionable patriarchy; men governed, men made the law and upheld it, they ruled the country, the church, the home and the hearth and they had the first and last say on everything. On the town council, Robert would have been used to hearing the words of men who were full of their own self-importance, desperate to put either their own interests forward or those of their political party. It is highly likely that by the age of 70 he would have been adept at seeing through an over-inflated ego, especially amongst those regarded as a 'young pup' (or indeed, a 'Young Turk'). On meeting Quilliam for the first time, perhaps he was reminded of the *Reporter* in 1874 which had criticised him – at a similar age to Quilliam - for not being old or fat enough in order to be a successful mayor.

Quilliam would have been a charismatic and commanding person to be around, even away from the spotlight of the press and visits from foreign royalty. The strongest influences in Robert's life until this point – men such as John Wroe, Joseph Rayner Stephens, David Urquhart and John Stanley – had displayed similar traits: a huge personality, large amounts of learning, evangelical zeal, controversial opinions and a strong backbone that could withstand the onslaught of criticism and even outright hatred at times.

Robert and Quilliam would have lived out quite different experiences in relation to family. Quilliam spent all his adult life in polygamous relationships. His first family consisted of his wife, Hannah, and their four children – Robert, Harriet, Elizabeth and William – each of whom were given Muslim names after his conversion. But he had another family living a parallel existence alongside them in a different house in another part of Liverpool. Mary Lyon was an actress who had been Quilliam's mistress prior to his conversion. After his conversion their relationship was formalised in a Muslim ceremony and, after Hannah died, he married Mary under English civil law. This union produced five children, who, like his first family, were raised as Muslims, although Mary remained Christian. In his later life as 'Henri de Leon', Quilliam married Edith Spray, who converted to Islam and recent research indicates that Quilliam married at least one other woman – said to be the first female convert, Fatima Cates.

As an adult, Robert juggled various jobs and businesses in order to make ends meet and until the move to Manchester he always lived in the small rooms above a business premises. So far as we can know, he only every enjoyed the one, lifelong monogamous relationship with Emma and he produced children who had respectable enough, but not well-paying, jobs. In fact, perhaps the only strong family similarity for Quilliam and Robert was that the women in their lives were very much living in their shadows; although, of course, Robert's wife and daughters had no choice but to work for a living.

Quilliam wrote and spoke a great deal about polygamous relationships. Some commentators feel that his excessive focus on this subject led to his downfall, the direct result of trying to defend a case where a woman was being treated unfairly under Britain's inequitable divorce laws. His attitude towards polygamy was pragmatic; he stated that the Qur'an permitted a man to have more than one wife and set of children only if the man could financially support them. He felt that it was better for society – and for women – if a man's innate need to express himself sexually was contained within committed and legalised relationships with additional wives as opposed to seeking out different women to have sex with -

often in risky situations. The threat of venereal disease and of unwanted pregnancy was very real in Victorian society. Perhaps Robert agreed with Quilliam on what seemed to be a logical solution to these huge problems, especially given his predisposition to believe that every family should have a right to privacy and the right to govern itself in its own manner, providing that no-one suffered as a result. Either way, Robert never expressed a public opinion on the issue of polygamy. It is not hard to imagine, though, that his children would have had a difficult time of agreeing with this particular element of what they heard about the Islamic faith, and it might even have been one of the reasons as to why his conversion was hushed up.

Masonic Similarities?

Jamie Gilham has demonstrated Quilliam's strong commitment to the Masonic movement; Quilliam even established his own Masonic 'Order' before he converted to Islam and continued to promote Masonic interests throughout his life. Contemporary British attitudes towards the Masonic movement have generally been mistrustful during the 20th and 21st centuries. Many in the Muslim community, too, have felt suspicious towards the Masons and other secret societies. Hundreds of books having been written about the origin of such groups, claiming them to be steeped in the Christian Crusader zeal of the early Middle Ages, or as being involved with Zionist conspiracies. Given these facts, Quilliam's involvement with the Masons might seem a rather peculiar affiliation for many. However, Gilham has carefully explained that Quilliam's involvement was indicative of his values, his class and was a common feature for men of his time. For Quilliam and other new converts, being part of these secret societies marked just another way of getting to join an old boy's network – a manifestation that bypassed the traditional elite systems of aristocracy of birth and which allowed men who had ambition, drive, and a curiosity for learning to buy into a new system of 'not what you know, but who you know'.

Robert was probably also a Mason. Many Masonic groups flourished in both Ashton and Stalybridge in the 19th century and membership was certainly a feature of our family. Masonic affiliation was often passed down from father to son and Robert's son, 'Unlucky Bob' Stanley, was a member and head of Stalybridge's Stamford and Warrington branch, as was Bob's son, Dean Stanley (who also became a mayor of Stalybridge), and who was a 'master' of the Lodge. Both then, and now, the Masons made an enormous contribution to local charities and causes and were often the first group to lend a hand when disaster or distress struck. During the Victorian era, the Masons were closely bound to local churches, with vicars and curates often found to be key members. It might be fair to say that at this time, for the average member of the Masons in the north of England, their involvement was nothing more than an older man's version of the Boy Scouts (without the need to get grubby in the great outdoors) mixed in with a less aristocratic adaptation of a gentlemen's club.

For Quilliam, who is described as "finding both a new religion and an old tradition when he embraced Islam", and probably for Robert too, an interest in Masonry was entirely compatible with, and complementary to, the practise of Islam and would have been just one more avenue of interest that they held in common.[99] Fraternity was a word used commonly by Quilliam to describe both Islam and the Masons and, ironically, on the very same page of *The Crescent* that celebrates the life of Brother Robert Reschid in 1898 there is an article by Brother John Yarker entitled 'Arab Masonry'.

Must Have GSOH

In addition to having similar social and political interests, Robert and Quilliam evidently shared a love of good humour. The recent revival of interest in Quilliam by academics has tended to portray him as a very serious man, a man interested in Sharia law and a chap who would issue fatwas and call for jihad when he felt the need to. Likewise with Robert: his life had been filled with solemn issues, social and civic and judicial matters along with grave concerns over British foreign policy. And yet from analysing Quilliam's publications and sources in relation to Robert we can see that both men had a sharp wit about them. In the council chambers, Robert seemed to be adept at pulling a joke from the hat when the occasion allowed for it and, although he was never one for hogging the limelight, he seemed to enjoy playing to the crowd and could dole out the odd sidewinder.

Quilliam, on the other hand, shows less evidence of verbal witticisms, but clearly felt the need to inject a bit of humour for his readers, deliberately including light-hearted moments in his columns. Granted, some of them would be deemed today to be rather offensive in their attitudes towards women and the Irish, for example – and they chimed with Robert's own rather offhand comment about women attending the meeting in Manchester about Armenia - but these were the socially accepted norms of the time. Perhaps we should not be too harsh on the two men with regards to this, given the fact that it is only very recently that 'mother-in-law' and 'blonde' jokes have become frowned upon. And in relation to their own lives, neither man displayed misogynistic attitudes; Robert encouraged his daughters to get a good education and did not feel the need to marry them off. Neither did he display any evidence of bias in the legal cases that he had to deal with (which cannot be said for some of his fellow magistrates). Similarly, Quilliam sought to help and support women who were being mistreated and, if anything, this proved to be his downfall.

It is a shame that, so far, no personal correspondence has been found as a record of the friendship between these two men; the only documents of Robert's that have been kept are receipts from his tea business, and Quilliam's personal papers were largely destroyed in a house fire which occurred when his third wife was living in the Quilliams' Isle of Man family home.

---

[99] Geaves, p.38.

CHAPTER 10

Glory Days and Manchester
1897 – 1907

Jettisoning the Pub

Robert's letters to *The Crescent* demonstrate that he was becoming more involved with Quilliam whilst still living in Ashton. Getting to Liverpool from the New Inn would have involved a 20-minute walk from the New Inn to Ashton train station, a train from Manchester to Liverpool and then another long walk to the LMI. And again, the same journey for returning home. Many of the events at the LMI that Robert was now becoming captivated by took place in the evenings and for a man

Six of Robert's children c. 1883 - left to right:
Thomas, Mary-Jane, Sarah, Emma, William and Alice

of his age such frequent journeys would have been exhausting. Shaving off some of the travel would have marked a welcome relief for Robert.

But was being that little bit closer to Liverpool a big enough reason for Robert to want to move to Manchester? Or did Robert feel, as he drew closer to Islam, that he needed to sell the pub? Muslim business owners who work in the food and drink industry today are faced with this sort of predicament and many manage to reconcile the sale of alcohol in their enterprises whilst refusing it for their own consumption. However, they often find that this route leads to a lack of trust and loyalty from other Muslims.

Before carrying out this research, I had presumed that Robert had sold the pub after becoming a Muslim, that he had somehow felt his position as a landlord would be wrong. However, we now know that Robert sold up and moved to Manchester some months before he said Shahada. I became aware of this thanks to *The Crescent*, because on 17th March 1897, his address is given as Ashton-under-Lyne. But by 25th August it has become 278 Upper Brooke Street, in the Chorlton on Medlock area in Manchester.

Was he increasingly becoming convinced that the sale of alcohol was wrong even before becoming a Muslim? Or did he sell the pub and move to Manchester for a non-Islamically related reason? Robert sold the New Inn in 1897 to Cardwell's Brewery, based in Hulme, Manchester and became a Muslim after this. This seems to indicate that he preferred not to be involved with the sale of alcohol at all. However, we have recently discovered that he applied for planning permission in 1904 to run a hotel, consisting of the properties of 28, 30 and 32 Stockport Road in Chorlton on Medlock, Manchester, which he owned. He made planning applications to develop this hotel in 1900 and then again in 1904 but was denied by Manchester Council, who stated that there were already too many licensed premises in the immediate area. Clearly, Robert was a practising Muslim at this time and, inevitably, setting up a hotel would involve the sale of alcohol. It seems, therefore, that Robert may have had a more practical outlook to the sale of alcohol. His planning application seems to reflect this; he wanted to set up a quality business - one that he obviously felt would be of a higher class than the usual pubs and guest houses in the area and where, perhaps, over-indulgence and abuse of alcohol would not occur. But he certainly seemed to feel that it was possible for him – as a Muslim – to be associated with a business that was licensed, even if he had decided not to run it directly himself or to be living on the premises.

Getting Settled

Because Robert and Emma moved to Manchester before he became a Muslim, it seemed likely that there were other motivations rather than just being a bit nearer to Liverpool. I noticed that their youngest son, John, had been listed in the 1881 census as working in 'tea' and after tracing him to the Chorlton area in 1891, I wondered whether his parents had moved to be nearer to him, and whether father and son were working together in the tea trade. This hunch proved to be correct, because I then discovered that John Stanley was listed as a tea agent and that he was partnered with his father, Robert Stanley, who was a tea trader at 16, The Old Corn Exchange. Surrounded by men trading in butter, sugar, cloth and other in-demand items, John would probably have acted as the seller of the tea, striking deals with buyers and promoting the Stanley teas, and Robert might have been the one in the partnership responsible primarily for seeking out new sources of leaves and negotiating with those bringing it from abroad: the perfect opportunity for him to broaden his knowledge of the world and to engage with those who had practical experience of living as a Muslim.

But what about Emma? We have no idea how she must have felt about this enormous change to her home life in 1897. Not only did she have to deal with the loss of the family pub and nest egg - and what had been their home for 19 years - but she would also have been witnessing her husband drawing closer to these unusual people in Liverpool.

By 1901, Robert and Emma had been together for 54 years and it is hard to imagine that Emma, at the age of 75, would have felt excited about the move. We do not know whether she had enjoyed being landlady of the New Inn, but after the respectable existence of being Lady Mayoress and owner of a well-established grocer's, it is hard not to imagine her feeling a little bit fed up by the elements of bawdiness and drunkenness that would have occurred from time to time at the pub. She – like Robert – may have found that the peaceful later years they had both been looking forward to were not forthcoming at The New Inn, no matter how hard they tried to make it a higher-end establishment. By 1897, they had been

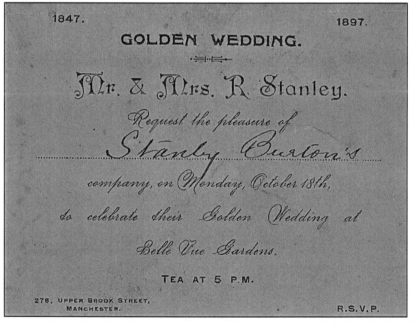

1847.   1897.

GOLDEN WEDDING.

Mr. & Mrs. R. Stanley.

Request the pleasure of

Stanley Burton's

company, on Monday, October 18th,

to celebrate their Golden Wedding at

Belle Vue Gardens.

TEA AT 5 P.M.

278, Upper Brook Street, Manchester.   R.S.V.P.

Invitation to Robert and Emma's golden wedding anniversary at Belle Vue Gardens in 1897 (addressed to their son-in-law)

living in the pub for nearly two decades and Emma may have been relieved to hear that Robert wanted to sell up and move closer to their son, John, and his family. During this same year, and probably not long after their move, the couple celebrated their golden wedding anniversary at Belle Vue Gardens, Manchester's most exciting entertainment venue. For some reason, an actual copy of an invitation was kept by a relative. It had been sent to a Stanley Burton, who was husband of their daughter, Emma, and family and friends must have enjoyed a wonderful celebration at the Gardens. However, within the space of a year, Emma's life would have changed dramatically.

The census of 1901 shows us that two of their daughters, Mary-Jane (aged 45) and Sarah (aged 40), were living with Robert and Emma at their home in Manchester. The sisters had both been teachers and there would have been more job opportunities for them in Manchester, but by now they were both middle-aged and a move to such a bold and brash city would have been rather daunting. In fact, the 1901 census no longer lists either of the sisters as being teachers; instead, they are described as 'at home' – perhaps marking a period of unemployment for them or even ill health.

Another strong 'pull' factor for Robert in relocating to Manchester would

Robert's home was in this row, Upper Brooke St, Rusholme - 1959

have been the fact that there was more access to libraries and different people from diverse backgrounds and therefore many more learning opportunities to fill his retirement with. Thanks to the work of Professor Siddique Seddon, we now know that the family's new home at 278 Upper Brooke Street, Chorlton, was close to an area with a significant Muslim population – and only eight years after Robert died, one of the first recorded places of worship had been set up close to their home.[100]

The New Neighbours
The Stanleys' new neighbourhood was based in the Rusholme area of Manchester. It must have been quite a culture shock for the women in the family, who would have been far less used to spending time on the streets of a great city than Robert was. And there would never have been a dull moment in Manchester at this period

---

[100] This was the home of Abdul Majid bin Jilloun, a Moroccan who had moved with his family to Manchester. His father opened their family home for congregational prayers at 47 Parkfield St, Rusholme. In Seddon, Siddique in *Early Muslim Communities in Manchester 1830-1950*, unpublished manuscript.

in time; King Cotton had evolved into the beating heart of new radicalism in England and, in particular, the question of female suffrage was dominating the political landscape. Indeed, a certain family named the Pankhursts lived at 62 Nelson Street, just around the corner from the Stanleys. Robert and his family could not have failed to have been aware of the actions on the part of the Pankhurst ladies, along with other well-known names from the suffragette movement, such as Hannah Mitchell, an Ashton woman, whose husband came from Stalybridge and who was also involved in the tea trade. Both would have been familiar figures to Robert and Emma.

Robert might well have disapproved of the growing levels of civil disobedience on the part of these women, and he would probably have been appalled on hearing the news that his young neighbours, Christabel and Sylvia, had been arrested in October 1905. They had assaulted a police constable during a Liberal meeting at the Free Trade Hall addressed by leading politician, Sir Edward Grey. It seems likely that Robert would have met Emmeline Pankhurst, who had moved back to Manchester from London just a few months after Robert and his family relocated. She had taken on the job of registrar for the Rusholme district where both families lived, so it is likely that the two were familiar with each other– if not in the debating halls and political meetings occurring in the city (as they shared similar domestic and foreign policy interests) then as a result of the sadder occasions of Robert registering the deaths of John, in 1898, and Emma, in 1902.[101] Indeed, after putting together the Stanleys' and the Pankhursts' timelines, we recently applied for a handwritten copy of Emma's death certificate and found that Emmeline Pankhurst had indeed presided over and signed the registration, listing the cause of death as 'bronchitis and senile decay' and writing that 'Robert Stanley, former tea dealer' was present at death and registered it with her.

Emma Stanley's death certificate, written and signed by Emmeline Pankhurst

Thanks to the railway boom and the flow of trade and commerce between Liverpool and Manchester, the city had attracted tens of thousands of migrants from rural areas, along with Irish, Jewish and Welsh people. The presence of these 'non-northerners' would have been less noticeable for the Stanleys, given the fact that the populations of Stalybridge and Ashton were not dissimilar to

---

[101] The proximity of the Stanleys to the Pankhursts has led to the creation of a script, an imaginary encounter between Robert and Emmeline and contained in the companion book to this one (*Imagining Robert – Scenes from the Life of a Hidden Victorian Muslim*, by Christina Longden, 2019).

Manchester's in this regard. However, the more 'foreign' elements of Manchester would have been enormously different to the previous neighbourhood experiences of Emma, Mary-Jane and Sarah. As international access to trading routes became even stronger during the 19th century, a significant number of Moroccan and Arab merchants were spending time in Manchester. The signing of the Anglo-Ottoman Commercial Treaty in 1838 had led to an increase in textile exports within the Ottoman Empire, opening further and faster routes into China and India for enterprising tradesman. Arab trading houses had existed in Manchester since 1798 and by 1890 there were at least 400.[102]

By the 1830's, Arab traders from Fez living in Manchester were exporting cotton to Morocco and in 1856 an Anglo-Moroccan Commercial Treaty reduced trade restrictions. Within ten years, British exports to Morocco accounted for over 50% of all imports to that country.[103] The two key regions from which King Cotton received its raw cotton were the USA and the Levant, and in 1838 the Anglo-Turkish Commercial Treaty, signed at Balta-Limason near Constantinople, led to the Ottoman Sultan importing more 'piece' goods from Manchester than the whole of the rest of Europe. This attracted 'wandering Lascars' to settle in Manchester, including Yemenis and Somalis. There were also significant Levantine Arab communities (from Syria and Lebanon) living towards the southern side of Manchester by the 1850s; although they were mostly Jewish and Christian Arabs, there were Muslims amongst them, too, and a great spirit of coexistence prevailed with the groups, who even set up an Arabic school together.[104]

The Ottomans also had an obvious presence in Manchester, living in the city and acting as clerks, translators and agents for European companies in the Levant. By 1860, an increasing number of Damascus and Fez merchants were in Manchester. The Ottomans also had a consulate in Manchester as well as in Liverpool, and a key figure involved with the consulate during this period was Abdullah Ydilbi, who had lived in Manchester since the 1850s, beginning his enterprises selling Chelsea buns but then moving into cotton exporting between Turkey and Manchester. The presence of an Ottoman consulate proved to be a reason for Quilliam's many trips to Manchester when he visited the city, and he undoubtedly looked to King Cotton as fertile ground to further grow the Muslim convert community.

In 1892, John J. Pool wrote *Studies in Mohammedanism* which focused on the new and increasingly famous British convert, Abdullah Quilliam. Pool provides a typically Victorian Christian outlook on Quilliam's work in Liverpool, which he said was, *'started and maintained by Englishmen, with the direct object of converting us all to the doctrines of Mohammedanism'.*[105] Siddique Seddon has noted that Pool inaccurately claimed that in Manchester there were, *'forty of the faithful, but only four of them are English converts'* and yet given the above information on Muslims living in the area, his figure was obviously far short of the mark. However, he was probably closer to the truth in terms of English convert

---

[102] Seddon, p. 3.
[103] Seddon, p.3.
[104] Ansaria, H. *The Infidel Within; Muslims in Britain since 1800*, Hurst, 2004, p38.
[105] Seddon, p.16.

followers although, of course, Robert would not have been factored into the count as he did not convert until 1898.

The Crescent informs us that members of the LMI also used to visit Manchester in order to give talks at the Secular Hall, just a few hundred yards away from Robert's home. Two other well-known British converts of the time - the artist, Walid Preston, and Djem Lester, one of the very first convert friends of Quilliam - were already living in Manchester. For Robert, having brothers Walid and Djem close by would have been most welcome: new friends and spiritual advisors for his change in beliefs and in aspects of his lifestyle. Another welcome feature of the area for him may have been the Turkish baths, which were located close to his home, although there was also another Turkish baths just a mile or so away in Salford, which Urquhart had been involved with. Even when living in Ashton, Robert would have been able to access the right sort of meat for any dietary requirements as a Muslim, with halal food being very similar to kosher and with John Stanley's and the other Christian Israelite shops all selling kosher products. Manchester would have been even easier for him in terms of being able to buy halal meat. There were clearly many attractive factors for Robert in moving to Manchester.

Robert's conversion in April 1898, probably marked a strange and perhaps an unsettled time for Emma, Sarah and Mary-Jane. Shortly after his conversion, tragedy struck the family when, on 3rd November 1898, and only a year after his parents moved closer to him, John Stanley died aged 35. John had been the baby son of Emma and Robert and their sorrow must have been all the worse for the fact that John's fifth child, his baby son, arrived some six weeks after his death. It must have been a terrible time for his widow; not only was she now left to bring up four children under the age of nine (her first child, named after Robert, had died at the age of one) but she would also have lost all family income. Robert had converted just seven months before the death of his son and perhaps the fact that they had made the move to Manchester would have felt very fortuitous to all the family. At least they were already close at hand to help John's widow and for Robert to be able to steer the tea-trading side of things.

The situation now facing the family illustrated itself more clearly when I noticed that a new little character had appeared on the 1901 census in Manchester. Living with Robert, Emma, Mary-Jane and Sarah was George Meredith Stanley, aged nine years old: the eldest child of John. The same census tells us that living with Alice and Joe Taylor, Robert's youngest schoolteacher daughter and her headteacher husband in Uppermill, was a girl named Marguerite Stanley. Marguerite was George's sister, aged eight years old. Both children seemed to have departed from their home in Chorlton following their father's death – leaving brother William and baby John with their now-widowed mother.

Marguerite's Aunt Alice and Uncle Joe effectively adopted her, because in the 1911 census she was still living with them, this time at Wakefield Road, Stalybridge and she was in school at Ashton Grammar School in 1909 – although she had previously attended Huddersfield Municipal Secondary School - a fair commute for a young girl but on a direct train line from Uppermill (perhaps she travelled with her teacher aunt and uncle). It seems likely, therefore, that when John died in 1898, Robert and Emma similarly adopted young George. Not an ideal situation for an elderly couple but having two middle-aged daughters living with them would certainly have helped with managing the new nine-year-old addition to the nuclear family.

Expansion – and Contraction.

The period from 1898, when Robert converted, to his death in 1911 marked a time of expansion and then rapid contraction for the community of Muslim converts in the north of England. In 1891, Quilliam recorded 50 converts; in 1895 this had grown to 121; in 1897 there were 152; and by 1899 he listed 182.[106] As the convert community grew in the Liverpool region, the Woking area also began to experience larger numbers of Muslims visiting Surrey's purpose-built mosque and it, too, began to be seen as a spiritual home to those practising Islam. During these years, Quilliam's meetings, lectures and visits both at home and overseas were quite astonishing in terms of their frequency and frenetic energy. However, this was also one of the most precarious periods for British foreign policy; there were grave concerns over the growing disturbances in the Balkans and, ultimately, this was one of the key elements in preventing any big increase in terms of convert gains for Quilliam. In all likelihood the international situation would have been the reason why my family chose 'not to remember' Robert's conversion after his death, just three years before the outbreak of the First World War.

Even before Robert had moved the seven miles to Manchester from Ashton/Stalybridge, several unpleasant episodes involving Quilliam and the Muslim community of Liverpool had occurred. The year of 1895 had proven to be terrible for many in the Balkans area. Reports claimed that around 1,000 Armenian Christians had been killed by the Turkish army. Deaths then occurred in Syria and in Constantinople as fighting between the two religious groups broke out. Even before he became a Muslim, Robert had experienced vitriol towards his views on the Bulgarian crisis of 1876, and Quilliam frequently began to encounter very aggressive sentiments. In August 1895, he was invited to speak on the subject of Armenia at a meeting in a Liverpool chapel. Passions were running high and, as he protested some of the abusive words being poured out against the Turkish race, he was met with shouts from the audience such as, "You should be burned alive!" and, "Strangle him!"

It wasn't just the audiences in Liverpool who expressed such views. During the same year, the Archbishop of Canterbury gave his take on Islam, *"it is a rock beneath which are volcanic forces of the most terrible kind ... the cultivation of its leaders is as marvellous as the fanaticism of its rank and file."* [107] Quilliam responded to the head of the Anglican church by citing examples of Christian atrocities in the Philippine Rebellion against the Spanish, the actions of the Rinderpest guards in the Waterberg district of South Africa and crimes against humanity against the Serbs and the Albanians. He stated that the reports of the atrocities against Christians by Muslims in Albania were greatly exaggerated and continued to claim that Abdul Hamid II was a great reformer and that the European powers should not seek to crush the Ottoman Empire as it would lead to the most destructive and

---

[106] Geaves, see his Chapter 3 for more details on convert numbers.
[107] Geaves, p. 248.

costly war ever experienced. He also slammed the British press, describing them as, *"intolerant, mendacious and unfair."* [108]

Geaves has pointed out that there appears to have been an inconsistency with Quilliam's attempt to defend the Islamic faith, per se, whilst being too closely associated with the Ottoman version of Islam. Many Indian Muslims, for example, did not feel a particular connection with the Caliphate and were also not comfortable with the thought of rebelling against their British rulers if it meant having to show solidarity with the Ottoman Muslims.[109] Quilliam's pro-Ottoman rhetoric seemed to have been contradictory at times; when the Lord Mayor of Liverpool introduced him as the representative of Turkey, he responded to him, *"I do not officially represent Turkey in Liverpool, but I do represent the Muslim Faith, and I am the Sheikh of Musselmans in the British Isles. I do not receive one penny from the Turkish Government."* [110]This must have been somewhat confusing to those who knew that he had accepted financial gifts from rulers associated with the region – not to mention the fact that he would often speak of loyalty to the British Crown. He had even composed a special prayer for the occasion of the coronation of Edward VII, following Victorian's death.

Nonetheless, Quilliam battled on during this period. He continued to rail against British foreign policy when he felt it was unjust towards Muslims or the Turks and he allied himself with the Sunni branch of Islam, yet he consistently sought to demonstrate that he was a loyal subject to the British monarch and government. Walking this tightrope will feel familiar to many British Muslims today; their loyalty to the country is all-too-often called into question if they are critical of British foreign policy and its actions overseas. It is as though British Muslims have always been forced to make choices that other residents are simply not expected to make.

As the situation in Eastern Europe and in the Middle East became even more precarious, Quilliam was faced with the problem of needing to grow a community of converts, continue his relationship with the Turks (who did, after all, despite his words, provide most of the funding for his work) and deal with damage limitation because of his views on British foreign policy. As Quilliam and the convert congregation came under more criticism and faced anger for refusing to condemn the actions of the Turks, it would have occurred to him that he needed to demonstrate that the British Islamic faith was not just a Liverpool phenomenon. He needed to show his critics that extremely rational, highly respected and fair-minded people were becoming converts. Manchester already had its own small Muslim community – primarily from the Levant – and it would have been useful for Quilliam to have someone like Robert living there and perhaps becoming a figurehead, in the same way that he had fulfilled the role in Liverpool.

A Decade of Islam
The year of 1898 proved to be a busy one for Quilliam's convert community, and for Robert. It seems likely that he would have attended some of the courses on

---

[108] Geaves, p. 248.

[109] The term Indian Muslims is used to reflect the fact that states such as Pakistan did not exist at this time and therefore all Muslims from this region would have been described in this way.

[110] Geaves, p. 249

Islam available at the LMI and to attend the prayers as and when he could. Travelling to Liverpool from Manchester would have been much faster than getting there from Stalybridge, and the journey does not seem to have been a problem for Robert; by all accounts he was a sprightly 69-year-old when he became a Muslim and looks very well for his age in photographs. His name crops up quite frequently during this year in terms of attendance at the LMI, but it seems that he also travelled backwards and forwards between family, friends and duties in Stalybridge. Some readers may wonder whether Robert ever went on Hajj, but this remains very unlikely; he would have lacked the capital available to do this and his family would probably have frowned upon it – especially with him being quite elderly. Instead, he probably enjoyed 'vicarious Hajj', hearing about the religious obligation through the writing of others and the stories that those attending the LMI would have brought back with them.

In May, Barnum and Bailey's world-famous circus appeared in Liverpool and members of the LMI attended, with Quilliam reporting back to *The Crescent* about the spectacular event; he was as keen as ever to prove that his convert community was happy to engage with the same sort of family fun and entertainment that the average British person looked forward to. Quilliam's loyalty to Queen Victoria, too, had been officially noted, which brought much joy and relief, given some of the pressure that the convert community was now under. He received a written acknowledgement - essentially a nod - from the Queen that year, when he was appointed as official to the Liverpool Turkish Consulate following a visit from one of the Sultan's VIPs. However, as media coverage became increasingly focused on the Ottoman Empire and the precarious situation in the Balkans, the convert community came in for even more attention and criticism; and not just because of their views on foreign policy. Just two months after Robert's conversion, a high-profile wedding took place at the Liverpool mosque where an Indian prince married Emily, a white 16-year-old convert. Many sections of the press were indignant at the event and barely attempted to disguise their sentiments, which quite transparently seemed to consist of 'these Muslims, coming over here, marrying our women'. Robert may well have attended this event - perhaps his first ever Islamic wedding.

Those involved with the LMI were extremely fond of celebratory parties and these early years of Robert's conversion were filled with them. In 1899, the simple fact of Quilliam leaving Liverpool to travel to the Sultan's Court at Constantinople was marked by an Osmanti parade and heralded by the sound of Turkish marches being played. *The Crescent* noted that the Muslims living in Manchester presented Quilliam with a blue silk robe to wear during his journey. The official vice-consul for the Turks in Manchester, Mustapha Karsa, was present at this event and it is likely that Robert would also have attended. *The Crescent* noted that another white convert, Mrs Robinson and her daughters, appeared wearing veils at the event.

During 1898 to 1899, the convert community in Britain was disturbed to learn that around 7,000 Muslims had been killed throughout Egypt and in Sudan as a result of the Battle of Omdurman; this was largely a result of Sir Herbert Kitchener seeking revenge on 'the dervishes' for the death of General Gordon in 1885. Quilliam reflected on the bravery of the dervishes, perceiving them to be fighting against colonial oppression, and he was roused to anger on hearing that the actual head of their fallen leader was in the possession of Kitchener: something which was never denied. After petitioning Parliament, Quilliam then decided to issue a proclamation – also known as a 'fatwa' – where he urged Muslims to isolate themselves from communication with the Christian world until the perpetrators behind this unjust war had been tried.

Following closely after this came news of yet more conflict in Algeria; this time the French were accused of slaughtering over 600 Muslims. By now, the sense

THE LIVERPOOL MOSQUE
Moslem devotion led by the Sheik ul Islam

In the Liverpool mosque: Quilliam in white, Robert behind him on the left

of alarm and probably of persecution on behalf of British Muslims must have been growing, thanks to a largely anti-Ottoman press. British press attention, however, soon moved from Egypt and Algeria and onto the Boer War in South Africa. Quilliam, though, felt that this war was a just one; like the Caliph, he sided with the British Government against the Boers. He believed that under the British, Muslims in South Africa would be treated with more freedom and that a British victory would open up the region to allow for more Muslim influence. Subsequently, he proudly noted that several members of the LMI had gone to fight in the Transvaal.

Quilliam – and Robert - remained loyal to Queen Victoria throughout her reign. This was a time in her life where the devotion of British Muslims to her would not have fallen on deaf ears. Her friendship with Abdul Karim, an Indian Muslim who had found himself in the strange position of becoming her closest confidante, had caused her to want to learn Urdu and to understand more about the Muslim faith.[111] Perhaps Victoria's own fascination with Islam, and the Indian subjects that she was never allowed to meet, protected Quilliam and his associates from receiving an even harsher backlash. Unfortunately, the presence of Abdul in court was not popular; he was associated far too much with simply having replaced John Brown, Victoria's closest male friend and servant who had passed away some years previously. But even worse than a gruff, outspoken Scotsman, here was a young, Indian Muslim who was clearly getting ideas above his station, and his favours from Victoria provoked much jealousy and racism within the Establishment. On the death of the Queen, her son, Edward VII – an unabashed racist - cruelly dispensed with her good friend, sending Abdul back to India and destroying all letters and intimacy that Victoria had shared with him and his wife.

In 1900, Quilliam realised that it was time to move beyond the more regional focus of his Liverpool Muslim Institute and he subsequently set up the British Muslim Association (BMA). This period was also marked by the growth of factions amongst the convert community, with increasing criticism being levelled at Quilliam from other convert leaders based in the West.[112]

Robert Stanley: A Jewel in the Crown?

It was important to Quilliam that a man like Robert had taken the decision to convert to Islam. This is evident through the fact that he constantly mentioned Robert's previous magisterial and mayoral status in his publications. For example, when he formally announced Robert's conversion to Islam in April 1898, Quilliam described him as 'Justice of the Peace for Stalybridge' and yet, thanks to the *Stalybridge Municipal Yearbook* 1907, we know that Robert requested his removal from the position of magistrate 'on his move to Manchester'. Quilliam's special regard for Robert, though, is best demonstrated when he chose to single him out for a feature on his life story within the pages of *The Crescent* in 1907, an accolade which comparatively few other converts ever received. It might seem strange at first to consider that for someone like Quilliam - a man who spent time with the fabulously wealthy and with royalty – that Robert Stanley was a personality who symbolised something rather important.

Geaves has noted that, "*British converts to Islam, especially those from educated or high-status classes, stood as iconic symbols not only for Muslims in Britain but also for those who remained living in Muslim countries.*" [113] Robert would definitely not have been considered of high-class status. However, there was something about Robert and about his life that seemed to indicate for Quilliam that he was perhaps a different sort of high class, maybe in relation to meritocracy as opposed to birth or a university education.

Quilliam, therefore, chose to describe Robert as, '*A Very Distinguished British Musselman*'. And it seems likely that as soon as Robert converted, Quilliam wanted him to become an active player in the LMI. Robert was quickly appointed as the vice-president of the LMI and was often there to meet royals and VIPs from

---

[111] S. Basu, *Victoria and Abdul,* The History Press, 2010. See also the excellent screenplay and/or the film of the same name by *Billy Elliot* writer, Lee Hall, 2017.
[112] Lord Headley, another famous white British convert, founded the British Muslim Society in 1914. Not all Muslims in Britain felt that Quilliam was the only leader for British Islam and he did receive criticism from other Western convert Muslims from time to time.
[113] Geaves, p.294.

overseas. When the Agha Adem Mesic of Tesanj, Bosnia, visited Liverpool in July 1900, the VIP stayed at the famous Adelphi Hotel and was taken on the 'usual' tour: the mosque and Muslim College, the Ottoman Consulate (presided over by 'Chancelier' Ahmed Quilliam Bey) and the Medina Orphanage – where, *'the children saluted the visitor in true Muslim manner, and several of them repeated in Arabic short extracts from Koran-Shareef'.* [114] Then the party went off to *The Crescent's* printing works, inspected the land acquired for building a new Jumma Mosque, visited Quilliam's home and finally saw a lecture at the LMI where a reception meeting was held. The list of the receiving line was reproduced in order of importance, *'the Ottoman Consul-General in Liverpool, Brothers Hasan El-Hadjwy (Fez, Morocco), R Stanley, Ahmed Quilliam'.* After this came another 50 names, many of them well-known converts such as the painter Professor Walid Preston, Djem Lester and all of Quilliam's family.

So, as far as Quilliam was concerned, it seems that Robert was 'top of the tree'. On 5th September 1900, Robert's letter to Quilliam was printed in *The Crescent*, where he apologises for being unable to,

> *...attend the ceremonies at the Mosque on Friday next in connection with the celebration of the Accession to the Throne of His Imperial majesty the Sultan of Turkey. Hoping the occasion will result in pleasure to all concerned. Yours truly – ROBERT STANLEY.*

However, it turned out that Robert was able to make the event after all, and this 25th Sultan's Jubilee was certainly a glittering affair, held at the Alexandra Hotel in Liverpool. Quilliam gave many speeches, using the event to remind those present that under Abdul-Hamid Khan, *"toleration to all sects and creeds of religion is to be found..."* He went on to describe at great length some of the atrocities of 'Jew-hunting' at the hands of Christianity and of the fact that, *"Jewry is starving in great masses in all parts of the globe,"* because of this.[115] After the fuss of presenting, *'a beautiful and costly gold English lever hunter watch,'* for the Sultan and to be passed to him by the Ottoman consul-general, there was plenty of cheering, the reading of telegrams and finally the procession into the banqueting hall. *The Crescent* then provides the reader with a list of who sat on the right and the left of the consul-general and who sat next to Mustapha Karsa Bey, Ottoman consul of Manchester: the seating order turned out to be Quilliam's son, Ahmed Quilliam Bey, and then 'His Worship R. Reschid Stanley, Esq., JP'. The magazine paints a vivid description of the occasion:

> *Over the head of the Consul-General was suspended an exceedingly well-written banner, on which was inscribed in letters of gold and in Turkish characters the well-known sentence Padishahim chok yarshah! Surrounded with a border of flowers and bearing the Crescent and Star as decorations at each corner. At the far end of the room, facing the Consul-General, and in full view of all present, was an excellent crayon portrait of his Imperial Majesty the Sultan in a handsome deep gold frame, draped with Ottoman banners and surrounded with a trophy of banners representing all the countries and*

---

[114] *TC*, 18th July 1900.
[115] *TC*, 5 September 1900.

provinces over which His Imperial Majesty holds sway... The tables were ornamented with a profusion of choice flowers, which had been so artistically arranged as to represent the Crescent and Star, the Star of the Medjidieh Order, and other pleasing devices. The menu would certainly not have been pleasing to a vegetarian; halibut, sole, shrimp, lamb's tongue, chicken, roast ribs of beef and boiled leg mutton. For pudding there was a lemon jelly, custard, and compote of fruits.

Certainly, a very English menu!

The list of the toasts was given on the opposite side of the menu, as printed in *The Crescent*; to the Sultan, Queen Victoria, The City of Liverpool, 'Our Visitors' – with each one being separated by a 'Pianoforte sole'. The final toast was to 'The Press' and proposed by 'Reschid Stanley, Esq, JP'. Unfortunately, we have no way of knowing exactly what Robert said, but trust that he was diplomatic in his words towards the media!

Queen Victoria died in January 1901. The grief expressed and the prayers made in her name on behalf of Quilliam and his congregation were undeniably genuine. During Edward VII's first year of rule, Quilliam spent a great deal of time out of the country on overseas visits, as well as receiving many visitors of Muslim royalty. Quilliam, however, continued to carry out his day-to-day duties – somehow managing to crank out his usual weekly editions of *The Crescent* and the monthly *Islamic World* whilst juggling his various work and civic commitments. He also presided over an increasing number of Muslim burials (see Chapter 11).

Meanwhile, Robert and his family suffered the sad event of Emma's death on 8th January 1902, at the age of 76. After 55 years of marriage, losing Emma from his life must have been a terrible shock. Having his two daughters living with him – and the presence of young George, as well – might well have brought some comfort to him, and certainly his Muslim friends in Liverpool and in Manchester would have done their best to support him during this enormous period of adjustment.

In 1903, Quilliam once again entered a sparring match with certain sections of the church and the press over the situation in the Balkans, and in a lengthy article in *The Crescent* defended himself, saying that surely denying the existence of God was far worse than merely dissecting the wrongs of British foreign policy. During the same year, Quilliam was introduced to Prime Minister Arthur Balfour. This was at the direct invitation of Lord Stanley, who had become a Muslim in 1869 – the first recorded white Muslim to be born and then to die on British soil. Lord Stanley's story has always struck me as being somewhat melancholy; his family continuously ridiculed his interests in 'all-things Oriental' and at times were downright horrible about his preoccupations, with even his nephew, famous writer Bertrand Russell, describing him as one of the most boring persons that he had ever met. It is difficult, however, to know what conclusion to draw on the life of this other 'Muslim Stanley'. He married a Spanish Muslim woman - whom the rest of the Alderley Stanleys were horrified to learn was already married - and after succeeding to the peerage, he ended up barring certain relatives from visiting the estate of Alderley. He may have been of a difficult character himself or felt himself wronged and misunderstood by the rest of his family. However, there was overwhelming sadness amongst the Muslim convert community when he passed away shortly after introducing Quilliam to the Prime Minister. British Muslims had lost their elder statesman, and, in his honour, the Turkish embassy sent both their ambassador and an imam to say the prayers alongside Quilliam at the Liverpool mosque in December 1903. Robert probably travelled to the mosque for this occasion and may well have accompanied the body back to the stately home of Alderley in order to witness the final burial. Perhaps all the 'Muslim fuss' at his funeral led to even more animosity on the part of Lord Stanley's family, because at his graveside his brother, Algernon, was said to have told Stanley's nephew, *"Not your hat, you fool, your boots"* along with saying that the peer had, *"lived like a dog, died like a dog."* [116]

In April 1901, Robert had ordered books from Quilliam and, by May 15th, he was still heavily involved in the affairs of the LMI, being listed at the annual meeting as 'Vice President in England'. This accolade was printed alongside the Ottoman Consulate General for Liverpool and Manchester, and Ismail Effendi of Southport and El Hassan El Hadjaway of Manchester. Robert is listed on this occasion as being from Stalybridge. In October, the convert community were invited to meet England's Turkish ambassador who was visiting from London and their names are all written in *The Crescent,* with 'His Worship R. Stanley, Esq., J.P' being right at the top of the list, followed by the artist Professor Walid Preston. In May 1902, the LMI was visited by the Shareef of Medina, with Robert being unable to attend and sending his apologies.

In 1905, Quilliam visited the Sultan again and came home bearing gifts from Constantinople. During these visits, Quilliam and his family were usually presented with awards, often as names and titles for achievements but also in terms of material gifts. Jewellery, provided as gratitude for loyalty to the Sultan, is mentioned in the pages of *The Crescent* and, unlike the declaration mentality required of today's politicians and religious leaders, was deemed to be a great cause for celebration and pride. It is likely that Quilliam also brought back gifts himself for some of his closest convert friends and, if not a gift from him, from the Sultan to be passed on. Although it is difficult to know for sure how far detached Abdul Hamid II was from dealing with his own written correspondence, given his closeness and regard for Quilliam it is highly probable that he already knew of Brother Robert 'Reschid' Stanley.

Robert had written to the Caliph on several occasions, dispensing words of advice and offering sympathies with the Caliphate (see previous chapter), and when my family first discovered the tie-pin found by Brian, after our gran's death in 2008, we wondered whether it had, in fact, been a gift from royalty for Robert himself; a thank you, perhaps, for Robert's services to the Ottoman Empire. A tiny crescent moon, set in gold, encircles a star containing rubies; it is clearly the symbol of Islam and would have been fastened into a man's lapel. It could have been that either Robert received it directly from Quilliam as a gift or it was passed onto him as a present from Ottoman royalty or the diplomatic service for this

---

[116] The allusion to 'boots' would have been in relation to Muslims taking off their shoes in a house or a mosque as a sign of respect – as opposed to removing their hat, as is the Western tradition. N. Epton, *Milord and Milady*, Oldbourne, 1962.

dedication. Yahya Birt believes that the pin was probably the symbol of membership of the LMI and worn by all converts.

Whatever its origin, given that my family are from a background that hardly has a cache of family jewels to pass down from one generation to the next, it is both astonishing and intriguing that it has been kept for over 100 years, with no explanation whatsoever, being passed down to us from Robert's son, 'Unlucky Bob', to his son, Dean, and then to Dean's daughter, Edith. For my family it will always be a priceless possession.

During 1905, Quilliam also visited Bulgaria, a country that had been so outraged at his opinions that it had banned his publications. Quilliam would have wanted to investigate the situation in the Balkans for himself; the Sultan was coming under increasing pressure from European powers and, for Quilliam, the crisis caused him to issue a fatwa against British actions of sending warships to the region in order to support naval manoeuvres against the Turks. At the celebration of the Prophet's birthday he told his followers, *"Islam is not like Christianity. It is a fraternity. He who strikes one Muslim injures every Musselman,"* and the full text of his speech against British action and the intentions of other European powers was sent to Prime Minister Balfour, whom Quilliam had recently

met. [117] He stated that the British were forcing 102 million Muslims in the British Empire to choose between, *"loyalty to an earthly ruler and loyalty to their religion,"* and his words were reproduced in the national press, causing a great deal of anger.[118] At the same time, another convert and close friend of Quilliam, Henri de Leon, made it his task to track every disaster in the newspapers that seemed to be unfolding in relation to failing British military manoeuvres and he attributed them to Quilliam's words.

Given the international situation, it became increasingly difficult now for Quilliam to promote conversion to Islam and, rather than pushing for positive publicity of Islam, he was instead trying to highlight the flaws of Christianity. Liverpool, like Stalybridge, had suffered grave sectarian ructions over the years and he took the opportunity to remind his readers of the violent religious riots of 1904, where Catholics were pitted against Protestants, *"whatever happened to turning the other cheek?"* he asked.[119] Despite the fact that the word treason was increasingly levelled against Quilliam by those who had a tendency towards British jingoistic sentiments, the LMI congregation battled on, determined to celebrate Eid al-Adha in their usual splendid style, complete with

Robert's tie pin – possibly a gift from Quilliam, or the LMI.

---

[117] Geaves, p.104.
[118] Geaves, p.104.
[119] Geaves, p.124.

wrestling competitions, fire-swallowing, music and slide shows.

Top Gear – to Manchester

During 1907 and in early 1908, Quilliam visited Manchester on many occasions in order to carry out various lectures and for his own source of entertainment, visiting the city's splendid Palace Theatre. Much ado was made about his trip to Manchester on 13th January 1907:

> He was met at the Central Station, Manchester by Brother Reschid Stanley, Esq., JP, the late Mayor of Stalybridge, and proceeded with him to his residence in Upper Brook Street. Later in the evening the Sheikh lectured at the Secular Hall, Rusholme Road, Manchester... Taking for his subject 'Morocco and the Moors', with the assistance of about fifty magic lantern slides, the Sheikh... pointed out many admirable traits in their character, and showed how it was through the interference of Europeans that a great deal of the troubles arose in that country.

Quilliam was very frequently on the road, delivering lectures to both Muslims and non-Muslims and by the 20th March 1907 edition of *The Crescent*, he had acquired a motor vehicle in order to aid him with his travels. The event had received considerable build-up in the pages of *The Crescent*; Quilliam was giving a lecture hosted by the Manchester Sunday Society on 'Constantinople', accompanied by 'magic lantern slides' and again held at the Secular Hall in Rusholme. The report of the day marks one of my favourite extracts in *The Crescent*. Seeing someone driving a car was still very much a strange site on most streets and *The Crescent* waxes lyrical about the car's prowess and mechanical wonders. The reader is informed that Quilliam was accompanied by his daughter, Hanifa, that the car was driven by Brother Osman Haton and that the, "*journey was accomplished in one hour and fifty minutes*" (not an unusual time, even today, for those of us familiar with the M62 from Liverpool to Manchester...) and that:

> On arriving at Manchester, the Sheikh was met by Brother Reschid Stanley, J.P., late Mayor of Stalybridge who entertained the Sheikh at tea ... A little after 10 o'clock pm, the Sheikh left Manchester again by motor-car, arriving home at his residence in Liverpool at half-past one in the early morning. The cause of the journey requiring more time in the evening was in consequence of the darkness of the night, as the way being mainly along lonely country roads, it was impossible to travel as quickly on the motor-car as in the daylight.

We can only wonder whether the task lay to Robert's daughters, Sarah and Mary-Jane, to provide tea at home for their father's rather unusual new friends on such occasions. No doubt Quilliam's arrival in his motor car would have made an unforgettable impression on their neighbours!

Quilliam was back in Manchester again on 15th December 1907. He had:

> ...motored over from Liverpool to Manchester, a distance of 35 miles (about 50 kilometres), the car being driven by Bro. Osman Haton. The Sheikh, on

arriving at Manchester processed to the house of Bro. Reschid Stanley, J.P.,
the late Mayor of Stalybridge, where they dined. After dinner, they proceeded
to the Secular Hall, Rusholme Road, Manchester where the Sheikh delivered
a lecture on 'Buddhism in Christianity', before a large and appreciative
audience ... we may mention that no less than sixty copies of his new book,
'Footprints of the Past', were sold at the bookstall in the Hall at the close of
the proceedings, and that if there had been more copies they could have been
sold, such was the demand for the same. Sheikh Abdullah Quilliam Bey
motored back in the evening, the journey being accomplished in one hour and
forty-five minutes.

The Poet
In the 30th January 1907, edition of *The Crescent*, an intriguing little poem
appeared:

WELCOME, AMERICAN COUSIN
(To my cousin Hannah Miller, on her visit from the Western States of America).

From Western lands beyond the sea
We meet, and kindly welcome thee.
Blood kinship hath a mystic tie,
Which none can fathom, none deny.
When seas divide, and time rolls on,
When youthful days are past and gone;
Remember then the pleasant time,
With kith and kin in Britain's clime.

RESCHID STANLEY, J.P., Ex-Mayor of Stalybridge

So far, we have no other examples of Robert writing a poem and having it
published (the local newspapers were full of this sort of thing at the time, so he
had ample opportunity to) and neither do we have any mention of his family by
him in anything that he was reported as saying in the press or in the pages of *The
Crescent*. What was so special about Hannah Miller? A woman whom he refers to
as 'cousin' even though we have scoured the family tree and have established that
she was actually a niece (the word cousin being employed frequently during this
period in history for a relative who was not a brother or a sister). It could have
been the simple fact that she had travelled such a long way to visit her family in
the north of England and that Robert wanted to honour this. He may even have
thought that Hannah would be amenable to considering Islam as a religious path
to follow. Certainly, many of the people who were increasingly choosing to migrate
to the USA were more open-minded to different religious paths and forms of
expression than many of the native British were. It was likely, too, that Robert felt
particularly touched by Hannah's visit given that he had only recently lost his
beloved Emma.

Quilliam allowed for the occasional romantically-inclined verse to be
included in *The Crescent*, and he was certainly no philistine when it came to the
arts (Yahya Parkinson was one of Britain's most well-known poets and a convert),

but in general the poems included in *The Crescent* were either about Islam or were love poems written by Quilliam under a nom de plume.[120] This makes Robert's poem even more intriguing and it indicates, by accepting and publishing the poem, a strong bond of fraternity between the two men. Of course, Robert may have persuaded Quilliam that he wanted an excuse to send copies of *The Crescent* to Hannah and her family in the USA and that including his poem would be a splendid opportunity for a bit of not-so-subtle evangelism.

A Last Interview

Quilliam's feature on Robert 'Reschid' Stanley took place in the 3rd April edition of 1907. After the death of Lord Stanley in 1903, he would have been seen by many as the elderly statesman of British Islam. The next few years proved to be filled with strife for the British converts.

By 1908, British relations with Germany were on a knife edge. Parliament was concerned that Turkey was edging towards a formal alliance with Germany. Quilliam and all the most well-known Muslim converts – including Robert – were seen as 'people of suspicion' and British Intelligence was keeping these individuals under surveillance. What we now refer to as 'Islamophobic attacks' on the LMI were ongoing. Right from the beginning, when the first British Muslim converts began to gather together in Liverpool at the Mount Vernon Terrace address, prior to purchasing the Brougham Terrace properties, they had suffered attacks and persecution: being pelted with stones and eggs, having the windows of the mosque broken and Frances 'Fatima' Cates – the first female convert under Quilliam – on more than one occasion was specifically targeted by local bigots who scooped up horse manure from the road, grabbed her, and rubbed it in her face. Various factions of the evangelical Christian church had always been unashamedly Islamophobic in their reaction to Quilliam and racist in their words towards Muslims; in fact, the low-level harassment experienced was one of the reasons that the congregation were asked to vacate the Mount Vernon address.

With the international situation looking graver than ever for those who practised Islam in Britain, Quilliam needed to do his utmost in order to convince the British people, the government and potential future converts that Islam was not a threat to the country. In the autumn of 1908, an exhibition in London entitled 'Muhammadan Art and Life - in Turkey, Persia, Egypt, Morocco and India' was put on and opened by the Turkish ambassador as an attempt to portray a more positive image of Islamic contributions to the world. However, Quilliam had always been convinced that the convert community were best placed to ensure that Islam could be incorporated into British cultural life, *"he believed that only British Muslims could achieve this, as Muslims originally from abroad would bring their own cultural baggage."* [121] Time and time again, Quilliam had tried to demonstrate that Islam was a moderate and peaceful religion and that, *"a Muslim had to practise their faith by conviction, rather than by birth."*[122] Robert 'Reschid'

---

[120] We do not know who Quilliam wrote his love poems about, but they strongly indicate a new infatuation as opposed to either of his two wives. They were written around the time that he made his visits to Manchester, and speculation has focused on his third wife as the interest in question (Henri de Leon's wife, Edith).

[121] Geaves, p.128.

[122] Geaves, p.130.

Stanley, a man who was so obviously distinguished and so loyal to the British way of life, had chosen to follow Islam. So why – Quilliam doubtlessly would have argued - would such a fellow have chosen to do so if Islam was a crackpot, violent and anti-British formulation of beliefs? Quilliam, too, would have been aware that Robert's story would have been especially appealing to those from a working-class background, unlike the Woking group of converts who tended to come from the upper class. In fact, Quilliam had been criticised by those such as the Christian missionaries who had visited the LMI for drawing together a congregation of converts who were, *"a very ordinary people ... drawn generally speaking from the lower ranks of life – persons, as a whole, neither of education, nor position."*[123]

Robert would have been aware of the importance of his own life story to Quilliam; he was no fool and would have known that Quilliam needed to validate Islam and that, in the current climate, publicity was needed to demonstrate that humble men of wisdom, learning and high intelligence were becoming Muslims. Perhaps he was also aware of the fact that Quilliam was notoriously reticent about his own life story, and he preferred not to speak at any length about his own conversion or private life. Robert might have felt that he was long enough in the tooth to be less concerned about going public about his own change in religious affiliations. Perhaps he felt that, because he was less of a controversial and flamboyant public figure than Quilliam, he could be an even better example to attract people towards Islam.

It is interesting to note, too, that Robert's story did not appear in *The Crescent* until six years after Emma's death. Perhaps by this point Robert would have become used to day-to-day life without her presence; he would have been a Muslim for nine years, certainly enough time for him to feel confident in his faith and perhaps less held back in terms of allowing the public to read his story as he sought to support Quilliam in upholding Islam in the British Isles.

---

[123] J. Gilham, *Loyal Enemies – British Converts to Islam 1850 – 1950*, OUP, 2014, p.101.

CHAPTER 11

The Empire Crumbles
1908 – 1911

This final chapter on Robert's life is somewhat slim in comparison to the others, simply because there is very little available material about the last two years of his life from 1909-1911. It is difficult to establish whether this paucity of material is related to Quilliam's hurried departure from Britain and the change in his identity, whether it was because of Robert's health declining or for another reason. It is hard not to assume that the last few years of his life were somewhat melancholy, but this conclusion should not necessarily be drawn.

The Flight of Quilliam

During 1907, Quilliam had taken up the case of a woman whom he felt was being unfairly treated by British divorce laws; he had prosecuted many such cases before on behalf of women. Over the years he had given numerous speeches and written many articles on the unjust nature of the British legal system when it came to the issue of women and the subject of property within marriage. He sought to compare unfavourable practises in Britain with what he argued were far more equitable rules and guidance within Islam. Quilliam's intention behind taking up this woman's case was to prove that the husband had committed adultery and was still doing so. English law required that the act of adultery be witnessed and Quilliam was accused of employing an underhanded tactic. He had been successful in finding a witness to stand against the husband and to declare that his adulterous behaviour had been witnessed, but it soon transpired that the man who took on this role was biased; he had previously been a clerk of Quilliam's.

In hindsight, we might struggle to judge this scenario too negatively, even if the accusations against Quilliam proved to be true and his methods of proving guilt were rather crafty. The woman was being deceived, after all, and Quilliam felt that she had been sorely mistreated; her husband was said to have quite a track record. He wanted to support her against the grossly archaic and sexist rules of the British legal system. However, it seems that some of his legal colleagues did not see it in the same light and, by July 1908, allegations of malpractice hit the press. Almost overnight, Quilliam's work in Liverpool was blackened by the charges against him. The last ever edition of *The Crescent* was published in May and it was announced that the Liverpool mosque was going to close. The death of his daughter, 11-year-old May Habibah from his relationship with Mary Lyon, had occurred only weeks before the divorce scandal case hit the press and by July 1908 Quilliam had disappeared from British public view.

From this point onwards, Quilliam's regular publications ceased, and his existence became shrouded in mystery. As the Ottoman Empire stood on the brink of collapse, the LMI announced that Quilliam and his eldest son, Ahmed, had been summoned to Constantinople, although for many, he was simply a guilty man grabbing a chance to leave the country so that he did not have to deal with the consequences of his actions. Before leaving Britain, though, Quilliam had informed his friends and colleagues that foul play and opportunism was afoot.

Prior to his departure, he had written to the press stating that he had never been in Glasgow, where the alleged adultery-entrapment had taken place. Some commentators find it strange, too, that the case was caught by the King's Proctor and flagged up all of a sudden when previously it had sailed through the courts without any sort of hitch. Whatever the truth behind the story, Quilliam had decided that it would be wise to leave Britain. He was struck off The Rolls in June 1909 and chose to stay in Constantinople: an extremely painful episode for him, as he was forced to witness the Young Turks rebellion and the final collapse of the Ottoman Empire. Not long after this, in September 1908, Austria annexed the Ottoman provinces of Bosnia and Herzegovina, in blatant violation of the 1878 Treaty of Berlin. Yet the rest of Europe seemed happy enough to turn a blind eye.

In November 1909, Quilliam's first wife, Hannah, died. By now, he had spent a year on the continent and whilst he was there two of his children with Hannah had also become gravely ill. In December 1910, he visited Britain, where he legally married Mary Lyon (who had never felt content with simply having undertaken 'just' the Islamic marriage ceremony in the mosque). But things were never going to be the same again for Quilliam; his glory days with the Liverpool convert community were over and, given the unstable situation on the continent, he became increasingly concerned as to how he was perceived by the British public and by the government. It was around this time that Quilliam decided to adopt a new identity: that of his old friend and fellow convert, Henri de Leon, who had recently died. Subsequently, it was the name of Henri de Leon that Quilliam carried to his own grave in 1932.

For many who admire Quilliam today, something seems to be rather strange – if not rotten to the core – about what he went through during those few years. Here was a man who cared little about British Christian morality – much of which he felt was hypocritical and oppressive – and who believed in equality and fraternity. Similarly, Quilliam had born no qualms about openly living with two different women and having two different sets of children with them. He had always had an excellent track record within the legal profession, as well as being highly regarded for his role within Liverpool civic life. Why would such a strong character suddenly feel that he had to slink away from British shores, simply because his professional reputation had taken something of a tumble? Of course, getting stuck off any professional register is deeply troubling for anyone, but for a man like Quilliam – who had access to powerful and rich friends overseas and who was easily operating a small but growing Islamic publication empire – would this be so absolutely devastating as to warrant his need to run away and to take on the new identity of a dead person?

Did Quilliam decided to leave Britain in 1908 for different motivations? Certainly, because of the situation in the Balkans and in the Ottoman Empire, and because of his close relationship with the Sultan and his pro-Turkish interests, Quilliam was deemed to be a person of interest to British Intelligence. Prior to the escalation of the situation in the various countries surrounding the Ottoman Empire, he would have already been under some sort of surveillance (like the Pankhursts and others deemed to be overly critical of the British Establishment) and perhaps now even more so. But whether he was a victim of conspiracy and the target of intelligence agents or not, his life was turned upside down from this point onwards.

Although we know that from 1908-11 Quilliam – now Henri – was living on the continent, and that in 1910 he also had a presence in England, we have no records that refer to Robert's participation in British Muslim society. Neither do we know anything about his life in Manchester for this period. In Liverpool, the convert community were now faced with an enormous problem; not only had they lost their leader, but there was the accompanying scandal and interest of the press. Quilliam's eldest son, Ahmed, accompanied his father to Turkey, whilst his next son, Bilal, remained in Liverpool. Bilal had recently qualified as a solicitor himself and Quilliam had given him power of attorney over all the property associated with the LMI. However, Bilal proved not to be the leader that his father was and certainly had less interest in nourishing the Islamic community within the city. He soon sold the properties on Brougham Terrace that were used as a mosque and community centre, leaving the converts lacking a place to gather. Over the years, with regards to Bilal's involvement, various financial irregularities came to light, too, with a missing funeral fund that many of the converts had paid into and with Bilal serving several prison sentences and finally being struck off by the Law Society in 1938.

This lack of leadership, and even of a sense of 'place', led to many members of the convert community drifting south towards the now-flourishing Muslim group in Woking and to the community under the figurehead of Lord Headley in London. Although Ahmed returned to Liverpool in 1912 and sought to revive the group there, the number of people following Islam in the area continued to dwindle sharply. The country teetered on the brink of the First World War as "an errant foreign policy had driven Turkey into the arms of Germany" and British Muslims at this time would have felt overwhelming pressure to go about their faith and lives quietly, with the minimum amount of fuss.[124] These, then, are probably the best explanations as to why we know nothing more about Robert's life as a Muslim from 1908 to 1911.

Going Home

In 1911, census data tells us that Robert had returned to Stalybridge. He was no longer living with his daughters, Mary-Jane and Sarah, but with his youngest, Alice, and her husband, Joe. Robert's granddaughter, Marguerite, aged 19, who had been brought up by her Auntie Alice, was also with them.

The family were living at 85 Wakefield Road and the house still stands there today, on a tight bend that takes the traveller past the top of Cocker Hill and onwards on the Huddersfield Road to Heyrod village. Given the national and international situation at the time and the impact that it had had on the life of Quilliam, it is hard not to imagine Robert's last couple of years as being somewhat sad, somehow disappointing. Over the years, he had spent his life trying to shine a light on injustices both at home and abroad, had risked his personal and professional reputation in pursuit of this and had done his best to juggle these intentions whilst still putting his family and his loyalty to the town of Stalybridge at the centre of things. In addition to the often-precarious nature of walking these

---

[124] Geaves p 247.

religious, political and social tightropes, he had also enjoyed great advantages: the benefits and distinction of corresponding and meeting with royalty, the thrills of being a close associate of such a magnetic personality as Abdullah Quilliam and of being deemed to be a wise and dignified elder statesman of British Islam. Not to mention the slow-burning fire of righteous anger which must have blistered in his belly against an all-too-often hypocritical Christian nation and its 'native' religion.

An account, published in 1912, by an Indian Muslim visitor who was keen to meet the Liverpool community and had travelled to the city in order to do this, mentioned the sorry state of the Islamic community there in comparison to what he had been told would be waiting for him. In this account, a direct reference is made to 'Brother Reschid' as being one of a small band of devoted Muslims who were still practising in Manchester. This would have been somewhat difficult (for Robert, at any rate) to achieve in 1912 – as he had passed away in 1911! But presumably his status and good works were living on as a legacy for British Islam and, of course, it was far more difficult to trace someone's whereabouts at this time, especially someone who was by now very elderly and living with his family who probably did not want others to know about his recent religious inclinations.

85 Wakefield Rd, Stalybridge – a final home

It is most likely that Robert relocated to Stalybridge soon after Quilliam left the country and the mosque in Liverpool closed. By this time, there would have been less cause for him to be living in Manchester. Not only was the Muslim community in Liverpool dwindling and no longer providing the vibrant hub and sense of fraternity as it had under Quilliam, but there would have been less need for the Stanley family to be living close to Robert's widowed daughter-in-law. His grandchildren were old enough now to fend for themselves. Emma, too, had gone, and it would have been a lonely time with painful memories, perhaps, for Robert, if he had remained in Manchester. We can presume that his health became more fragile and that, if he was ill, he may have been nursed by Alice and Marguerite during his final weeks. Certainly, most of us want the familiarity of home when we feel that we are coming to the end of our days.

Robert died on 6th September 1911, with the cause of death being noted by the doctor as 'senile decay', a term commonly used in the period as simply implying old age rather than any presence of senile dementia. He was buried at St Paul's churchyard and there is no indication that there had been any form of Muslim ceremony. When Brian located his great x 2 grandad's final resting place at St

St Paul's graveyard, Stalybridge – Robert's grave is the flat one

Pauls, he was horrified to learn that the area was due to be dug up and turned into a car park. Despite many pleas to the local authority, my family's request to at least save the headstone was turned down. We were told that we had not put a request in within the timescale required in order to save it, clearly an impossible thing for us to have achieved given that we had only just discovered the truth about Robert's life. We were only permitted to photograph the stone before it was smashed to pieces and the plot was flattened over to make way for the 21st century.

A Death. A Janazah?
The destruction of the family gravestone was more than a little upsetting. But the subject of Robert's burial has also become a cause for concern for many Muslim friends and relatives too; did the family overlook his desire for an Islamic burial? Was he unable to express his requirements lucidly? Some have wondered whether he decided to change his mind and turn back to Christianity in his final days. After all, there were certainly plenty of examples of Muslim funerals and janazahs carried out by Quilliam in Britain. *The Crescent* lists most Muslims being buried in Liverpool within a Muslim portion of the cemetery, but some Muslim burials also occurred in Manchester's Southern Cemetery; there does not always seem to have

been a straightforward practise in terms of who was buried where. For example, in 1897 Selim Muhamad Idielbe, a Syrian Muslim merchant living in Manchester, was buried in Liverpool by Quilliam. *The Crescent* noted that Christian onlookers gathered outside of the mosque and followed the cortege to the grave, where they behaved very well – apparently an unusual experience for such occasions.[125] In 1902, a 79 year old Syrian merchant named Mahomed Hollarby, died in Manchester and - like an Indian sailor who was on board a vessel on the Manchester Ship canal when he passed away - Hollarby was buried at Manchester's Southern Cemetery.[126] Hollarby had come to live in the city in the 1870s and had been close in age to Robert. A janazah was held for him at Manchester's Southern Cemetery, led by Quilliam whom, *The Crescent* reported, wore a robe of, *'chocolate colour, striped with green and gold and topped off with fez and turban.'*[127] The other mourners wore traditional black suits and wore their scarlet fezzes. Robert lived very close to the cemetery and would probably have been one of these mourners

Quilliam had also performed funerals elsewhere, too. A Turkish Muslim soldier had died at the coronation of Edward VII and Quilliam took the decision to head a procession with hearse throughout the streets of London, taking in an impressive and very deliberate stop-off at Westminster Abbey where, rather boldly, he stood outside of the doors and chanted a passage from the Qur'an, before travelling on to Woking for the burial.[128]

But so far as we can know, Quilliam did not preside over Robert's burial and, yet again, we are left having to guess at another important cornerstone of his life and times: why his final resting place lay in a Christian graveyard, as opposed to a cemetery where those of other faiths might be buried. The most likely answer seems to combine several factors.

The rise of what we refer to today as 'Islamophobia' in Britain at this time, would have caused Robert's family to proceed cautiously whenever faced with discussing his religious or political affiliations. Rightly or wrongly – and despite many other examples of Muslims who did not tie their colours to the mast of the Ottomans – Robert had consistently defended the Turks, and they were now German allies. As a provincial Northern town, Stalybridge lacked the cosmopolitan air of neighbouring Manchester. It lacked the confidence of 'daring to be different' and it would have been a frightening and unnerving time for an extremely conservative and respectable working-class family who felt that their loyalties to King and Country might be questioned: even more so, if Robert himself had been

---

[125] Funerals during the 19th and early 20th centuries were always a spectacle to behold and most attracted interested members of the public. This was even more so when the funeral was of a different religion, attended by people of different cultures and presided over by someone like Quilliam, who wore Ottoman robes. Inevitably, some of the Muslim funerals attracted troublemakers, but Quilliam hit on an ingenious method in order to deal with this. In 1902, at the funeral of Sheikh Ram-Jan in Liverpool cemetery, he ensured that the children from the orphanage attended, where they distributed hundreds of copies of *The Crescent* to the onlookers. Using cute children to stem off any violence, whilst at the same time evangelising Islam, proved to be a clever tactic.

[126] See Seddon. Southern Cemetery has a very old portion where Jewish and Muslim graves from this time period lie very close together.

[127] TC, 17th September 1902.

[128] See Geaves, pp 159-163 for more information on the funeral rites used by Quilliam.

under surveillance. Although there are no records of correspondence between Quilliam and Robert at this time it would not have been implausible for such letters to have been tampered with by those who wanted to keep an eye on Quilliam and his followers.

Indeed, all Quilliam's own personal papers were destroyed in a strange house fire at the home of Edith de Leon, his third wife, following Quilliam's death.[129] In 1910, we know that Quilliam - Henri de Leon - was living (ironically) on Christian Road in Preston, just some 40 miles from Stalybridge. Unfortunately, we have no information as to whether Quilliam/de Leon and Robert ever met up after his return to England. Of course, we have no evidence that Quilliam/de Leon visited Robert in his last few months or whether other members of the LMI stayed in touch with him. It certainly seems unlikely, though, for such a caring and close community to have suddenly forgotten Brother Reschid once he had moved home to Stalybridge.

None of Robert's children followed in his footsteps, in terms of becoming a Muslim, although the interest in civic affairs and politics has proven harder to break and, arguably, the pull towards Islam simply skipped a few generations. At the time of his death, most of Robert's children and grandchildren still had ties to Stalybridge. It is likely that they preferred to remember the days when their father was mayor of the town and received respect and accolades rather than recall a time that hinted of treachery and national disloyalty. We have no way of knowing if Robert's words and actions ever brought any discomfort home to his own family in Stalybridge, whether there were any Islamophobic attacks, or any form of prejudice experienced by them as the country tottered on the brink of war. It is likely, therefore, that his children simply wanted as little fuss and controversy as possible: a quiet, traditional burial and simply remembering his more British achievements.

There is also a practical reason, too, that explains his burial in a Christian graveyard. Robert and Emma had purchased a family grave, back in the early stages of their married life at St Paul's. Their one-year old son, George, had been interred there, followed by Emma herself, whose body would have been brought back from Manchester. The couple's adult son, John, had also been buried there – far from his own wife and children in Chorlton. It is not difficult to imagine both Robert and his family declaring the oft-said Lancashire truism of 'waste not, want not' when it came to the matter of gravesites. Graves were of huge cultural importance during this era. The family plot would have had a lot of time, effort and money put into it and many relatives would have been greatly upset if convention was ignored and if a family member could not be visited easily in their final resting place.

Whilst there is a possibility that Robert may have paid into the Muslim burial fund that the LMI had established it would have still been problematic for him to have been interred in Liverpool or in Manchester's Southern Cemetery alongside other Muslims. To begin with, the physical transportation of his body to the place of burial, plus the organisational factors of carrying out a janazah, would have had

---

[129] Edith had been married to Henri de Leon, Quilliam's friend. Quilliam took on Henri's name after his death and also married his widow. Sometimes the truth is stranger than fiction.

to have been overseen – with the necessary family agreement. Robert had not only physically moved away from the Manchester and Liverpool Muslims, but Quilliam was no longer keeping a public profile. It would have taken a strong personality to approach Robert's family and persuade them to follow his Islamic wishes. In short, it is unlikely that Robert would have had a Muslim advocate either with him or for him at his time of passing. In practical terms, the only religious supplicant available to him in his final moments, particularly if they were quite sudden, would have been Christian. Sadly, the Muslims in Liverpool were experiencing significant problems after Quilliam's departure, and the allegations of misappropriation of the LMI's funeral funds, whether accurate or not, would have negated any further chance of an Islamic burial.

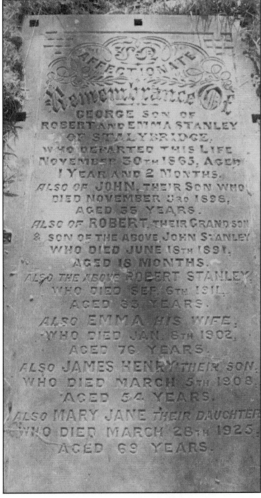

Robert's family grave – just days before it was destroyed in 1999

Whilst all of this might be cause for sadness on behalf of some readers as we close this final chapter on Robert's life, it need not be so. Robert very much remained a proud local man for whom family and faith were paramount. Even if his Islamic faith was not reflected after his passing, he would have been comforted by having the familiarity of his hometown around him and his family close to him at the time of death. Whilst we have no concrete evidence currently available to us with regards to this, it seems likely that in his final hours his devotion to Allah and to the Islamic faith remained.

The Last Word

We have no record of Robert's words from 1908-11. However, his life and achievements – we hope – are recognised and honoured every time someone picks up one of these two books about him, hears his story or refers to him in a speech, a class or a publication. With reference to Quilliam, Ron Geaves states that, *"British converts to Islam, especially those from educated or high-status classes, stood as iconic symbols not only for Muslims in Britain but also for those who remained living in Muslim-majority nations,"* and this remark precisely demonstrates the difference between Robert's life and the vast majority of other British converts. It reminds us why he is someone who deserves to be honoured and remembered. [130]

Robert 'Reschid' Stanley was not born of these classes, and he was not buried as those converts were. His views and opinions were - if not overtly camouflaged – subtly clouded over, probably as a result of the fear and misunderstandings of his family. His very being was woven into the fabric of these conservative mill towns and moulded into the tension and tragedies of a First World War just about to erupt. Unlike practically all the other well-known Muslim converts of this period, he was never able to venture abroad to visit a country with a predominantly Muslim population; his understanding of – and ultimately love for – Islam came from the good examples of people that he met on the streets and in the workplaces of Manchester and Liverpool.

And yet, thanks to the sheer strength of his personality and as a testament to his bravery, tenacity and convictions, the spirit of this proud Northerner found its way towards the Muslim faith. And today – despite being silenced for over a century – the life and beliefs of this Most Distinguished British Musselman have found their way through the darkness. And back into the light.

---

[130] Geaves p. 294.

Below are words recited in both English and Arabic by Sheikh Abdullah Quilliam at the janazahs of other LMI members that he presided over. If Robert could not hear them at the time of his passing, may he hear them now:

In the Name of Allah, Merciful and Compassionate
Know then, that this present life is only a toy and a vain amusement
A world of pomp and affection of glory anyhow ...
God permits man to come from an insignificant thing not greater than a drop of water ...
Death, like birth, is but a milestone of life ...

Out of the earth God created you and to the earth
thou art returned again, but of the earth God shall raise you again.
Thou wert created by God to receive the reward of this life, and to it, and to the worms art thou returned, and out from the soil of the earth shalt thou be raised to give an account of thy doings in the flesh.
May God, the One, the True, bestow mercy and peace upon you as you lie in your grave, for He is the Merciful and the Compassionate and the Forgiving God. Amin!

APPENDIX 1

AS PRINTED IN *THE CRESCENT*, 3rd APRIL 1907

note – using the exact grammar and spelling of Quilliam etc.

A DISTINGUISHED BRITISH MUSSELMAN

Bro. Robert Reschid Stanley, Esq., J.P.,
Late Mayor of Stalybridge.

We have pleasure today in presenting to our readers a photograph of Brother Robert Reschid Stanley, J.P., formerly Mayor of Stalybridge, but at present resident in Manchester.

Our earnest and worthy brother was born at Cardiff in September 1828. He subsequently left that town and settled down in Stalybridge about the year 1847, he then being about 19 years of age, and has been engaged in commercial pursuits from then until now.

About fifty years ago Bro. R. Stanley made the acquaintance of that distinguished traveller and writer, David Urquarht*, who had been for some time Secretary to the British Embassy at Constantinople. Mr Urquarht was then conducting an agitation in England warning his countrymen of the disastrous policy of some of the British statesmen in favouring the advance of Russia in Asia and Europe, and the attempts to destroy the Ottoman Empire and thus advance her own interests at the cost of her neighbour.

The arguments of Mr. Urquarht convinced Bro. Stanley that many of the British statesmen were under the influence of Muscovite agents, both male and female, and Bro. Stanley therefore threw in his own lot with Mr. Urquarht, and assisted in every way he could in advocating the interests of Turkey, and in active English interposition to prevent further Russian aggression against the Ottoman Empire.

In the years 1875 and 1876 our brother, who had for nearly a quarter of a century taken an active part in political life, was unanimously elected Mayor of the Borough of Stalybridge. Mr. Gladstone was then agitating the country by delivering most inflammatory speeches on what he termed "The Bulgarian Atrocities." Some of the deluded followers of Mr. Gladstone drew up a requisition, signed it, and presented the same to our Brother Stanley in his capacity as Mayor of the Borough of Stalybridge, requesting him to call a meeting of the inhabitants of Stalybridge to protest against the conduct of Turkey and support Mr. Gladstone in his agitation.

Our brother carefully considered the matter, and having read for himself the various Blue Books with reports that had been published upon the subject, he arrived at the conclusion that the Gladstonian agitation was promoted by Russian agents, and that the so-called Bulgarian atrocities were manufactured by newspaper correspondents simply for political purposes, and he accordingly wrote a dignified but emphatic letter to the promoters of the requisition refusing to accede to their request or to call a town's meeting on the subject. This letter was couched in vigorous language, and was filled with the soundest of arguments, and was widely published and circulated at the time, and created a great sensation, and induced other Mayors throughout the country, particularly the chief magistrates of Cork and Belfast and Wolverhampton, to follow the example shown by our worthy brother.

When the matter came on for discussion in the House of Commons, one of the speakers referred to this letter written by our brother as "a masterly exposure of the policy of Russia and the art of vilifying the Turk which had become so rampant in certain sections of the British Press," and the Right Honourable Benjamin Disraeli, afterwards Lord Beaconsfield, who was then Prime Minister of Great Britain, stated in Parliament that the Czar of Russia denied on behalf of his Government that he or they had had anything to do with either the atrocities in question, or the promotion of agitation in England.

The public, however, took a different view of the question, and Mr. Gladstone was mobbed in his own house by a large number of supporters of a Turkophile policy.

This emphatic action on the part of Bro. Stanley met with considerable disfavour in the minds of that section of the public of Radical tendencies, and some violent speeches condemning his action were made against him at the time, on both political and religious grounds, by persons with whom up to that period he had been on terms of the greatest friendship; but at the conclusion of the Russo-Turkish war, our brother had the satisfaction of finding that several of the persons who had condemned his action in a most violent manner, had now come to the opposite conclusion, and they were as warm themselves in condemning the cruel manner in which Russia had concluded the war, and the extortionate demands made by the Czar and the Russian Government upon the Ottoman Empire, whilst they were charmed and amazed at the heroic advance that had been made by the Turks under martial Ghazi Osman Pasha at Plevna, and they admitted to Brother Stanley, and on some instances even publicly declared that he was quite justified in the course he had taken in refusing to assist in the agitation against the Ottoman Empire.

A little later an attack on Penzah in Afghanistan opened the eyes of a number more of those who had supported the Gladstonian agitation, and they admitted that Mr. Gladstone had undoubtedly been simply made use of as a cat's paw and a tool in advocating Russia's interests in the manner he had done.

A few years later, after George Ville, a distinguished French chemist, had been commissioned by Napoleon III., Emperor of France, to investigate the subject of agricultural chemistry, he published a book demonstrating how the soil became exhausted of its fertility by cultivation, and how it could be restored by means of the use of certain mineral substances which were abundant in most countries, the soil of the same being practically inexhaustible, and that by this means the most barren soils could be rendered profitable for the cultivation of suitable plants or vegetables, and the result of his discoveries the French Government had adopted the same, and were able to derive and still receive, a large revenue from what was formerly barren and arid sand. Our esteemed brother, in his desire to assist the Ottoman Empire, sent a copy of the work in question to the Caliph of the Faithful, H. I. M. Ghazi Abdul Hamid Khan, Sultan of Turkey, accompanied with a letter showing that if the policy advocated in that work could be carried out in Turkey, the agricultural population could be assisted and more persons could derive a living from agricultural pursuits in that Empire; and this work being provided for a larger population, the number of persons available for military service in defensive warfare would be considerably augmented, probably to the extent of at least fifty thousand persons, and had this policy been carried out, say, for a quarter of a century prior to that date, at least fifty thousand soldiers could have been added to the army and the treaty of peace would probably have been signed on the other side of the banks of the Danube instead of at St. Stefano. Our brother received a letter of acknowledgement from the Imperial Chancellery, and, as showing the interest which His Majesty takes in all matters concerning the welfare of his subjects, an Empire Irade was shortly afterwards promulgated directing that these young Turks should be selected from the Imperial civil school and sent to study in the agricultural schools of Germany in order to qualify them for the posts of inspectors of agriculture in the Ottoman Empire

In order to become more fully acquainted with the tenets of the Islamic faith our brother read and re-read Sale's Translation of the Koran-Shareef, and was much impressed by the same.

He also was struck by the doctrine set forth in that holy work and with the manner in which Christians persistently misrepresented the teachings thereof, and also with the manner in which in some of the footnotes to that work a construction was attempted to be put upon the passages thereof in a manner which the sense of the context did not reasonably allow. Our brother therefore wrote to the noble and exalted Caliph of the Faithful, suggesting that it would be wise to have an authentic fresh translation of the Koran made at as early a date as possible, so that English people who desired to know the principles of Islam could study the holy book of the Mussulmans in their own language; as the present translations were written by Christians and were calculated to create prejudice in the minds of persons reading the same.

Our brother is firmly convinced that such a work if completed would carry conviction to any unbiased mind who read the same and would do much to remove the misunderstanding unfortunately so prevalent at the present time amongst English speaking people as to the life and teaching of our holy Prophet.

A few years ago another agitation was instituted in the British Isles by fanatical Christians and others with respect to the alleged disturbances in certain provinces of Turkey inhabited largely by Armenians, and it was stated that several bands of men disguised as Kurds invaded that province, and had compelled some of the inhabitants thereof by menaces and threats to commit outrages and rise in revolt against the Government. Such conduct of course, could not be allowed to continue, and the Ottoman officials who were in charge of these provinces, were obliged to take vigorous measures to suppress such risings and disturbances. Stringent measures were taken and a great outcry arose in the British Isles that outrages were being committed by Turks upon Christians, whereas in truth and in fact, they were simply the necessary precautions which it was absolutely essential for any civilised government to take for the suppression of murder, rapine and outrage which the Armenians were carrying on every side.

As is usual in England when it was possible by any pretence to attack the Mussulman and his creed, meetings were held in many villages and towns throughout the country. One of these were held in Manchester, and our brother attended thereat and vigorously protested against the misrepresentations which were made against Turkey and its Government, and subsequently wrote to the Marquis of Salisbury, Prime Minister of England, pointing out to him that the meeting in question had really no political significance inasmuch as it was only attended by females, curates, Dissenting ministers, idlers, and persons of that ilk, and that what was most conspicuous of all was that the leading members of the Armenian community and the principal inhabitants of the City of Manchester were conspicuous for their absence from the meeting.

A copy of this letter was written by our esteemed brother to the Marquis of Salisbury, was published verbatim in the columns of the "Crescent."

During this agitation some of the members of the British House of Commons and several editors of Turkophobe newspapers brought forward a scheme which they advocated for a division of the Ottoman Empire. Our esteemed brother at once wrote to the principal promoters of this foolish project and to the editors of the paper in question a satirical letter saying that if Turkey was to be divided in that way, he trusted that some portion thereof might be presented to himself. This was also published in extenso in the columns of the "Crescent." One result of the publication of this letter broadcast in the manner described was that the foolish project was covered in ridicule.

Some time ago after Professor A. Vambery paid a visit to H. I. M. the Sultan of Turkey, in describing the result of his visit he ended his remarks with some uncalled for and somewhat disrespectful allusions to His Majesty. Our indefatigable brother at once wrote a letter to the Press, a copy of which was also published in the "Crescent," in which he pointed out the injustice and unfairness with which Professor Vambery and many of the English newspapers had spoken of the Sultan, and showed how they endeavoured to make His Imperial Majesty responsible for any alleged fault, however small, that might be committed by a Turkish official, even although he occupied a subordinate position in some remote province of the Empire, and knowledge of which action it could not be possible for the Sultan to have. At the same time it pointed out that no one ever thought of charging the Czar of Russia or the King of England in a similar manner; and that where the newspapers in England commented upon the necessary precautions which were taken to guard the safety of the valuable life of H. I. M. the Sultan they appeared to forget how often the life of both the late Queen of England and the present King had been attempted, and how many presidents, emperors, kings, rulers, and other public men had from time to time been assassinated.

At another period, in the interests of the Ottoman Empire, Brother Reschid Stanley wrote to the Sultan pointing out that two hundred years ago Damascus and Baghdad were the greatest commercial centres in the world, and that at that time manufacturing certain goods by machine was unknown, work having to be done by hand labour.

The advent of machines enabled goods of this class to be made at much less cost than they could be made by hand, and the treaties of commerce existing between Turkey and the other European Powers, whereby certain goods were to be admitted into the Ottoman Empire free of duty, practically destroyed the home trade in hand made goods, the result of which was that the home manufacture of these articles in the Ottoman Empire had been practically killed, and thus the means of livelihood of great numbers of the inhabitants of Turkey had been taken from them and they were rendered unable to get their living by the labour of their hands.

The object of our brother in writing his letter was to suggest to the Ottoman Government that every encouragement should be given to promote the manufacture of the class of goods required in Turkey itself, in order thereby to increase the resources of the Empire and thus to provide a means of living to a large increased population.

At the same time our brother did not forget that existing treaties with foreign Powers prevented the Ottoman Government from increasing certain imported duties on articles manufactured by some of the European nations; but he pointed out that there was nothing in these treaties to prevent the Ottoman Government giving bounties to their own people to encourage a greater production of home-made goods; and our brother felt that if a few young men were sent from the Imperial Civil School at Constantinople over to England, particularly in the Lancashire and Yorkshire districts, to study the manufacture of cotton and woollen goods in Technical schools in this country, that on their return to Turkey there would be little doubt but that the matter could be taken up, and the Turks, by establishing manufactories in their own Empire, would become independent of foreign manufactures, and thus employment be found for a large number of inhabitants of that country.

We have already alluded in this article to the fact that our esteemed brother has filled the chair of Mayor of the Borough of Stalybridge in the years of 1875-1876, and that he had been created a Justice of the Peace for the Borough in 1867. The Jubilee celebrations of the existence of half a century of Stalybridge as a borough were celebrated this year and our distinguished and esteemed brother was invited to partake in the celebrations, and as the senior surviving Mayor of the Borough was given a prominent and distinguished place at the celebrations; and the Stalybridge Year-Book for this present year not only contains an excellent photo of our brother in his Mayoral robes, but also contains the following biographical sketch of his career which we have pleasure in reproducing;-

FROM THE STALYBRIDGE YEAR-BOOK 1907
ROBERT STANLEY, ESQ., J.P.
Ninth Mayor, 1875-76

Mr. Robert Stanley was born at Cardiff in the year 1828, and at ten years of age came to Ashton-under -Lyne, being engaged in a grocer's shop kept by his uncle, John Stanley, in Stamford Street, known as the old Johanna Shop. He afterwards went to a grocer's shop near the Town Hall, Stalybridge, now occupied by Burgess and Sons, *and in 1848 commenced business for himself in Princess Street, now called Melbourne Street.*

Mr. Stanley was elected to the Council to represent Dukinfield Ward in 1863, was elected for Staley ward in 1869, was appointed Alderman and Mayor in November 1874 and re-elected Mayor for a second term. He was appointed a Justice of the peace in 1867, was chairman of the Building Committee for the Market Hall during its construction, was one of the original Trustees of Stamford Park before it was taken under Municipal Control and was Deputy Chairman of the Joint Waterworks during the construction of the Yeoman Hey Reservoir at Greenfield.

During his connection with the Council, Mr. Stanley was called as a witness before the Parliamentary Committee appointed under the chairmanship of the Marquis of Hartington with reference to the desirability of adopting the Ballot Act for parliamentary and Municipal Elections. He was under examination for nearly three hours, answering over 300 questions. The under-secretary for foreign Affairs left his seat on the committee and personally thanked Mr. Stanley for his evidence, and it also formed matter for a discussion in Parliament.

A requisition was presented during his Mayoralty asking that a meeting of the inhabitants be called to urge the Government to interfere to prevent the Turkish Government from suppressing the disturbances in Bulgaria. This Mr. Stanley refused do, on the ground that the outrages were the work of hired ruffians prompted by Russian agents, and that the measures taken by Turkey, are only in those interests of good order which every government is bound to uphold. For taking this view of the matter Mr. Stanley was freely condemned more particularly perhaps because of the statement made by Mr. Disraeli, as Prime Minister, to the effect that he had the word of the Russian Emperor that his Government was in no way concerned in the outrages. At the conclusion of the Russo-Turkish war however, the cruelty of Russians and their exorbitant demands proved that Mr. Stanley's view of the matter was not very wide of the truth.

Mr. Stanley retained his position in the Council as Alderman till November 1880, when his connection was terminated by removal to Manchester, where he now resides.

The earliest appointed of the ex-Mayors who are still living - is a distinction he can lay claim to."

(*Note – Quilliam's spelling of 'Urquhart' in the above article is incorrect).

APPENDIX 2

INFORMATION ON PROPHET JOHN WROE AND THE SEVEN VIRGINS DEBACLE IN ASHTON-UNDER-LYNE, 1830–31.

Most of the information on the 'Seven Virgins scandal' has been taken from the Manchester-based newspaper *Voice of the People* and used verbatim – as fact - by other historians during the last century. The *Voice* was considered by most in polite society to be something of a rabble-rouser and more a tabloid than a quality broadsheet newspaper. Other regional newspapers reported on the debacle, of course, with the *Sheffield Courier* also providing more detail than others. However, the *Voice* stands head and shoulders above the rest for the degree of enthusiastic – and explicit – information that it shared with its readers.

The names of the women involved in the hearing were given on page 72 in the 4th March 1831 edition of the *Sheffield Courier*, which stated that the women making the allegations against Wroe were Ann Hall of Doncaster, Sarah Pile of Devon and Mary Quince (also probably from the same area as Sarah). The *Voice* and the *Courier* reported that Wroe had appointed the seven virgins as servants but that, in the late summer of 1830, one of them came forward to accuse Wroe of impropriety after she accompanied him on a missionary tour throughout the North. She accused him of *'indecency and things not fit to be spoken'* and the accusations were replicated by the two other young women who worked for Wroe and declared against him.

The *Sheffield Courier* stated that these were three of the seven virgins and that they all said that the source of the problem had been Wroe's obsession with wanting to generate the birth of the Shiloh; that he had told each of them that he was to be honoured as the, *"holy instrument for bringing about this glorious event"* and that they were threatened with judgement if they told anyone else of their purpose. The *Voice* also went the extra mile in terms of titillation for its readers, stating that Sarah Pile had told those assembled at the hearing that Wroe used to, *"suck on her breasts and declare that he could live on them"* and that he caused her, *"to inflict a peculiar punishment upon him which he had appointed for disobedient and offending females"*, which the newspaper at that point decided was, *"too gross to be mentioned."* More than a little bit racy for your average Victorian audience, even those who chose to read the tabloids!

These same newspapers reported that the presence of the seven virgins within the new home, built for Wroe in Ashton, had caused Mrs Wroe to want to spend most of her time in their Bradford house and that allegations had been made that Mrs Wroe had previously caught her husband 'in the act' at their Bradford home with one of the women. This woman had apparently been asked to transcribe Wroe's words as he was not a strong writer, and the story goes that Mrs Wroe had found them up to no good and that the 'transcription' was simply a ruse for Wroe to spend time with the servant. This was also the same servant who brought forward the initial allegations in relation to Wroe taking advantage of her whilst on a mission across the North. Wroe, however, dismissed all of this, saying that she had been angry with him because his son, Benjamin, had caught her stealing jam from the pantry and that, consequently, he had told her she must be demoted and become servant to his wife instead. Certainly, Mrs Wroe did tend to stay away from the home in Ashton, preferring the Shepley Gatehouse and the Bradford home, and Wroe had noted her jealousy in his own private diaries; he had even prophesied her feelings, predicting that their unborn child would die because of it.

Whatever the truth, no other female servants came forward to make allegations against Wroe and there was never a legal case lodged against him, just a lengthy church hearing. The problem for the Christian Israelite church, however, was the fact that there were already whispers of suspicion against Wroe and his behaviour which was deemed to be very outlandish and eccentric, and it was not the first time that Wroe had been accused of scandalous behaviour. In Bradford, in 1827, a warrant had been drawn up for his apprehension when it was rumoured that a 13-year-old apprentice at his Tong Street home had fallen pregnant. It must have been horribly upsetting for the girl to have been internally examined by a doctor (on three separate occasions) but, perhaps to set the balance straight, the doctor at least also insisted on checking Wroe out, too (presumably for venereal disease). Either way, Wroe was not prosecuted in a court of law and in the end the girl was formally discharged from service at the Wroe home. There is no record, either, of her ever giving birth.

To add to the sexual nature of the seven virgins scandal, in 1831 one of the particular – and very outlandish - criticisms levelled at the Christian Israelites was that they placed emphasis on physical punishment for sinners. A book by a former Scottish Presbyterian minister was published in 1857, a good amount of time after the 1831 case and after he had left the Christian Israelites on very unhappy terms. This author tore into John Wroe, who he thinly disguised as a character in the book leading a sect, which was clearly meant to be the Christian Israelites, and whom he called 'John the Jew'. The author continued to rail against the church and alleged that the strange physical punishments did take place, that at Wroe's direction a 'cleansing room' was built underneath the ground floor of the Sanctuary. It was stated that men who had sinned were immersed in water seven times and beaten on the buttocks by women, who cupped the men's genitals as the thrashing took place. The men were apparently forced to record each strike with a piece of chalk on a chalkboard. These allegations were said to have continued as a practise within the early establishment of the church in Australia but were outrightly rejected then – as now – by the Christian Israelites, whose response was that the author – and many others, too – detested Wroe and wanted to blacken his name with a detailed sexual scandal.

Over the years, other rumours developed in relation to a marriage which was said to have taken place between Wroe and Sarah Lees. Sarah was the daughter of the wealthy widow Hannah Lees and sister to Henry Lees (one of Uncle John Stanley's fellow Number Four). The marriage was said to have been hushed up after it took place in 1823 in order to produce the Shiloh. But the Christian Israelite church in

Australia state that this tale was simply a misinterpretation by an earlier historian of a newspaper report of such a marriage between a church leader for this purpose and that it had gone on to become a (wrongful) local legend. The church states that the bridegroom was not Wroe but instead a man with the name of Twigg, who was one of Wroe's rivals for prophetic leadership and who felt sure that he could generate the birth of the Shiloh. When the child was born to Sarah it turned out to be a girl, which clearly was not the intended gender for a Shiloh.

It is incredibly difficult to untangle the truth of the matter and determine whether Wroe was indeed a rogue and a sexual predator or simply a man who was hated for his personality and his desire to lead the church, a man who suffered from the most appalling blackening of his name. Either way, Robert Stanley remained silent on the subject. He was happy enough to get married at the Christian Israelite church in 1847 but by the 1860s was worshipping at the local Anglican church. This may have had something to do with the publication of the book in 1851 that declared against Wroe, and the death of Uncle John Stanley, but on the other hand it may have simply been that Robert's spiritual journey had moved on and away from the Christian Israelites.

As with many aspects of Robert's life, the background of the Wroe scandal and the impact that it had on his life is something that we will never know; and yet it is important not to continue a version of history relating to the Christian Israelite church that has remained, until now, almost completely unchallenged.

(See Chapter 2 footnotes for further information on the Christian Israelites).

APPENDIX 3

EXAMPLES OF ROBERT'S MAGISTRATE CASES

As with the town council meetings, thanks to *The Stalybridge Reporter*, which had a permanent desk in the courtroom, we can read Robert's words verbatim, the speech of all who came before him, as well as the reaction of the courtroom. Most of the cases in this chapter are taken from the period 1872-76, with more cases represented from 1874-76 due to Robert being chief magistrate at that time. Rather than adding endnotes to each case, the edition of *The Stalybridge Reporter* that they appeared in is mentioned as the date of occurrence. I have indicated where Robert was not mayor and chief magistrate when a judgement was made.

The Violent Adults
Over the years, Robert had to deal with hundreds of cases of fighting in the streets. Many of those mentioned that the culprits were 'Irish' (although no other ethnic group is ever mentioned!). The typical sentence that Robert gave for street fighting was 14 days and hard labour with the choice of a fine instead. Robert also had to deal with at least one unpleasant case of violence against women at the hands of men on a weekly basis. Other examples include:

-    A police officer who was escorting two women home at night was attacked on 1st August 1874. A neighbour approached the group and, when the constable joked, *"we've all been turned out of the workhouse"*, the neighbour – clearly not a fan of the police – attacked him. Robert took a harsh view of this and sentenced the man to four months in prison with hard labour.

-    On 17th April 1875, a man beat his wife so severely, by kicking her in the mouth and then the rest of her body, rendering her incapable of walking, that Robert told him he, *"ought to have a severe punishment"*. He was sentenced to three months with hard labour and no fine option.

-    A large amount of money was stolen from The Fleece Inn on 26th September 1874. Robert sentenced the man; a week later the *Reporter* told of a related story, entitled 'A forgiving wife and a brutal husband'. Because the woman had given evidence in the previous week's case, which was presided over by Robert, her husband, a good friend of the thief, had beaten her. The prosecution against the man was not brought by the woman; in fact, in the courtroom she refused to talk about it to Robert. She was clearly terrified of the man and his cronies. Even though the female examiner present at the police station had seen her horrific bruising and gave witness to it, the woman refused to accuse her husband. There was little that Robert could do in these circumstances; no sentence could be made.

-    On 28th November 1874, the *Reporter* introduced 'another wife beater,' who had badly kicked his wife. Robert told him, *"the magistrates throughout the country are generally inflicting severe penalties for kicking women. We shall fine you 20s 6d and costs, or 3 months imprisonment with hard labour"*.

- A less traumatic and rather more colourful episode occurred in September 1874, when a husband and wife were arguing over the issue of their collective debt and started walloping each other with a brush.

- On 21st November 1874, an argument had developed between two women, who ended up taking swings at each other and then began hitting each other with brushes, because the first woman spat on the shoulder of the other woman whom, she claimed, had been bullying her child. Robert gave both the women a good ticking off and simply dismissed the case.

- In the *Reporter*'s 'Early Trouble In Married Life,' on 16th March 1875, the newspaper outlined that Robert had heard a case where a young married couple were arguing fiercely (see Chapter 5 for more information).

- On 7th November 1874 (during the local elections when Robert was also elected as mayor) a man was killed after being hit with a beer bottle during an attempt to bribe him to vote in a certain way (see Chapter 4 for more on bribery during elections).

- A case reported on 21st November 1874, involved a man kicking his eight-year-old child. Robert listened to the evidence at length, with the *Reporter* yet again choosing the title of 'A Forgiving Wife'. At the end of the hearing, Robert dismissed the case, saying that he felt convinced that the kick administered to the child was indeed an accident, but he warned the man, *"I hope I shall not see you here anymore."*

- *"A fast-young man,"* as the *Reporter* described him on 6th February 1875, was making a bad habit of attending 'public ball fights' every Saturday night. Robert's sentence was simply a fine.

The Thieving Adults

Small business owners and shopkeepers are always the hardest hit by petty theft; it is, therefore, perhaps reasonable to expect a magistrate who is drawn from this background to be quite merciless when it comes to prosecution and sentences. As a grocer, Robert would have been acutely aware of the impact theft and larceny could have on his own livelihood, but he also showed himself not to be too hard in terms of his sentencing:

- The theft of a fowl by Thomas Booth on 2nd March 1874, from a grocer. Despite telling the man, *"if you had not told such a lie, you would not, very likely, have been here,"* he decided that, *"the prisoner should be set at liberty".*

- On 20th March 1875, the *Reporter* told its readers that a woman had stolen glasses and four eggs from a shop. Robert, rather kindly, let her off with a small fine only, telling her, *"we were inclined to believe you were tipsy and you did not know what you were doing,"* but another time, on 21st November 1874, for the theft of a shawl from another woman, he gave an old woman one month's imprisonment with hard labour. Perhaps he thought that going hungry and taking eggs, as opposed to hankering after clothing, was deemed to be a more reasonable excuse for light-fingered behaviour.

- The *Reporter* took great delight on 3rd April 1875, in declaring a 'Filthy Dirty Thief'. Bacon was the object of this man's desire and, after being found with the meat tucked away on him, everyone who encountered the thief was of the same mind: not only was he a robber, but he was a rather smelly one, too. Robert announced to the courtroom that the man was in, *"a filthy state"* and felt that prison would be the best course for him, *"it will give him the opportunity to get cleaned".*

- A woman stole mackerel from a fishmonger, slipping four of them into her apron. She was discovered in Samuel Peeke's Tripe Shop and was arrested. She told Robert, *"I did not know where I was until the next morning, I was so drunk".* Before she was sentenced, it is interesting to note that the police in Stalybridge had obtained a list of all the previous crimes that she had committed in Ashton, a long list of larceny, theft and 'drunk and riotous' behaviour, and these were read out in court: not something that would be permitted in today's modern courtrooms.

The Misbehaving Adults

The newspapers were filled with the bizarre – and sometimes amusing – cases that Robert had to hear and to rule on:

- A drunken man got onto a train and ended up in Stalybridge, far away from his intended destination, without having a ticket. On 20th March 1875, Robert (who was not a fan of the Manchester, Sheffield and Lincolnshire Railway) let the man off with a small fine and told the court that it was the railway company's fault.

- A very elderly man had been left 'abandoned' in Ashton's workhouse and, on 17th July 1875, his two sons were summoned before the mayor for refusing to maintain him. There appeared to have been some sort of disagreement between the brothers as to who should support the father's bed and board in the workhouse, with both claiming that they couldn't afford it. Robert, however, had little sympathy, telling them that if they could not take their father into their own home then they would be ordered to pay his costs at the workhouse.

- A case of begging was heard on 21st November 1874, when a man walked all the way from Liverpool to Stalybridge. Perhaps some wag had told him that the streets were paved with gold there. Robert seemed to feel some empathy for the Scouser, telling the man, *"We shall let you off, but you must leave this town."*

- Adulterated tea was a big problem during this era and the Government had recently taken efforts to address it under the Adulteration Act. Robert had to deal with one of his fellow shopkeepers being accused of this and appearing before him (see Chapter 8 for case details).

- A weights and measures case occurred when a grocer owning a shop on Princess Street (just yards from Robert's shop and whom he no doubt knew well) was accused of overcharging for potatoes. The chief constable had found that the scales were 14 drachms against the purchaser. The mayor, however, decided to, *"take a lenient view of the case,"* with the *Reporter* quoting him on 16th February 1875 as saying, *"the bench could not expect shopkeepers to clean their scales every time they were used, and it was a practice in the greengrocery trade to make allowances for any dirt by giving extra weight".* The man was only ordered to pay a fine of 1s or seven days hard labour. Hoorah for the small shopkeeper!

- Gambling – or 'tossing', as it was then known - was a huge problem in Victorian society. Taking bets was illegal unless within a registered betting establishment and, on 8th May 1875, a 'tossing on Sundays' case occurred, with the *Reporter* describing the young men involved as *"blackguards"* and one of them *"a rogue and a vagabond".* Robert had no choice other than to take the matter seriously and sentence them to six weeks in prison.

- On 3rd April 1875, the *Reporter* recounted a strange tale that involved a police constable 'befriending' another man. (See chapter 5 for more.)

The Drink. And 'More Drunken Women!'

Alcohol abuse was perceived to be one of the biggest social problems at the time. In many areas of the country, beer was cheaper than the cost of clean drinking water and it was a sad truth then – as now - that those who are the most down-trodden and the most unhappy in society were driven towards the need to drink. But inevitably it was the issue of women and alcohol that caused the most outrage.

- On 21st November 1874, Robert told a drunk and disorderly man that, *"as it was Sunday, we shall fine you more than for any other day."*

- On 24th April 1875, Robert had to hear the story of "Drunk at 15 years of age!" and chose to discharge the boy, telling him this was because, *"you are so young - but don't get in such a hobble again."*

- On 19th September 1874, a case related to a woman visiting from another town who got so drunk at the Stalybridge Agricultural Show that she couldn't find the man who had accompanied here there, or even find her way back to Stalybridge train station. Robert fined her 1s or seven days hard labour.

- On 28th November 1875, a woman had turned up to the courtroom, having oiled her wheels with a rather substantial amount of Dutch courage. Robert told her, *"if you had come here sober, we would have let you off with half a crown and costs, but we will fine you 5s and costs or 7 days hard labour".*

- Of all the various repeat female drunken offenders, the notorious Rosanna Fox made most of the news headlines (see Chapter 5 for more information). Below is the full editorial taken from the *Reporter* on 21st November 1874:

There is an old saying that it is 'bad enough to see a drunken man, but it is ten times worse to see a drunken woman'. If some of the women of Stalybridge appeared at the police court in the same percentage – one to every ten men – [as they do for all other crimes] we should have a much happier state of things in the borough than we have at the present time. It is seldom a trio of prisoners are placed in the dock on charges of drunken and disorderly conduct but that a woman is one of the three. And for the most part they present a wretched and careworn appearance which is repulsive in the extreme. They are not only the worst of drunkards, but they are the breeders of thieves and pests to society. In Stalybridge we have a circle of them. Who have lost all shame and who think nothing of being taken before a magistrate time after time – witness the fact that an old woman named Fox has this week made her twentieth appearance before the borough bench for drunkenness and other offences. What would be the state of the homes of most of these women if they could be visited and publicly described? To procure some of the rooms would cause the most careless to shudder. We can imagine them being almost bereft of furniture, except the filthy rags or straw which form the common resting place ... so dirty and unwholesome as to be almost sufficient of themselves to breed disease; the inmates being scantily clothed with such rags only as the poorest pawnshop would not receive; the mother squalid, wretched and careworn, without a ray of hope to cheer her misery, except the prospect of such alleviation as occasional visits to the gin shop will supply; the children emaciated with hunger, and shivering with cold, and often one or more amongst the number suffering from a painful and perhaps incurable malady, rendered the more distressing and the more dangerous by the utter want of cleanliness, which seems the invariable rule. Is not such a state of things ruinous to health, pernicious to morals, and altogether disgraceful to any civilised community? Can we be surprised that such a home offers no attractions which can induce the husband to give up his absence?

The Suffering Children

At a time when children were to be 'seen and not heard' and even though the likes of Joseph Rayner Stephens had managed to reduce the number of hours spent by tiny children in horrific working conditions, it was still very much the lot of Victorian children to have their rights ignored and to be treated with little regard.

- On 17th April 1875, Robert was horrified to hear the case of a man and woman who ran off together, abandoning their children and leaving them with no food in the house. He sentenced the woman to a month with hard labour and the man to six weeks with the same.

- A woman employed at William Leech's mill as a frame tenter was caught stealing bobbins from her workplace. On 26th February 1875, Robert said that such thefts were occurring quite frequently in the town and he let the woman give her side of the story. She told the court that she simply needed them for firewood, and he replied, *"We are sorry to see you in that position, but it is a thing which cannot be overlooked. It is carried on to a great extent and an example must be made. In consequence of your little baby, we shall only give you fourteen days without hard labour – if it was not for your child, we were inclined to give you a much larger punishment".*

- On 6th February 1875 an 18-year-old woman named Esther Powell was accused of murdering her new-born baby. Robert felt that she had not deliberately killed her child, but a Manchester jury subsequently gave the girl a harsh sentence: six months imprisonment with hard labour (see Chapter 5 for more on this.)

Children and Crime

At first, finding some of the cases that involved children was shocking but sadly, after a while, the sheer volume of cases can have the disturbing effect of desensitizing the reader to their plight. Examples include;

- A boy stole a florin from an old lady and with it bought buns, coffee, tobacco and pipes on 15th August 1872. Robert remained unimpressed with young William Windsor, saying that he was, *"...giving crocodile tears".* He sentenced him to one month in prison without hard labour. After the month, he stated that the child should be sent to reformatory school (and for some reason he asked the constable present what religion the child followed, receiving the answer that he was Roman Catholic. Perhaps that was Robert's diplomatic way of asking whether the lad was Irish or not).

-      Two boys were found to have been stealing oranges from the new market hall (built/managed by Robert), on 20th February 1875. The parent of the youngest (aged seven) told Robert that the little boy had recently lost his 'half-term job', perhaps hoping that the magistrate would understand that the lad had been used to having a bit of cash previously. Robert discharged the case and told the parents that the boy, "*had better work as a half-timer than get into mischief. If there was a promise that he should go to work, the case would not be pressed against him this time, but if either of them is again brought up he would be sent to prison*".

-      On 26th January 1875, a youth had taken a fancy to some cigars in a Stalybridge shop. The shopkeeper told the court, "*I was just going to box him and let him go when the constable came in and took possession of him. I did not wish to press the case against him, as he is so young.*" Robert seemed to have a particular aversion to young people stealing things; as a small business owner himself, he probably would have felt that taking such acts lightly would only lead to reoccurrences and certainly sympathised with the shop owner who wanted to give him a good 'boxing'! He said, "*It is your first case, and we are sorry we can't order you a good flogging and let you go. Taking into consideration your parents are respectable people and hoping you will never appear in that box again, we shall let you go.*"

(See Chapter 5 for more information on the 'sending children to prison with hard labour' case)

APPENDIX 4

WHERE WERE THE WOMEN?

Note to the reader: this appendix was originally meant to be the final chapter of the book. However, ending with Robert's life and then moving onto a chronological discussion of all the women in his family did not sit well with a narrative approach. It was important to me, though, given that the lives of working-class women have been so overlooked in history, to try and retrieve the experiences of 'Robert's Women', even though the companion book to this one, 'Imagining Robert', provides a greater glimpse of women and their perspective. So, in trying to decide what approach to take, I sought out the opinion of the two most important women in my own life - my mother and my daughter. Both felt that it would seem artificial to try and shoehorn in a special chapter on women and that this might even come across as being a bit patronising towards our female ancestors. But surely, I said, it would be worse for me to simply shove the issue of women in as an appendix? Haven't women always suffered from being dumped into the appendices of history? At this point, my daughter pointed out that I was overthinking the matter, and my mother added that there are only so many times in a book about a man's life that you can write the phrase 'of course, none of this would have happened without the women in his life.'

As always, I appreciate your directness, 'ladies'.

The Women

One of the most frustrating aspects of researching Robert Stanley has been the impossibility of finding out more about the women in his life. History has been harsh to the voices of women but when carrying out this research I did not expect to be met with such a silence on behalf of the Stanley women. However, if a working-class born man like Robert Stanley, who became a successful grocer and tea trader, who rose to become a magistrate, mayor of Stalybridge and vice-president of the Liverpool Mosque, left virtually no paper-trail behind him, how much more so in the case of the women in his life?

Practically all that we have had to go on, in terms of the women to date, are birth/marriage/death (BMD) certificates and census information. When we first discovered Robert's conversion, my gran, Edith Stanley (great granddaughter of Robert) was as surprised as any of us. She had heard nothing about Robert's life other than him having been mayor, owned a grocer's shop and having been a 'Rechabite'. As explained in a previous chapter, this terminology for someone who practises temperance might well have been the family's choice of words for glossing over the Islamic aspects of Robert's life.

The Mother

We know next to nothing of Robert's mother, Ann: just her name and date of birth in 1795. It seems highly likely that she became pregnant with her first child when she was just a child herself and she stayed loyal to William, Robert's father, bearing him at least another nine children who survived infancy. She lived to the age of 61 and must have had a remarkably hardy constitution. If we take what my distant relative in the USA told us about the personality of William Stanley - that he was not too careful with his money and that he placed no value on the education of his children - it seems likely that it was Ann who pushed for sending their sons John, Robert and James up to Ashton in order to gain the advantages that Uncle John Stanley could provide them with.

The Wife

One of the questions my family is often asked is what Robert's wife must have thought of his conversion to Islam. Sadly, we know next to nothing about Emma Stanley, nee Meredith. No photographs exist of her; this might be indicative of an involvement with the Christian Israelite church (where no images of humans were permitted by Wroe), suspicion of the new practice of photography or simply that no pictures managed to survive.

Emma Meredith was born in 1825 in Tewkesbury to Thomas and Margaret Meredith. Thomas was described on Emma's marriage certificate as a bricklayer. In the 1841 census she was living in Ashton as a domestic servant to a family with the name of Knott. Perhaps, like Robert, she was sent away from her family to an area where there was a greater chance of employment so that her wages could be sent home. She may have met Robert in Ashton at the Christian Israelite Sanctuary. This is a strong possibility, given that the Knott family lived close to the Sanctuary, as many Christian Israelites did. But they could also have met in a more secular setting; Robert's home with his brother, John, on Oldham Road, Ashton, was in the middle of Ashton's entertainment area.

However the couple met, we can be sure that at least one of them had connections with the Christian Israelites and that they married in the Sanctuary. We know that Emma was literate, as she was able to write her name on her marriage certificate, and that she went on to give birth to at least eleven children, losing one child (George) when he was a year old: a low rate of infant mortality for the times. Here was another woman with an exceptionally robust constitution, bearing her last child at the age of 45 and living until the age of 77. Like most women in Stalybridge during the Victorian era, Emma would have had to manage a large family, living in only three or four rooms with no running water, electricity or household gas supply. Putting housework and cooking to one side, the washing for such a large family – with no mod-cons - must have been hellish and, in all likelihood one, if not more, of her eldest daughters would have been second in command.

On meeting Robert, Emma had been a domestic servant and, whilst not as grim as many of the factory jobs doled out to women at this time, the occupation was a hard slog. Marrying Robert meant a tough life – non-stop pregnancy, birth and child-rearing – but it also permitted her to become mistress of their own shop: extremely liberating for her in many ways, preferable to mill-work as she could be around her family, and certainly of higher status. She would have needed to use her intellect to order, run and liaise with suppliers and to keep on the right side of the customers, many of whom would be coming into the shop in order to reach Councillor Stanley via Emma in terms of local moans and groans.

The clubs and societies in Stalybridge during Emma's life were almost exclusively 'by men, for men', whether they were the political parties, special interest groups, improvement and educational groups or masonic lodges. There was a Women's Institute on Ridge Hill Lane and there were various church groups for women, but in the main there was neither the time nor the opportunity for a non-middle-class woman to socialise in such a way. From time-to-time, Emma may have enjoyed occasions associated with municipal affairs, such as her overseeing a stall as Lady Mayoress at Stamford Park Bazaar, and it is likely that the prestige associated with Robert's position might have made all the hours of Robert's absence whilst attending council committees seem worthwhile.

When Emma's son, John, passed away at the age of 35, she was 73. The fact that Robert and Emma had already moved to Manchester may well have been a silver lining for Emma, now that she had greater proximity to her grandchildren and could try to help her widowed daughter-in-law. Subsequently, grandson George came to live with them at their house on Upper Brooke Street, whilst his sister, Marguerite, went to live with Emma's daughter, Alice, and her husband, Joe, in Uppermill, who did not have any children of their own. Marguerite attended Huddersfield Secondary School – presumably because Alice or Joe would have been teaching there - and then managed to pass the entrance exam for Ashton Grammar School. No doubt Emma would have been proud of her granddaughter's achievement.

In 1897, Robert and Emma celebrated their Golden Anniversary and a tea party was held for their friends and family at Belle Vue, Manchester. Reaching this milestone was a remarkable achievement and the sign of a couple who were devoted enough to their relationship to want to share it with others - and at a considerable expense.

Emma died in Manchester in 1902 and her death was officially registered by Emmeline Pankhurst (see the *Imagining Robert* book for more on creative interpretations on the part that the Pankhursts may have played in her and her daughters' lives). She was not buried in Manchester, however, but in the family grave, where she was preceded by her children, George and John. It must have been with a very heavy heart that Robert accompanied the body of his wife of 54 years back home to Stalybridge.

The Daughters
Thanks to census information, we know that Emma and Robert's daughters received a good education. Apart from Annie (who emigrated to New Zealand and whose occupation we do not know), all the girls worked; Emma junior was a confectioner and Mary-Jane, Sarah and Alice all entered the teaching profession. Teaching was a typical occupation for women from the lower middle class of that time. Given Robert and Emma's own working-class origins, this would have been something to be proud of and indicated that Emma, too, wanted her daughters to

be responsible for bringing income into a household rather than simply just being wives and mothers.

It is interesting to note that most of the couple's sons did not focus on education as a career and all of them were listed at one time or another as a 'traveller', meaning a commercial travelling salesperson; most likely they were involved in the tea or grocery trades in partnership with their father. Business was more of a suitable and 'manly' occupation for men in the family, whereas teaching was a more respectable job for women.

In the 1901 census, two of Emma's daughters, Mary-Jane and Sarah, both qualified teachers, were living with their parents in Manchester and were listed as 'not working.' This could have been because they could not find jobs (teaching jobs being more difficult to find for middle-aged women), or because an elderly parent may have needed looking after. Either way, when it came to her daughters, Emma must surely have been pleased with their work and station in life; she would have felt that they had made something of themselves and, in comparison to her own lowly birth and her first occupation in life as a servant, Emma would have achieved the old adage which most parents cling to: 'we want something better for you.'

Because Mary-Jane Stanley was the only daughter of Robert and Emma's who never married, I have found her personality to be the most intriguing and have included her perspective as a full monologue in the companion book to this one. She worked as a teacher and always lived with her parents until Robert's final years, when he moved in with his youngest daughter, Alice, and his granddaughter, Marguerite, in Stalybridge. I could not, though, find out what had happened to Mary-Jane at this point, as she did not appear on the census with anyone from her family. However, the census for 1911 shows her to be living in lodgings in Scarborough, with her occupation given as 'commercial traveller' - a very unusual trade for a woman to be in at this time in history and particularly a woman of the age of 56! Perhaps she was selling Robert's teas for him.

Robert: On the Female Question

Examining the context of Robert's reflections during the school board education case of 1872, and when considering that his daughters became teachers and that his granddaughter went to Ashton Grammar, it seems certain that he was not opposed to the education of women.

It is, of course, impossible to know much on Robert's overall attitudes towards women. On first researching his life, it was rather dismaying to read the dismissive comment that he gave in *The Crescent* with regards to his 'Unmanly Meeting' letter. However, having now discovered more of his personality and politics, this comment does not represent anything more than a casual acceptance of the lower status of women in society, and he was just as offhand in relation to male dissenting ministers and curates.

Although from time-to-time there had been a rare speaker in Stalybridge who gave a talk on 'the electoral disabilities of women,' the mill towns to the east of Manchester were slow to wake up to the cause of women's suffrage. Robert was not involved in any form of campaigning for women's rights that we are aware of. But, in some respects, he may well have had more progressive opinions with regards to the role of women than many men during this era. For example, during his time as a magistrate, despite trying hundreds of cases that appeared in the press, Robert never treated a woman more harshly than he would a man; if anything, he showed himself to be more merciful towards women than his fellow magistrates were when the Stalybridge reporters were railing against the horrors of 'more drunken women!' Robert agreed not to send the notorious Rosanna Fox to prison if she gave 'the pledge', he would not give prison and hard labour to a woman because of her 'little baby' and he stated that the girl who gave birth to the illegitimate baby that died, and which she then tried to hide in the toilet, was not guilty of murder.

As someone who had always been taken with the issues surrounding the wider enfranchisement of the population, it would have been interesting to learn his views on extending the right to vote to women. It is likely that in his younger adult years he would have held concerns that this action would be premature, probably believing that women were not sufficiently in control of their emotions in order to check their voting behaviour. On the other hand, given his exposure in later years to more female-focussed dialogue with the likes of William 'Abdullah' Quilliam on the unfair British legal system when it came to the rights of women and the double standards employed by men, he may have changed his mind, recommending them as a more sensible-minded and trustworthy portion of the electorate than many men were.

Once the Stanley family had moved over to the Chorlton area of Manchester, they would have been aware of the activities of the Suffragettes. Emmeline Pankhurst, who lived just around the corner from them at 62 Nelson Street, had been a member of the Independent Labour Party (ILP) and although the suffrage bills of 1870, 1886 and 1897 had shown signs of more progression for women, they had been defeated. By 1903, Pankhurst had had enough; she now believed that mainstream political parties would never take the issue of women's suffrage seriously and she broke with the ILP, deciding instead that direct action needed to be taken. In October that year she set up the Women's Social and Political Union (WSPU), declaring, *"Deeds, not words, was to be our permanent motto"* and, in October 1905, Emmeline's daughters, Christabel and Sylvia, were arrested for their involvement in assaulting a police constable during a Liberal meeting at Manchester's Free Trade Hall.

All of this was happening on Robert's doorstep. The civic unrest employed by the WSPU both in Manchester and London caused an explosion of headlines across the world. It is very likely that Robert and the Pankhursts' paths crossed in relation to other issues that were being frequently debated and discussed in the meeting halls across Manchester. In fact, Emmeline Pankhurst's own politics were perhaps not that far removed from Robert's; later on in life she joined the Conservative Party, standing as a candidate for them, so whilst Robert would no doubt have disapproved of Emmeline's campaign of civil disobedience he may have appreciated the fact that she had been a tormentor of both the Liberals and the ILP.

Emmeline certainly met Robert on at least one occasion: when he registered Emma's death with her in 1902 (see Chapter 10 for the death certificate and

Emmeline's signature.) Despite Emmeline's increasing fame as the leader of the women's movement, this was a time when she had been struggling to pay the bills following the death of her husband. She had taken on the job of registrar for the Chorlton area. Christabel worked as an assistant to her mother. An imaginary meeting between Robert and Emmeline is included in the companion book to this one, *Imagining Robert*.

Quilliam: On the Female Question
This book has compared the similarities and differences between Robert's life and that of Quilliam's. One thing that they both had in common was the fact that the women in their lives all very much lived in their shadows. Later in Robert's life, his perception of a woman's role in society may have been influenced by his friendship with Quilliam and by his conversion to Islam. Little has been written on the attitudes towards women amongst Quilliam and his peers, or of the lives of the women who lived as part of the convert communities, but examination of copies of *The Crescent* and *The Islamic World* demonstrate a philosophy and practical approach to 'the female question' that would have been quite staggering for its time. Perhaps the best examples of this are some of the reasons behind the founding of the Medina Orphanage and the manner in which working class and downtrodden women were treated in Liverpool.

Polygamy was a subject that Quilliam spent a great deal of time writing and talking about. He had two wives and separate families and he frequently justified such practises by looking to Christian society and its despicable treatment of women in relation to the law and male predatory sexual behaviour. For Quilliam, polygamy provided a logical answer to this Christian inequality: allow a man access to another woman's arms, which also gave legal security for the women involved, and this would eradicate the deception of illicit affairs or dangerous liaisons with prostitutes, plus all the accompanying risk of disease and pregnancy that these involved.

Quilliam always underscored the fact that a woman should have the final say in agreeing whether a man should take another wife. He also emphasised that the Qur'an stated that a man should only take another wife where he was able to fully financially support her and more children. A contemporary critic of polygamy, however, would counter all the above by arguing that no matter how 'fair' these rules appear to be, they cannot occur in a society where men and women do not have a truly equal status. Victorian society, of course, could never offer any hope of this; a man's views would always prevail over a woman's. Plus, many would argue that in Islam there is not a similar arrangement for a woman who may be able to financially afford – and want – to take on another husband.

It would have been fascinating to know what Emma and her daughters thought about the subject of polygamy and Islam. Whilst putting the idea into practise was probably the furthest thing from Robert's mind, the women in his life would no doubt have heard rumours about polygamy amongst Muslims. They would have been aware that Robert's new friends (both the poorer Levantine Muslims in Manchester and the wealthier white converts like Quilliam) often ran two separate households with more than one wife. The community that Emma lived in and in which her daughters had grown up, like all small towns, could be subject to both silly and cruel gossip. Allusions along the lines of, "I wonder what old Robert is up to over there in Liverpool..." may well have been a reason why his family decided that they didn't want to discuss the issue of Robert's new religion, either with outsiders or even amongst themselves before or after his death.

To add more fuel to this fire, the end of Quilliam's glory days in Liverpool were surrounded with rumours involving his acquaintances with women. Quilliam had made the subject of women's lack of legal rights a key mission in his life and, sadly, his work to support them invited dubious scandal-mongering after he left the country. For example, locals living close to his Isle of Wight home preferred to misunderstand the fact that both of his families spent time together, choosing to tell outlandish tales of 'harems' and women coming and going. The 'harem' accusation is one which, even today, more bigoted and ignorant sections of the media enjoy levelling at Muslim communities, along with the 'poor, downtrodden women of Islam' prejudiced rhetoric.

Quilliam's chosen lifestyle in relation to his marriages would probably have unsettled the women in Robert's life, particularly after he left Britain for Constantinople surrounded by the divorce scandal rumours. Robert's daughters would not have been used to this sort of thing; men in Stalybridge did not involve themselves in such strange behaviour. The maxim 'there's no smoke without fire' would have prevailed; surely this Quilliam must have done *something* wrong in order to flee the country? And if Robert had mentioned anything about the converts being under British Government surveillance then his daughters would have been even more wary about keeping any connections with this religion and with the people who practised it after Robert's death.

Unfortunately, to date, the lives of the women in Quilliam's life have been neglected or simply side-lined by historians who have focussed on the life of Quilliam himself. Women are always harder to trace in history, this is true, but the weight of interest certainly needs to be redistributed. Hopefully this will be addressed by both Quilliam academics and community activists in the years to come; we now know for example, that Quilliam hosted a debate in 1926 (as Henri de Leon) where Emmeline Pankhurst herself was the key speaker. The rights of women certainly seemed close to the heart and mind of Abdullah Quilliam.

A Final Word: Granddaughters and Beyond
The building that Robert had owned on Princess (now Melbourne) Street in Stalybridge, and which housed his home and his grocers, was, by a strange twist of fate, later used as a shop where both my granny, Edith, and her sister, Joan, had once worked. In fact, Joan married the manager of the shop and went on to produce Michael Oliver, great-great grandson of Robert Stanley. We cannot be sure whether either of them was aware that their great-grandad, Robert, had owned this very shop. It is difficult not to feel frustrated at the lack of information that my family have held onto with regards to Robert; it tends to be women in a family who 'keep' and who are 'keepers' of the oral memories of other relatives and it is hard not to make the presumption that, for the above reasons, subsequent generations deliberately chose not to remember Robert as a Muslim. However, to

be fair to our ancestors, it must be remembered that Robert's descendants were 'respectable working class' and practically all of them (Brian aside) have been Conservative voters who would have been more interested in making a living, keeping their children alive and getting through two world wars. Little wonder, then, that the more colourful and outlandish tales of 'What Robert Did' were not kept.

In a country where women are not equal, where legal, economic and social conventions actively oppose their emancipation, women are forced to seize whatever they can in terms of power. For working class women, this usually manifests itself in relation to the family story: what can – and cannot – be spoken of. A new narrative is created where women, often behind closed doors, are finally in subversive control, albeit subconsciously. My family may well be a good example of this.

The likeliest scenario that occurred when Robert died, some three years after Quilliam had fled the country, was that one or more of his daughters decided that it was best never to talk about that chapter of his life, i.e. let's remember dad as he was; mayor – not Muslim.

I hope that the companion book to this one, *Imagining Robert*, goes some way to honouring the lives of the women who loved and supported him throughout the course of his life.

APPENDIX 5

ON FAMILY HISTORY

If reading this book has inspired you to try and build a better picture of your own ancestral background then the good news is that researching family history has never been easier. There is some bad news, however; genealogy can be utterly addictive.

Some of Robert's descendants today

Now that we have the internet, it has never been easier and faster to examine your ancestral roots. The discipline of family history has been rapidly embraced by the, predominantly older, white working classes of Britain, as records become easier to access and people retire at an earlier age. However, there has been far less take-up of family history interest amongst non-white groups and younger sections of the community. So, it would be excellent to see more of these amateur-expert groups passing on their knowledge and support to these other sections of the community. In particular, people who hail from immigrant backgrounds need more help than others; many are often filled with trepidation at the thought of investigating what can often feel like highly complicated trails to navigate.

Thanks to the sheer wealth of information online that now exists, a beginner embarking on their family history research can feel completely overwhelmed. So, my first piece of advice for a newcomer to family history is not to attempt to 'go it alone.' Practically every local authority in Britain has its own local history studies and archives section and this is where you will nearly always find a group of devoted genealogy enthusiasts, eager and willing to share their experience with you. Face-to-face contact is very important when delving into your family history and gaining the support of volunteers through physical meetings will be more helpful to you than just relying on email.

The kindness and generosity of the family historians in the locations that I am the most familiar with (Tameside and Kirklees) has been staggering. Many of these people work alongside local history studies and archives sections and offer hour-long (or more) slots a week where they will sit with you and help in your research. So, if you happen to live in an area which offers such an incredible opportunity, grab it with both hands and get your hours booked in with them!

One of the overall intentions of this book about Robert Stanley is to encourage people from different backgrounds and communities to work with each other through the pursuit of family history. This book is not the place to begin to tell you how to conduct family history (and knowing the sheer expertise of the Tameside genealogical experts, for example, I would never dare to be so presumptuous as to try and do that), but I thought it might be useful to provide a few tips for those readers who are curious about this wonderfully enriching pastime:

o **Family Tree** – If you already have possession of a family tree (no matter how scruffily produced) then this is your first port of call. If you don't have one, then ask around; you might be pleasantly surprised and find that a lot of the groundwork has been done already and that 'just the gaps' need to be filled.

o **Interviewing** – Learn from my own family's mistake with Robert: when they're gone, they're gone. There are plenty of books and online resources on the best way to interview other family members but don't forget that it might also be useful to interview close family friends (who often know a side to a person that a family is not aware of). The younger generation, too, can be brilliant at mining information from the older generation (my daughter is an expert on ferreting out information from her grandparents that I never seemed to gain access to!).

o **Visit your Local Studies/History Archives** - The local authority-run ones are free, but they sometimes charge a small amount for printouts, photocopies etc. Some local areas run family history/genealogy centres that are not part of the local council and they may need to charge you a few pounds for going along and getting advice. I would recommend that you visit both if you are fortunate to have them in your area; building up a bank of helpful, friendly volunteer experts is crucial and the more people that know about what you are trying to research, the better.

o **Read Books** – There are too many books on genealogy and starting your family history to mention, but before you go anywhere near a computer, and before you begin to chat to your local experts, buy a simple book (the 'Dummy's Guides/Idiot's Guides are good enough but ironically can provide more detail than you will want to know in the beginning). Better still, borrow a book on the subject from your local library.

o   **Get Help with your Family Tree** – There are many different approaches to creating and developing a family tree. You can buy all sorts of software to help you to do this but get advice from one of the experts before you part with your credit card number.

o   **Online Research Portals** – There are literally hundreds of free and not-so-free databases that you will want to head for once you have fleshed out your family tree and you want to pursue more B/M/D (birth, marriages, deaths) information. Perhaps the one website that every family historian in the world owes a great debt to is the free www.familysearch.org which was set up by the Church of the Latter Day Saints. This website is really staggering in terms of the volume of information that it contains and for the service that it has given to family historians. However, as well as needing to access BMD information, you will probably find that you also need items such as immigration records, newspapers, legal cases, wills and probate etc. and this does not come free of charge. There are many 'pay for' services online but most people plump for the excellent www.ancestry.co.uk or www.findmypast.co.uk where you can pay as you go or subscribe annually. Both also offer a 'free day' most years for those who want to try them out. But most local history archives will also give library members free access to them through their own computers. Phone ahead and find out exactly what they have on offer, because booking a space on their computers normally needs to be done several days in advance.

o   **Family/Local History Groups** – You don't necessarily have to join one of these groups, but by simply being aware of their events and talks you might stumble across some fascinating and useful links for your own research. Get on their email/newsletter list as soon as you can.

If you are interested in looking at a basic family tree for our connection with Robert 'Reschid' Stanley, it can be seen at our website – www.robertreschidstanley.wordpress.com

Good luck with your hunting

Family visit to the Abdullah Quilliam Mosque in Liverpool

BIBLIOGRAPHY

Al-Djazairi, S. *A Short History of Islam*, IIH, 2006.

Al-Djazairi, S. *The Myth of Muslim Barbarism*, Bayt al-Hikma, 2007.

Ansaria, H. *The Infidel Within; Muslims in Britain since 1800*, Hurst, 2004.

Arnstein, The Murphy Riots: A Victorian Dilemma, in *Victorian Studies* (1975) 1991.

Bagley, J. *A History of Lancashire*, Phillimore, 1976.

Basu, S. *Victoria and Abdul,* The History Press, 2010. See also screenplay by Lee Hall, 2017.

Birt, Y. The Quilliams, Popular Conservatism and the New Trade Unionism in Liverpool, *Islamic Review Special Edition*, 2019.

Chamberlain, J. *Speeches of the Right Hon Joseph Chamberlain,* 1918.

Chapman, *The Cotton Industry in the Industrial Revolution*, Macmillan, 1979.

Clark, P. *Marmaduke Pickthall: British Muslim,* Beacon, 2016.

Denby, P. *Two Into One Will Go – A History of the Parish of St George, Stalybridge,* Trinity Press, 1990.

Dennis, *English Industrial Cities of the 19th Century*, CUP, 1988.

Diamond, M. *Victorian Sensation: Or the Spectacular, the Shocking and Scandalous in Nineteenth Century Britain*, Anthem Press, 2003.

Dinwiddy, J. *Radicalism and reform in Britain 1780-1850*, Continuum, 1992.

Disraeli, *Sybil, or The Two Nations,* OWC, 2017.

Edsall, N. *The Anti-Poor Law Movement,* MUP, 1971.

Engels, *Condition of the English Working Classes in 1844*, CIPP, 2017.

Epstein and Thompson (ed) *Chartist experience: studies in working class radicalism and culture 1830-60*, Palgrave, 1982.

Epton, N. *Milord and Milady*, Oldbourne, 1962.

Forrest, D. *Tea for the British*, Chatto, 1973.

Foster, J. *Class Struggle and the Industrial Revolution*, Methuen, 1974.

Gammage, R. *History of the Chartist Movement, 1837-1854*, Forgotten Books, 2012.

Geaves, R, *Islam in Victorian Britain – the Life and Times of Abdullah Quilliam*, Kube, 2010.

Geaves and Gilham, *Abdullah Quilliam and Islam in the West,* (ed) Hurst and Co. 2017.

Gilham, J. *Loyal Enemies – British Converts to Islam 1850 – 1950*, OUP, 2014.

Green, E. *Prophet John Wroe: Virgins, Scandals and Visions*, The History Press, 2005.

Haidt, J. *The Righteous Mind: Why Good People are Divided by Religion and Politics,* Vintage, 2012.

Harrop, S. *Victorian Ashton*, TLAC, 1987.

Hill, *Bygone Stalybridge*, Rigg, 1987.

Holyoake, G. *The Life of Joseph Rayner Stephens*, Weidenfield, 1981.

Hopkins, E. *A Social History of the English Working Classes 1815-1945,* Arnold, 1979.

Locke, (ed) *Looking Back at Stalybridge*, see Harrop's 'Why was Stalybridge First?' TMBC, 1989.

Locke, (ed) *Looking Back at Ashton,* TMBC, 1997.

Longden, B. *The Life of Robert Stanley*, 2012.

Longden, C. *Popular radicalism in Ashton, Stalybridge and Hyde, 1828-1842*, Dissertation, 1994.

Longmate, *The Hungry Mills,* Maurice T Smith, 1978.

Mitford, M. *The Stanleys of Alderley,* Hamilton, 1968.

Nevell, M. *Tameside 1700 – 1930*, TMBC, 1993.

Nevell, M. *People who made Tameside*, TMBC, 1994.

Probert, Rebecca (ed) *Catherine Exley's Diary,* Brandram, 2014.

Pugh, *The Pankhursts,* Vintage, 2008.

Rogers, J. *Mr Wroe's Virgins,* Faber and Faber, 1991.

Rose, J. *The Intellectual Life of the British Working Classes*, Yale, 2001.

Said, E. *Culture and Imperialism,* Vintage, 1994.

Seddon, Siddique in *Early Muslim Communities in Manchester 1830-1950*, unpublished manuscript.

Squires, P. *Anti-Social Policy*, Wheatsheaf, 1990.

Thompson, D. *Chartists,* Breviary, 2013.

Thompson, D. *Outsiders. Class, gender and nation,* Verso, 1993.

Tobin, P. *Southcottians in England,* UoM, Thesis, 1978.

Urquhart, D. *Russia and Turkey*, Ridgway, 1835.

Waller, P. *City and Nation*, OUP, 1983.

Ward, J. *Popular Movements 1830 – 1850,* Macmillan, 1990.

Wild, J. *Black Gold*, Harper, 2005.

Williams, G, *Ruling Britannia. A Political History of Britain 1688 – 1988,* Longman, 1992.

Wroe, J. *Divine Communications*, Christian Israelite Press, 1822.

Wroe, J. *Revelations on the Scriptures*, Christian Israelite Press, 1849.

Manuscripts and Papers

Ashton Town Council Minutes 1849.

Ashton, Stalybridge and Dukinfield District Waterworks Committee, 1872 – 1878.

Declaration of Councillor Interests, Stalybridge Town Council, 1871 – 1876.

Overseers of the Poor Accounts book, Ashton, 1853.

Parliamentary Papers, Select Committee on Parliamentary and Municipal Elections, 1869.

Stalybridge Town Council Minutes 1863 – 1876.

Stalybridge Town Council Sub-Committee Minutes 1863 – 1876.

Report of the Committee on the Conditions of the Working Classes in Dukinfield, Ashton and Hyde, MSS, MCRL, Oct 1836.

Tameside Archives – newspaper cuttings of Ashton-under-Lyne pubs 1877 – 1897.

Printed Sources

Ashton Reporter (1855 – 1906).
Islamic World (1895 – 1908).
Manchester Courier (various, 1824 – 1911).
Manchester Guardian (ditto).
Manchester Times (ditto).
Sheffield Courier (1831, 1876).
The Crescent (1895 – 1908).
The Stalybridge Reporter (1872 – 1911).
The Voice of the People (1831).
Trade Directories (various from 1848 – 1911).
Wheeler's Manchester Chronicle (1830 - 1848).

Recommended Reading

For those interested in finding out more about British Muslim convert communities, to begin with, I recommend any publications or books by Birt, Geaves, Seddon and Gilham. Riordan Macnamara is currently carrying out research into the history of the Manchester Muslim community. Many of the more locally-focussed books in this bibliography will appeal to those mostly living in the north west of England and further reading can be found at the various local studies libraries in the region. For those interested in family history, see the Appendices for further information.

QUESTIONS FOR READERS

1. Robert was from a poor background, but he had a hand-up from his wealthy uncle. With this in mind, should we still think of him as being working class?

2. The Christian Israelites in many ways were closer to the Jewish faith than to Christianity. Do you think that this had a bearing at all on Robert's perception of God/Allah?

3. Prophet John Wroe: was he a charlatan or the victim of 'fake news'?

4. What would you say were the main drivers of Robert's desire to see justice carried out?

5. Do you think that Robert believed that 'all (men) are equal'?

6. Did Robert chase local power and prestige for the sake of it or because it was the 'right thing to do'?

7. We don't have any evidence of what the women in Robert's life thought about him. How do you think that they may have perceived him?

8. Do you think that Robert wanted to move from the pub because he was growing closer to Islam?

9. Would you say that Robert's relationship with Quilliam was intellectual, spiritual or more fraternal?

10. Do you think that Quilliam's fleeing the country in 1908 was for a more sinister reason than the legal scandal? And do you think that it was a contributing factor to Robert's death in 1911?

11. Do you think that Robert's views about the role of women in society changed as he aged? If so, was this because he became a Muslim or for another reason?

12. Why would Robert's family have chosen to have him buried in a Christian graveyard, rather than in a Muslim plot in Liverpool or Manchester?

13. Do you think that Robert's family deliberately covered up his conversion?

14. The keeping of the fez, the tie pin and the copy of *The Crescent* for over 100 years by a Stanley relative with no accompanying explanation: was this mere coincidence or was something else at play?

ABOUT THE AUTHOR
Christina Longden

Christina grew up in the Tameside area of Greater Manchester. She studied History at the University of Birmingham and went on to complete an MSc in Social Housing at the University of Salford. She worked in social housing, becoming a consultant to Whitehall on social policy. In 2003, she moved to Namibia, Africa, where she lived with the Kalahari Bushmen, writing two books about them and giving birth to her first child there.

On returning to the UK, Christina settled in the Colne/Holme Valley area and wrote two Northern comedy-dramas, '*Mind Games and Ministers*' and '*Cuckoo in the Chocolate*'

Christina is the great x 3 granddaughter of Robert 'Reschid' Stanley, the 'Hidden Victorian Muslim Convert' and sister to Steven, who is a teacher, activist and also a Muslim. She has written the biography of Robert 'Reschid' Stanley ('*His Own Man*') and a work of creative nonfiction, based on his life and times ('*Imagining Robert.*') She is married with two children and her family are one of the three founding families that set up the ethical coffee roastery, Dark Woods Coffee in West Yorkshire.

Christina is Director of an international charity, the Lorna Young Foundation and is founder of Past Truisms CIC – a social enterprise that works to overcome barriers between communities, using the arts as a medium to bring people together. Christina was appointed Writer in Residence for Kirklees in 2020, as a result of her passion for supporting more people to discover public libraries and reading.

www.robertreschidstanley.wordpress.com
www.funnylass.com

Books – Links to Christina's books (paperback and eBooks) can be accessed via the websites above.

Speaking engagements - Christina carries out speaking engagements and workshops in relation to her writing, books and her family's remarkable story.

On behalf of Robert's descendants – thank you for reading this book.

Brian Longden playing his ancestor in Arakan's trailer about Robert Stanley

If you enjoy being entertained by fiction and if you want to find out more about the fascinating life of Robert and the incredible historical events that he lived through - why not read the creative nonfiction book, based on his life story?

Christina Longden, Robert's great x 3 granddaughter has created a work of fiction based on his life and times. *Imagining Robert* is accessible to all and is written primarily in dialogue - in the style of a series of one-act plays and monologues about him. Deliberately created with all age groups in mind, it can also be performed by theatre groups, students, community groups, faith groups and reading groups.

Imagining Robert

Scenes from the Life of Robert 'Reschid' Stanley 1828-1911

by Christina Longden